"JUNE 22, 1941"

Soviet Historians and the German Invasion

"JUNE 22, 1941"

Soviet Historians and the German Invasion

By Vladimir Petrov

UNIVERSITY OF SOUTH CAROLINA PRESS
COLUMBIA, S.C.

Contents

"*JUNE 22, 1941*"

Soviet Historians and the German Invasion

PROLOGUE

This volume deals with a controversy centered around Aleksandr Moiseyevich Nekrich, one-time prominent Soviet historian and a corresponding member of the Academy of Sciences. Part I consists of a translation of his book about the origins of the Second World War, *June 22, 1941*, published in Moscow in the summer of 1965, which was at first praised but which later came under a barrage of official criticism. In July 1967 Nekrich was expelled from the ranks of the Communist Party of the Soviet Union (CPSU). This drastic punishment presumably terminated his associations with the Institute of Marxism-Leninism and the Institute of History of the Academy of Sciences. Whatever else may have happened to him, his career as a historian may be considered finished.

The importance of l'Affaire Nekrich transcends the fate of one man of whom we know little. It is directly related to the most burning issue in the Soviet Union in the late sixties: the persistent attempts on the part of the post-Khrushchev leadership to restore the late Joseph Stalin to a place of respectability in the communist pantheon from which he was ejected at the Twentieth Congress of the CPSU in February 1956. The reversal of the policy inaugurated in Khrushchev's Secret Speech has such far-reaching implications for the whole direction of Soviet society that it has aroused a determined and sometimes vociferous opposition in many influential quarters. Most of the struggle around the issue of the de-villaini-

1

zation of Stalin goes on beneath the surface, forcing foreign observers to resort to conjectures and speculations. The unique value of
the Nekrich controversy is that so much related to it has become
known and that it deals with history, traditionally the most political
branch of knowledge in the communist world.

History has always occupied a special place in the Soviet cultural
life. Unlike arts and even literature, where manifestations of unor-
thodoxy were on occasion tolerated even during the darkest years of
the Stalin era, history has at all times been chained to politics. The
party has been extremely reluctant to permit diversity in the interpretation of politically sensitive historical events, and there have
been precious few historical events in the recent past which have not
been considered sensitive. As Merle Fainsod said a few years ago:

All Soviet historians to some degree, and historians of the recent past
in particular, are expected to operate within the framework of Marxism-
Leninism, as its requirements are currently interpreted by the party
leadership. . . . These requirements shift with changes in the party line,
so that Soviet historians face the occupational hazard that yesterday's
heroes may become tomorrow's villains, and books which meet every
canon of orthodoxy when they are written may become politically un-
acceptable shortly after they appear. This means, among other things,
that scholars . . . must develop a keen sense of the direction of impending change and be able to gauge its limits as well as the potentialities
which it unfolds. Periods of transition . . . are periods of crisis for historians. When an uncertain trumpet blows, there will inevitably be some
historians who fail to catch the tune.

The misfortunes of Nekrich have befallen him precisely because
he "failed to catch the tune." He wrote his *June 22, 1941* early in a
period of transition, the true direction of which he did not detect.
By the time the book appeared, the change in the political climate
was well under way, and within a few months after its publication
all copies were withdrawn from the bookstores and libraries of the
Soviet Union.

The chief interest of Nekrich's book and of the storm it caused in
certain Soviet circles lies in his treatment of the issue of responsibility for the tragedy of the Soviet-German war, known in the Soviet

Union as the Great Patriotic War. This emotion-charged issue, by its very nature, has been of minor interest to Western writers who have been much more concerned with the Soviet contribution to the Allied cause than with the war's human and material cost to Russia. Yet insofar as this issue has obviously evolved into a major factor of the Soviet political scene in the last few years, it deserves further critical study. In addition, Western scholars interested in the Soviet side of the war's political and military background can benefit substantially both from Nekrich's revelations and the attacks upon him by the official party critics; these attacks offer us for the first time valuable insights into Stalin's thinking and his attitudes towards the Western democracies from Munich and until Hitler's invasion of Russia on June 22, 1941.

In order to appreciate the significance of the Nekrich controversy, we must put it into the context of the policy of de-Stalinization and its tremendous impact upon the masses of the Soviet people. We must recall that the Secret Speech which Khrushchev delivered at the Twentieth Party Congress in February 1956 was meant to augur a new era. By denouncing the "cult of personality" and indicting Stalin for his many crimes and errors, Stalin's heirs sought to reassure the rank and file of the party that never again would a single man concentrate such awesome power in his hands and that "socialist legality" would protect them from then on from the arbitrariness and capriciousness of the state security establishment, the dreaded secret police. In a calculated and seemingly irreversible step, the new leadership cast Stalin in the role of a scapegoat, solely responsible for the horrors of the past, and proclaimed its determination to start with a clean slate.

The decision to cast out the demi-god who had ruled Russia and world communism for a quarter of a century was not an easy one to reach for the men whose own claim to power was based on their faithful service to Stalin. We do not know how they arrived at this decision, but we do know that the more orthodox Stalinists in the Soviet Union and most of the leaders of other communist parties and regimes in Eastern Europe and Asia opposed it. They had strong and, as the subsequent events proved, well-founded reservations about the wisdom of throwing the communist world into a state of confusion in this manner. Their objections, however, were overruled: at that time, the consensus in the Kremlin was that nothing short of a frontal attack on the "cult of personality" would give the new leadership a credible new look. The hope apparently was that the likely political damage would be more than offset by a positive and enthusiastic response of the Soviet masses, and by the exciting opportunity for new communist initiatives abroad.

Yet there was one aspect in Khrushchev's Secret Speech which invited speculation that the decision to throw Stalin off his lofty pedestal was made under pressure from one particular power group motivated by an entirely different set of considerations. Khrushchev's sneering remarks about Stalin's fatal misjudgment of Hitler's intentions on the eve of the Great Patriotic War and his grotesque descriptions of Stalin's fantastic blunders in directing military operations could not be explained in terms of the need to demolish the "cult of personality" and to expose the dead Leader's vicious paranoia. In these terms, this line of attack was clearly counterproductive. In the minds of the Soviet people, Stalin had been closely identified with the triumphant victory over Germany. Even allowing for Khrushchev's personal bitterness and the natural vindictiveness of all those who had chafed under Stalin's heavy hand, there seemed little to be gained by portraying him as a simpleton who was outwitted by Hitler, who planned military operations on a globe, and whose pigheadedness resulted in tremendous losses to the Red Army in the first great battles of the war.

In taking this harsh line, Khrushchev was paying a political debt to a group of men who then had an unusual influence at the pinnacle of Soviet power, namely the celebrated war heroes, the "fighting marshals," grouped around Minister of Defense Marshal Zhukov. These men, who had long and unsettled accounts with Stalin and his uniformed cronies, had gained an upper hand in the military establishment after Stalin's death. Their belated "victory" was sealed when they replaced the old political generals and admirals in the Central Committee at the Twentieth Congress and when, defying precedent, professional soldier Zhukov was elevated to the position of senior candidate member of the Presidium itself.

A close reading of the Secret Speech shows that the concessions which the military extracted from Stalin's heirs only partially dealt with the need of giving the "fighting marshals" their well-earned credit for defeating Germany, a credit wholly misappropriated by Stalin. Their chief concern, which became quite evident in the following years, was to find a suitable scapegoat for Soviet unpreparedness on the eve of the German invasion and for the humiliating retreat of the Red Army all the way to the Volga.

To every living Soviet citizen, June 22, 1941, is a date which marks the greatest national disaster in the history of Russia. It was on that day that Hitler's hordes crossed the Soviet frontiers and unleashed the war which left a large part of the country in ruins, caused colossal dislocation of population, and brought death to over twenty million people. Almost every family lost at least one member; many families perished altogether; and almost everybody who is today thirty years old or older remembers personally the unbelievable suffering he and others lived through for four long years.

For two very special reasons the date of the German attack has become infinitely more memorable for the Russians than, say, Pearl Harbor has been for generations of Americans. One was the lightning-like initial advance of the German armies deep into Soviet territory, an advance which shattered the belief of a people conditioned by years of concerted—and largely successful—propaganda that the Soviet Union was omnipotent and invincible. The Soviet armed forces which had been for years supplied with everything on a top priority basis were universally expected to have no difficulty in repelling foreign aggression. The contingency plans of the Soviet General Staff itself assumed that the fighting would take place on enemy territory. Another assumption of the military planners, an assumption deeply rooted in the communist *Weltanschauung*, was that the toiling masses enslaved by capitalism would promptly side with the motherland of socialism and sabotage the efforts directed against it. The Red Army command had no alternative defensive strategy; the notion that the enemy might, however temporarily, occupy part of the Soviet Union bordered on high treason.

The second reason why the German invasion came as such a shock was that the nation was psychologically unprepared for it. Up to the very outbreak of hostilities Germany had been regarded as a friendly and even allied nation whose victories elsewhere were to a large extent made possible through the benevolent Soviet neutrality. To the Soviet Union, the two preceding years had also been fruitful and rewarding. It had annexed the vast lands of eastern Poland, the three Baltic states, and Bessarabia, without firing a shot. Because Germany had become a friend, Japan ended its bellicosity in the Far East. The Winter War with Finland was a painful episode and, to the informed military, it was a test of strength which the Soviet Union barely passed. But the significance of this campaign was played down by the press; it was short; and once it was over, few could doubt that the Finns lost the war. Economic difficulties which the population experienced during the years of the Nazi-Soviet cooperation because of the excessive trade commitments to Germany were not acknowledged in official statements; the information regarding these deliveries remained secret, and the difficulties themselves were not extraordinary by Soviet standards. Otherwise, the Soviet Union appeared to be getting stronger by the day. The Axis powers seemed to be treating it as an equal and, as Hitler's fortunes advanced, so, it appeared, did those of Stalin. There were no limits to the exultant glorification of the Leader by communist propaganda, to its praise of his wisdom and statesmanship.

Against this psychological background the German attack came like a bolt out of the blue. Its very suddenness produced a most traumatic effect upon the Soviet people, an effect which the magnificent victory over Germany four years later failed to erase.

Because the success of Hitler's volte-face had raised questions about the farsightedness of the Soviet leadership, communist historians and propagandists in the immediate postwar years treated this episode gingerly. Its embarrassing significance was vaguely acknowledged through the use of the word *verolomstvo* (literally, a breach of faith) in reference to German perfidy. Otherwise, the initial defeats of the Soviet armed forces were minimized and uniformly ascribed to the tactical advantage the Germans achieved through their sudden attack. The great retreats of 1941–42 were de-emphasized by portraying them as the preliminary stages of ultimate victory. Mass desertions and defections from the Red Army were not even acknowledged. Stalin was presented as being at all times in full control of the situation, cunningly forcing the enemy to overextend his communications and to spread his armies thinly over the endless steppes of Russia in order to finally deal him a crushing blow at Stalingrad.

The legend thus drawn was too false to take root. It clashed so profoundly with the knowledge and personal experience of so many people that no amount of propaganda could make it stick. No matter how diligently historians tried to emphasize the glorious march of the Red Army to Berlin, the monstrous defeats of the 1941–42 campaign and the deprivations of eighty million Soviet citizens in the Nazi-occupied regions simply could not be forgotten.

Under ordinary circumstances a Soviet citizen does not challenge communist historians. He wants to know the truth but does not hope that the truth, at least the whole truth, will ever be told. He accepts, and learns to live with, half-truths, distortions, and plain untruths if the concoction is sufficiently palatable, because he has been taught not to question the party-endorsed versions of historical events. In this instance, however, the gap between his actual knowledge and the legend proved to be unbridgeable. This particular gap had acquired major political significance because of colossal dimensions of the calamity which had befallen Russia on June 22, 1941, raised in many minds the question of responsibility for it.

Had the party admitted in so many words that the German initial successes were due to the overwhelming superiority of Hitler's military machine, this question would have probably been dulled. But the party could not admit this. For one thing, such an admission would have required another one, namely that the Soviet people had been consistently misled into believing that the Red Army was invincible. For another, an explicit recognition that any foreign country could be more powerful than the Soviet state and that therefore Soviet citizens could not count on absolute protection against a foreign foe was politically intolerable. Finally, an admission that the Soviet leaders had been lulled by Hitler into such unbelievable complacency would have required, in line with the established Soviet tradition, the identification and punishment of the culprits.

No such admissions appeared necessary at the end of the war. Describing the glorious Soviet victory in his biography of Stalin, Isaac Deutscher wrote:

Stalin now stood in the full blaze of popular recognition and gratitude. Those feelings were spontaneous, genuine, not engineered by official propagandists. Overworked slogans about the "achievements of the Stalinist era" now conveyed fresh meaning not only to young people, but to skeptics and malcontents of the older generation. The nation was willing to forgive Stalin even his misdeeds and to retain in its memory only his better efforts. Since nothing succeeds like success, even his errors and miscalculations, including those of 1939–41, now looked to many like acts of prudent statesmanship. Even the cruelties of the thirties appeared in a new light, as salutary operations to which the peoples of the Soviet Union owed their survival.

The intoxication with the triumph did not last. As the millions returned to their miserable normalcy in the devastated country, the enormity of the price paid for victory began to dawn upon everybody. In an effort to mute their reaction, thousands of articles, memoirs of partisans, movies and plays, and history books emphasized Stalin's wisdom and heroism of the Russians. Most of what was said and written dealt with history of the war after the magnificent battle of Stalingrad. The preceding defeats and the nightmare of suffering, both under the German occupation and under Soviet rule, were played down. The masses of people who gained little from victory and who were toiling, half-starved, at rebuilding roads, factories, and mines rejected this version of history. Those who had suffered the most or had personal grievances of one kind or another —and their numbers were great—saw through the falseness of the propaganda. The regime seemed to have lost touch with the masses, and with reality. And the people started to speak up.

As long as Stalin was alive, even those people who had lost most of their docility in the trials of the war prudently abided by the familiar Stalinist conformity. There were riots here and there by crippled war veterans and hungry mobs, but most of the population remained bound by the habitual discipline still effectively enforced by the secret police; subversive discussions were usually restricted to small groups of intimate friends. But the death of Stalin in 1953 and the sharp reduction of the secret police power in the wake of the first clash among Stalin's heirs unleashed tongues.

The change came imperceptibly. It was barely noticed abroad because for a while nothing new appeared in print. The party continued to exert effective control over the press, enforcing as before the uniformity of treatment of all sensitive subjects. But in party and Komsomol meetings, in classrooms and army barracks, and in private gatherings all over the country the heat was on.

It was not very surprising that in the search for answers to the painful questions relating to the guilt for the calamity for 1941 most people condemned the military establishment. Some spoke, in general terms, of the blunders of the impersonal government; very few accused the party; and almost nobody blamed Stalin. This reluctance cannot be attributed solely to the effects of protracted brainwashing, to the "cult of personality." In the minds of people, Stalin even in his grave remained above the mortals. He was a symbol, not an ordinary human being. The more prominent members of the party familiar with the inner workings of the regime might have had a different opinion. But since the early thirties, the masses tended to blame their sufferings and misery on Stalin's evil underlings, on the secret police, on the criminally negligent bureaucrats, on the stupid and inept generals, in short on anybody but the Leader himself. While the Leader was alive, they often wrote him long letters reciting their grievances and begging for justice, as indeed their forefathers used to do in petitioning the Tsars. Now that he was dead, his memory remained sacred to all but the sworn enemies of all things communist and Soviet.

The questions people asked about the defeats of the early years of the war had ominous implications. Was the Red Army high command guilty of boastfulness, rank unpreparedness, of gravely underestimating the enemy? Were Soviet generals inferior to German generals? What kind of strategy had they followed which permitted the enemy to conquer, however temporarily, over a half of European Russia? If the Soviet Union was powerful enough to crush Germany in 1945, why had it not been able to stop the invaders in 1941? The enormous complexity of political and military factors which determined the course of the war escaped the questioners because they had traditionally been kept in ignorance of them; it is rarely realized how little even an educated Soviet citizen really knows about anything outside his immediate experience, how inadequate and distorted is his information. In this instance, precisely because the questions were so straight and simple, they were more difficult to answer.

The "fighting marshals" and all the others who had carried the main burden of war and led the Soviet armies to the heart of Europe, bitterly resented the accusations directed against them. In the fluid conditions of the first post-Stalin years they succeeded, in part by forming personal alliances with some of the influential party leaders, in coming close to the source of power. After a fierce struggle they wrested the control over the armed forces from the old-line political generals and by the beginning of 1956 they were able to confront Stalin's heirs with far-reaching demands: (a) to strip Stalin of his "historical role" as the sole architect of victory; (b) to enhance the stature of the armed forces by rehabilitating posthumously and glorifying anew the renowned military leaders who had been shot on Stalin's orders; (c) to absolve the military establishment of any blame for the catastrophe of 1941 by placing the whole responsibility for it on Stalin.

At the Twentieth Party Congress these demands were essentially met. Khrushchev's spectacular revelations were subsequently reported at public meetings throughout the country. Stalin's portraits and statues vanished from public places, and the cities, streets, and kindergartens bearing his name were renamed. Teachers and professors of history were put through crash reorientation courses. Since most of the old history books reflected the "cult of personality," they were either withdrawn or declared erroneous. On orders of the Central Committee communist historians were put to work, digging out of the memory hole the ghosts of the Red Army heroes executed by Stalin, rewriting the history of the war and sharply downgrading the Leader's role in it.

A special division of history of the Great Patriotic War at the Institute of Marxism-Leninism (entrusted with an absolute monopoly in interpreting the Faith) came up in time with six volumes of a "definitive" history of the war in which everything was carefully balanced according to the new party directives. As they appeared one by one, these volumes served as a guideline to other writings which began to pour out in profusion.

In one sense, most of this literature constituted an anticlimax: the impact of the removal of Stalin from his heroic pedestal appeared strangely cushioned by the absence of any meaningful political analysis. The "fighting marshals" (and the surviving influential members of the post-Stalin leadership) were given full credit for their accomplishments. The new works were considerably more accurate in their accounts than the old ones and thus more informative. But in their political content, all of them were only a pale reflection of the Secret Speech. It was evident that the latter, rather than serving as a starting point for breaking new ground, imposed instead stringent outside limits for historical-political revisionism.

The old military leaders, still concerned with the task of explaining away the disasters of the early period of the war, viewed this limitation as the party's refusal to honor the IOU issued at the Twentieth Party Congress. But in the fluid, and confusing situation of the sixties there was little they could do about it. Their bargaining position had deteriorated; after 1957 there was no more Marshal Zhukov in the Presidium of the Central Committee; and most of the old towering figures themselves had gradually been retired.

In spite of these adversities, the disgruntled military found an opportunity to have their say. They took advantage of the relative diffusion of power characteristic of the Khrushchev years, when the party lost a great deal of its control over historical writings and publications. It became difficult for an editor to deny a bemedaled hero the publication of his memoirs; some editors in fact encouraged famous heroes to put their recollections on paper.

Encouraged by these opportunities, retired generals and admirals went to work. In an outflow of war memoirs timed to coincide with the twenty-fifth anniversary of the beginning of the war, they made a bold effort to amend the official record. Using the Secret Speech as their license to probe into the circumstances of the German attack, some memoirists ventured onto politically sensitive ground. There were no real sensations in the Western sense of the word, and not a single member of Stalin's inner circle produced as much as an enlightening article. Nevertheless, these writings evoked extraordinary interest among the Soviet public—and Soviet historians.

Some of the memoirists, while writing about their own limited experiences, assembled their facts in a way which amounted to a theretofore unheard-of questioning of the wisdom and judgment not only of Stalin personally but of the party leadership collectively. To anyone who remembered the contents of the Secret Speech there were few major revelations. But the cumulative effect of their writings in Russia was enormous, for they afforded the Soviet citizen, conditioned to believe that anything that passes censorship and appears in print has official blessing, an unusual opportunity to discuss openly matters of high policy and the decision-making processes in the forbidding sanctuary of the Kremlin.

Even more interesting was the reaction among some of the historians professionally concerned with the history of the war. They had had for years at their disposal a variety of Western sources—German, American, British—including rich collections of documents published since the war. Although never devoid of "Marxist" interpretation, a number of their studies dealing with Western political and military strategies displayed a high quality of scholarship. But in their attempts to reconstruct critical diplomatic and political developments involving the Soviet Union, they were gravely handicapped by the lack of access to the secret archives of the Central Committee of the CPSU. The public record, including the old files of *Pravda*, was singularly unrewarding as a primary source. To these historians the appearance of the scores of memoirs by retired Soviet diplomats and generals, and their authors' availability for interviews, was a real bonanza. It not only permitted an expansion of research but also an interpretation of important events of the past in ways not necessarily consistent with the straight party line.

Professor Nekrich's book may not be exciting by Western standards. It sounds in places unscholarly and oldfashioned in its Soviet patriotism. But it must be remembered that *June 22, 1941* was written for a Soviet audience which has not been spoiled by the frankness and originality of communist historians. What makes the book exceptional both to its Soviet and Western readers is that Nekrich went further than anybody else in presenting the issue of responsibility for the Soviet defeats in the war to the liking of the dissident generals—and against the party's view on the matter, as it had evolved by the mid-sixties. Outwardly, Nekrich's criticism is limited to Stalin's multiple "errors" as specified in the Secret Speech. But in many instances his Stalin appears not merely as an individual but as a symbol of the party leadership as a whole. Among other things, Nekrich goes on record in showing (a) that the purge of the Red Army command in 1937–38 had gravely weakened the Soviet armed forces; (b) that in order to execute Marshal Tukhachevskiy and his comrades-in-arms Stalin knowingly utilized evidence fabricated by the Gestapo; (c) that Great Britain (particularly under Churchill's leadership) was not as devious in its dealings with the Soviet Union in the summer of 1939 and afterwards as had been alleged by official communist writers and that the United States was not devious at all; (d) that contrary to the official version, Stalin's decision to conclude a deal with Hitler did not result in an improvement of the overall Soviet position vis-à-vis Germany; (e) that Stalin's commitment to Hitler was so deep and sincere that he rejected all the evidence of the imminent invasion and prevented the military leadership from taking the most elementary defensive measures.

The Secret Speech stunned everybody in the Soviet Union. It pleased Stalin's enemies and filled the diehard opponents of the regime with glee. It was welcomed in the West by those who ever since Stalin's death had hoped for an East-West detente on some new basis, as well as by those foreign communist leaders who had been trying to get from under the heavy hand of Moscow. At the same time it deeply upset the faithful of all nationalities for whom Stalin had been the embodiment of the might and glory of the Soviet Union, and of the international communist unity. But whatever its other effects were, the Speech failed in one respect: it did not succeed in turning Stalin into the sole scapegoat for the disasters of the war. The average Soviet citizen could not believe that one man, no matter how wicked and powerful, could be held accountable for the political and military blunders of the Soviet government. Since, however, blunders themselves had been admitted, everybody felt suddenly free to apportion the blame according to his own judgment.

This inexorably led to an escalation of the whole issue. The people were now wondering what kind of men were all those who advised Stalin, who had helped him to devise and carry out his policies and strategies. After all, they knew that, with the sole exception of Beriya, Stalin's principal comrades-in-arms were quite prominent at the Twentieth Party Congress. Perhaps the most disquieting question was where was the Party, wise and infallible, this collective ruler of Russia since the revolution, while Stalin performed his evil deeds? Could it cast out the Leader and still claim its untarnished purity throughout its whole existence, including the years when Stalin ruled supreme? The public readily agreed that Stalin did not deserve the exclusive credit for victory; most of them felt that way all along. But they could not accept Khrushchev's thesis of Stalin's exclusive responsibility for the monstrosities of the past and for the unbelievable failures of the Soviet government.

This skepticism was only one element in the unsettling situation which the Soviet hierarchs had to face. Having delivered the fatal blow to the "cult of personality," they set in motion great forces over which they quickly lost control. Faced with all kinds of problems, they applied brakes, determined to proceed with de-Stalinization as slowly as possible. The Secret Speech itself has never been published in the Soviet Union, and during his visit to the United States in 1959, Khrushchev blatantly declared it to be a vicious concoction of the CIA. As they struggled with one crisis after another, Stalin's heirs gave up attempts to draw either definite limits for de-Stalinization or to determine a reasonably consistent "mixture" of good and evil in Stalin's record.

There is no doubt that many of the Soviet leaders began very early to have second thoughts about the wisdom of the new course. But for the time being damage done to Stalin's image (and to the image of the party) appeared irreparable. Even if they wished to reverse the policy, there had already formed two identifiable groups in the Soviet Union which had developed a strong vested interest in keeping Stalin out of the communist pantheon and which had to be reckoned with. One encompassed prominent intellectuals—writers, scientists, artists, scholars, and a part of the technical-managerial elite—for whom any notion that the liberties they had acquired after 1956 might be taken away was anathema. Another group, in part overlapping the first, consisted of an important segment of the military establishment. Its members were less numerous but more homogeneous. They also were recognized as belonging to the power structure of the regime. Not as vocally, but perhaps with a greater tenacity, these men continued to view Stalin as a butcher who decimated the Red Army leadership in the thirties and they insisted that the great act of the Twentieth Party Congress was final and irrevocable.

The party leadership, however, was running into such difficulties along the unfamiliar path of liberalization that before long the consensus in the Kremlin began to shift in favor of tightening the ideological screws. The brakes were at first applied without much consistency, thus giving the observers of the Soviet scene a hard time in correlating the various moves in Moscow. What baffled many people was that in spite of the signs of re-emerging orthodoxy, there was little suggesting that a restoration of "Stalinism" was in the making.

The answer was, of course, that the rehabilitation of Stalin was not initially an integral part of the ideological change. The issue of Stalin's place in history existed separately, having less to do with ideology than with a problem arising from a very pragmatic and apparently acute necessity for re-establishing the historical continuity of leadership in the Soviet Union. The managers of the Twentieth Party Congress soon discovered that their attempt to claim direct lineage from Lenin, bypassing the last fifteen to twenty years of Stalin's rule (in the Secret Speech Stalin was declared to have been "good" until the mid-thirties) had failed. The chronological gap turned out to be too great not to raise the question of legitimacy of succession, i.e., the right of Stalin's heirs to occupy the seat of power.

While Khrushchev was on the scene, even a limited de-villainization of Stalin was not feasible. It is in the nature of politics (and not only of Soviet politics), that leading politicians cannot reverse their positions on major issues without inviting trouble. Therefore, for the time being the ideological offensive launched by the party did not appear, except by implication, as a departure from the position it had taken at the Twentieth Party Congress. Nevertheless, by late 1962, the trend away from The Thaw and towards orthodox communist conformity had become unmistakable. The main thrust of the offensive was initially directed against the so-called liberal intellectuals, primarily from the literary and artistic circles, who defended what they regarded as their rights more doggedly than anyone else. At first, the issues appeared narrow, as if the party were pointing out that whatever stand it had taken on Stalin, there was no free license for anyone to challenge its leadership in other respects. By 1965, however, with the demise of Khrushchev, the attack had noticeably broadened; the unreconstructed party hacks who had been sitting on the sidelines, were encouraged to criticize the excesses of de-Stalinization; and in the public eye the issue of Stalin's place in history had become inextricably linked with all other ingredients of ideological orthodoxy. This was not an unfounded view: we have clear evidence that the party leadership was set to rehabilitate Stalin at the Twenty-third Party Congress in March–April 1966, abandoning its resolve only at the last moment under immense pressure from the opposition, both domestic and external.

This particular episode represented merely a temporary setback; in all other directions the offensive continued unabated. There were arrests and trials (mostly secret) of prominent intellectuals and other adherents of the short-lived "liberalism." The identifiable Stalinists in the party, the government, and in the cultural field, were having a field day. Before long, another ominous development took place. As Patricia Blake (in the *New York Times Magazine*, March 24, 1968) wrote:

The year 1967 saw a major attempt to rehabilitate the secret service, which, for the Soviet people, is quite properly associated with revolutionary violence, the bloody horror of the great purges, and the 20-year Stalinist terror. All the vast propaganda resources of the Soviet state were mobilized for this purpose. Countless books and articles glorifying the exploits of secret-service agents were cranked out by the state publishing houses. . . . If this campaign was intended to popularize the KGB, it was naive, to say the least. Its main purpose appeared, rather, to rebuild the morale of the secret service and thus increase its efficiency.

Although the restoration of the secret police to a place of honor it had not occupied since 1953 went hand-in-hand with the continuing efforts to de-villainize Stalin, there are no reasons to believe that the two were organically related. We may even reasonably speculate that the party leadership would have been satisfied with a relatively modest degree of Stalin's posthumous rehabilitation, e.g., with a recognition that whatever wrongs were done by him were done with good intentions; that he was basically a good Soviet patriot and a dedicated communist; and that therefore his successors, having exposed the record of Stalin's excesses and abuses, were still legitimate heirs to power in the party.

By 1967, however, important segments of the public had been

aroused. Having acquiesced with most of the other aspects of the emerging hard line, the opposition took a surprisingly strong stand on the issue of the "cult of personality." The reason for this last-ditch resistance was probably rather simple: the resisters could fight back without appearing disloyal and thus without taking excessive political risks. After all, the denigration of Stalin *was* one clear-cut decision of the Twentieth Party Congress and the people could assume that the party could not alter its stand without repudiating itself.

Additionally, the whole issue of Stalin's place in history had acquired an almost irrational symbolic significance to the opposition. The men who had been unable, and often unwilling, to criticize the party as such, or the Soviet system of government, including its secret police branch, rallied in resistance to anything suggestive of a restoration of the "cult of personality." Whatever current complaints they might have had they related to this (in practical terms irrelevant) issue, attacking the "cult of personality" not unlike a Don Quixote attacking his windmill. To illustrate, we may look at a typical document, an appeal to "the leading personalities in the fields of science, culture, and arts of the USSR," circulated in Moscow in February 1968, in which three intellectuals (I. Gabai, Yu. Kim, and P. Yakir) declared:

The term "cult of personality" has become almost forbidden in our press. The scholarly and artistic writings criticizing Stalin and the crimes of the Stalin period cannot appear in print any more. These include many books which had reached the typesetting stage, such as the memoirs of B. Vannikov, the book by L. Slavin about Marshal Yegorov (executed on Stalin's orders in the Red Army purge), the wartime diaries of K. Simonov, the memoirs of E. Ginsburg, and many others. We have reached a point where a high-ranking ideological bureaucrat, Fedoseev, recommends applying the term "cult of personality" exclusively to Latin American dictators or to Mao Tse-tung. . . . A large number of Soviet citizens have been forced again into despicable and humiliating spying and reporting to the authorities on their friends and neighbors. We warn that the tacit acquiescence to the deeds of the Stalinist bureaucrats who deceive both the nation and its leadership [*sic*] and who suppress every complaint and protest will logically lead to the most dreadful consequences, to lawlessness and savage reprisals against the people.

What the future holds for the "cult of personality" in the Soviet Union is anybody's guess. It is possible that as the ideological confusion in Eastern Europe increases, the CPSU might make an attempt to rehabilitate Stalin even if it would require making Khrushchev and his comrades-in-arms of 1956 into scapegoats. There have been no such precedents, but it cannot be ruled out either that the current leadership would try, in one way or another, to repudiate the decisions of the Twentieth Party Congress. In the face of the growing disarray in the communist camp and the challenges to the leadership at home, Moscow may conclude that no price is too high to pay for restoration of the traditional ideological conformity. Whether such a restoration is possible is another matter, but that a major effort in this direction might be made is not such a wild thought as may appear at first glance.

Historians have traditionally occupied a special place among the Soviet elite. The party has regarded them as an integral part of the propaganda apparatus, entrusted with the important task of giving a "Marxist" interpretation to history, ancient and modern, and adjusting the presentation of the past to current political requirements. Historians have always had to pass a particularly exacting test of loyalty; almost without exception they have been members of the Communist Party; usually they have been among the first to receive The Word, the latest secret directives of the Central Committee in the ideological field.

During the post-Stalin years, however, some of the historians also came to value their professional competence and their reputation as serious scholars. While still laboring within the confines of Marxism-Leninism, they looked for sound scholarship and sought to achieve a measure of objectivity in their studies and writings, perhaps hoping one day to obtain the kind of international recognition their colleagues the scientists had succeeded in obtaining. A few of the historians—those who specialized in the remote past or on the histories of far-away nations—elevated themselves above the levels of propaganda. But those who were primarily preoccupied with modern history, especially Soviet history, could never make the mark.

Even with full license to explore the Stalin era within the spirit of the Secret Speech, the Soviet historian finds himself in an impossible predicament. To appreciate it, we should compare him with a patriotic German historian who is trying to find a proper place for Hitler in modern German history. The German's task might be unpleasant, but it is not hopeless. He can, if he wishes, cast Hitler in the role of an unmitigated villain. After all, many good Germans resisted the Fuehrer at the time, and the more prominent Nazis have either been executed or reduced to social and political insignificance in postwar Germany. Much as most Germans resent accusation that they had acquiesced to Nazi rule, they can, if they wish, admit that such was the case without necessarily appearing unpatriotic. They are at liberty to denounce Hitler and his regime as well as to score the ultra-nationalistic fever which had brought the Nazis to power.

The policy of de-Stalinization did not create analogous opportunities in the Soviet Union. Only a few odious figures associated with the grimmest aspects of Stalin's rule met punishment for "violations of revolutionary legality." While Stalin's closest collaborators have left the scene, their departure had nothing to do with Stalin's crimes; they either became victims of Kremlin power plays or simply of old age. Stalin, and Stalin alone, was permitted to be blamed for whatever went wrong, and these "wrongs" were far from all-encompassing by any fair standard; the record of the party itself, unlike that of the Nazis in today's Germany, had to be maintained unblemished at all times.

In his *June 22, 1941* Professor Nekrich was anything but unpatriotic, certainly by the yardstick of the Twentieth Party Congress. He duly praised Stalin for his concern for industrialization and for expanding the Soviet frontiers at the expense of the neighboring countries. Nekrich strictly abided by one of the major taboos in Soviet historiography by not even hinting that this expansion came about thanks to the understanding with the Nazis spelled out in the secret protocols of August 23 and September 28, 1939; the very existence of these protocols has never been acknowledged in the Soviet Union. Equally cautiously, Nekrich skirted the ticklish subject of Soviet economic aid to Germany, so crucial for the build-up of Hitler's military machine. Even in his relatively favorable appraisal of the British and American attitudes and policies during 1939–41 he was not out of line with Khrushchev's treatment of them in the Secret Speech.

In spite of his irreproachable patriotism, Nekrich in his study clashed head-on with a host of other, less independent-minded, historians, especially those who had never really graduated from the ranks of party propagandists. The latter had stayed away from the whole issue of the "cult of personality" even during the Khrushchev years, limiting themselves to the omission of the Leader's name and to glorification of the currently approved heroes. Whether they did that out of habitual caution or out of conviction, these traditionalists continued to draw political support among Stalinists in the party hierarchy and retained control of most of the periodicals and journals of history.

June 22, 1941 was noticed immediately after its publication in the summer of 1965. But while it provoked lively discussions among the reading public, historical journals gave it the silent treatment. The book was reviewed only in the "liberal" monthly *Novyi mir* (No. 1, 1966) and, for some obscure reason, in *Komsomolets Tadzhikistana* (January 9, 1966), a daily in remote Central Asia. But the contents of *June 22, 1941* quickly became the subject of heated debates in the division of history of the Great Patriotic War of the Institute of Marxism-Leninism and in military and academic circles.

It was a measure of the insecurity of the present protectors of the communist faith that it took them some time to recognize publicly the controversial nature of Nekrich's book and to mount an attack on its author. He continued to write (an excerpt from his latest book, *In the Labyrinths of the Secret War*, was published in the

January 1966 issue of the journal *Novaya i noveyshaiya istoriya*),
and in June 1966 he was elected corresponding member of the
illustrious Academy of Sciences.

By the spring of 1967, however, the party's struggle for a return
to the communist orthodoxy was already in full swing. Books and
articles portraying Stalin in a favorable light were cropping up.
Finally, the party decided to set new guidelines for historians concerned with the history of the Great Patriotic War. The army
political organ, *Krasnaiya zvezda*, published on May 30, 1967, an
article entitled "The Memoirist and History" in which it severely
condemned those writers who unduly concentrated on the early
period of the war and on the "errors and miscalculations" of the
Soviet leadership. At the same time it warmly commended the
memoirists who stressed the overwhelming importance of the ultimate Soviet victory over Germany. And, without going into specifics, it admonished the writers to keep in mind that "the Supreme
Commander, J. V. Stalin, showing great fortitude, guided combat
operations correctly on the whole, and rendered considerable services in the field."

It has been a Soviet tradition that in order to emphasize a new
policy, one or several men guilty of following a discarded one, must
be "disciplined" for all to see. Thus Aleksandr Moiseyevich Nekrich
had become a candidate for punishment. Apparently his connections in military and academic circles were substantial enough to
delay the day of reckoning; for a while the party itself appeared
hesitant to exercise its full ideological authority in the field of
history.

The heavy blow to Nekrich came in July 1967, when the Control
Commission of the Central Committee of the CPSU ousted him from
the party. This act was not announced in the Soviet press but was
established by several Western newsmen in Moscow (see *The Times*
of London, July 8, 1967, and *The Christian Science Monitor*, July
27, 1967). Finally, in September, as a kind of post-mortem, *Voprosy istorii KPSS*, on the supreme authority of the Central Committee, attacked the hapless historian directly, viciously assailing
item after item of Nekrich's findings and interpretations. What has

happened personally to Nekrich since, we do not know, but his career as a historian has doubtless come to an end.

The collection offered here includes full translations of A. M. Nekrich's book *June 22, 1941*, of the transcript of the debate at the Institute of Marxism-Leninism on February 16, 1966 (text courtesy of *Survey*), and of two critical articles (one praising and another attacking the book). To this I have added an excerpt from my article, published in ORBIS (Winter 1968), in which I relate, for the benefit of those who may have forgotten the story, the background of the Nazi-Soviet Pact.

THE BOOK

The book by A. M. Nekrich, the full text of which follows, is clearly the work of a *Soviet* historian. Its Part One appears verbose, in places naïve, and it contains nothing new for a Western scholar familiar with Hitler's period. Its Part Two is equally verbose and contains lengthy passages which appear barely relevant to the subject, such as the story of the Soviet industrial growth, complete with statistics which may or may not prove anything. It is full of statements designed to prove the author's passionate patriotism. And only the last two parts contain information which is new and revealing to Western Sovietologists; it is here that the author takes his controversial stand most prominently and makes his case.

Taken as a whole, however, this is still a product of communist scholarship, containing errors by omission and commission, for the most part politically motivated. Above all, the book is addressed to the Soviet, not foreign, audience, and must be read with this understanding in mind. To the Soviet reader, Part One, for instance, written as it is on the basis of Western primary and secondary sources, *is* very new and very revealing.

June 22, 1941 has caused so much controversy in the Soviet Union only because Nekrich's version of the events described in it and his interpretation of them deviated considerably from the orthodox, partly-approved version, and was too close to that subscribed to by a certain group of Soviet military leaders and wartime intelligence chiefs who had been chafing under the charge that they were responsible for Soviet unpreparedness for the German invasion. More importantly, while aiming his big guns at Stalin—seemingly within the limits of the de-Stalinization policies laid down by the Twentieth Party Congress—Nekrich, in effect, accuses the Soviet government as a whole of being inept, nearsighted, and inefficient in meeting the Nazi menace.

Chronologically, the author limits himself to the period of the Nazi-Soviet partnership, inaugurated during Reichsminister von Ribbentrop's visit to Moscow in August 1939. He does not, however, discuss the background of the Nazi-Soviet Pact and does not go into an analysis of the Soviet-German relations: no Soviet historian has yet touched this politically damning subject. The reader interested in it might profit from reading the Appendix to this volume.

Nekrich states the purpose of his study in his brief introduction and pursues it throughout the book with a fair degree of consistency. His true message, however, is more implicit, for he could not announce that it was really the failure of the Soviet government that he wished to expose. This message was nevertheless detected by the readers of *June 22, 1941* in the Soviet Union, including the party hierarchs who judged the book heretical and politically damaging to the interests of the regime. It is in this context that the book should be read and appreciated.

In his Part One, Nekrich develops his major premise that Hitler had always been committed to the idea of Germany's territorial expansion in the east and that he had always been implacably hostile to the Soviet state. He needs to prove this thesis in order to strengthen his implicit contention that the Soviet government's decision in the summer of 1939 to join the Nazis in a common venture did not take Hitler's underlying hostility sufficiently into account, and that the resulting policies which governed the Soviet Union's attitudes towards the Third Reich were erroneous. Nekrich's rambling talk of Hitler's villainy contains little new to a Western reader; like many Western historians, he sees in *Mein Kampf*, published in 1926, Hitler's program for conquest from which he never deviated.

Although hindsight seems to confirm this, I consider such a supposition debatable; at the very least, the subject deserves a more critical and detached study. The evidence presented by Nekrich is vast but in places it is contradictory and at times doctored. For example, referring to Hitler's speech before the principal military commanders of the Reich on November 23, 1939, Nekrich translates one sentence as follows: "We can move against Russia only when we are free in the West," i.e., after defeating France and Great Britain. In fact, Hitler said "We can *oppose* Russia only when we are free in the West," adding that Russia was of no danger to Germany so long as Stalin was alive because its interests were elsewhere (in the Balkans and in the direction of the Persian Gulf) and because its communist internationalism "has retired to the background." There was no hint in this discourse that Hitler thought of a conquest of Russia.

Hitler started talking about the Eastern campaign only after the defeat of France. But even then, as Nekrich himself does not fail to show, Hitler viewed it as an auxiliary operation aimed at discouraging England from further resistance and at preventing a formation, at some future date, of a British-Soviet-American alliance; it was not a question of securing a *Lebensraum* for the German race or freeing mankind from the Communist Peril. Hitler's peroration at the Berghof conference leaves no doubt on this score.

It is true that contingency plans for the Eastern campaign were developed in the German General Staff in the following months. But then there was a plan for invasion of England which was never carried out; there were plans for invading Spain and French Morocco, and even plans of sorts for the conquest of Turkey, Syria, the Suez Canal, and even of Afghanistan and India. For a long time Hitler could not make up his mind what should come first. On the eve of Molotov's visit to Berlin in November 1940 he ordered preparations for the invasion of England "in the spring of 1941" to be resumed—something that simply could not be carried out if the Soviet Union was to be attacked in May of the same year, as Hitler specified in his Directive No. 21, dated December 18, 1940.

The actual merits of the case Nekrich is trying to present against

Hitler notwithstanding, we must note that he does not take full advantage of all the materials at his disposal. Since his main purpose is to show the gullibility of Stalin and his associates in dealing with the Nazis, he could have found a great deal of ammunition in the records of Molotov's conversations in Berlin. The titular head of the Soviet government was unquestionably in his best form as he discussed with Hitler and Ribbentrop the terms of the formal association of the Soviet Union with the Axis powers, and much of what he said could have strengthened Nekrich's argument. To utilize this information, however, would have meant to go beyond the limits set for de-Stalinization at the Twentieth Party Congress. To Molotov's talks in Berlin—which, in all likelihood, were decisive in firming Hitler's intent to attack the Soviet Union—Nekrich devotes less than a paragraph. He is silent about the terms which Molotov presented as the Soviet price for joining the Axis, and he falsely states that the Soviet government "turned down the German proposals." In fact, it was the other way around.

Nekrich's super-patriotism handicaps his efforts to prove Stalin's lack of vigilance in other ways. For example, he enthusiastically approves all the steps which Stalin took in order to aggrandize the Soviet Union after the conclusion of the Nazi-Soviet Pact. He barely mentions that it was this deal that permitted the Soviet Union to "liberate" forty percent of Poland's territory; he ignores completely the plight of the Polish state as he talks about the "liberated Western Ukraine and Byelorussia" and the presumed strengthening of the Soviet strategic position through this expansion. Bessarabia, to him, was simply "returned" to the Soviet Union. Northern Bukovina "became part of the USSR" because its people had presumably "taken a decision to reunite with the Soviet Ukraine as early as November 1918." To take this province from Romania also seemed justifiable because this country had become a "cruel dictatorship." The Baltic states of Estonia, Latvia, and Lithuania were, according to Nekrich, converted into Soviet republics because such was the wish of their toiling masses, alarmed as they were by the anti-Soviet schemings of their reactionary rulers. But then it could be asked, that, if things were going so well for the Soviet Union during the years of friendship with Germany, was not Stalin justified in valuing this friendship and behaving loyally towards Hitler? Deeply suspicious as he was, he could not mistrust both Germany and Great Britain with the same intensity, and he had hated the Western democracies for too long to be able to change his opinion of them. In addition, he was firmly convinced that the German General Staff feared a prospect of a two-front war above anything else, and he was sure that Hitler needed Soviet benevolence as long as Great Britain, backed by the United States, continued to fight. As to the evil plans of Hitler to invade Russia Nekrich talks so much about, Stalin had no knowledge of them. The real drama was that when, in the spring of 1941, Stalin began to receive information that something ominous was brewing, it turned out to be psychologically difficult, if not altogether impossible, for him to readjust his thinking and admit that he had placed his bet on the wrong horse.

Unlike other super-patriotic Soviet historians, Nekrich appears to trust, and justify, Churchill's policies and motives. Although he condemns Daladier, Neville Chamberlain does not appear in too bad a light, even in conjunction with the Winter War with Finland in which British sympathies were on the side of the Finns. On the subject of the Winter War itself, Nekrich's feelings appear mixed. On the one hand, it was necessary in order to "strengthen the security of the Soviet state." On the other, he calls it a "sad episode . . . particularly since Finland had obtained its independence thanks to the Great October Revolution," which, of course, is not quite true but then Nekrich probably had not read any but the official Soviet version of Finland's history. Be that as it may, he assumes that the Finns should have adjusted to the losses of territory resulting from the Winter War: he condemns the Finnish "fascist-leaning circles" for aligning later with Germany in pursuit of their "revanchist" plans.

Nekrich devotes his Part Two to the issue of Soviet unpreparedness for war. He gives due credit to the "gigantic organizational work of the Communist Party" and to the deep-seated patriotism and unity of the peoples inhabiting the Soviet Union, which were so much underestimated by Hitler. He devotes a great deal of space to a discussion of the growth of industrial production in Russia in the prewar years. And it is at this point that he makes his first critical comment about Stalin by saying that "the economy of the Soviet state could have developed faster still and achieved an even higher level by the time the war started, if the situation in the country had not been adversely influenced by the cult of personality and, in connection with it, by the mass, baseless repressions conducted by J. V. Stalin against party and Soviet officials." He goes on, describing —not without eloquence—Stalin's purges and their effect on industrial production, the atmosphere of suspicion and "spy-mania" in which "unprincipled careerists" advanced their fortunes by denouncing good and competent officials and technicians to the NKVD witch-hunters. Nekrich also cites instances of Stalin's personal interference in the production of vital weapons, which resulted in inadequate equipment of the Red Army on the eve of the war.

As Nekrich progresses, the "cult of personality," broadly understood, strongly emerges as the major factor in Soviet military and political weakness. He criticizes Soviet military doctrine which, on the assumption that in case of a war the working masses of capitalist countries would render the Red Army their wholehearted support, excluded the possibility of military operations on Soviet territory. This rejection of the idea of having an alternative defensive strategy apparently led Stalin and his advisers to a decision to dismantle the fortifications along the old Soviet-Polish border. Nekrich also laments the construction of military airfields and the location of the major army warehouses too close to the new frontier, another mistake for which he holds Stalin personally responsible.

In considerable detail Nekrich probes into the bloody purge of the Red Army commanders in 1937–38, which left the armed forces without competent leadership in the time of crisis. Drawing upon foreign sources, he describes the devilish scheme of the Gestapo to implicate top Soviet marshals and generals, a scheme in which Stalin knowingly concurred in his drive to crush this last pocket of resistance to his absolute rule. Nekrich's revelations are unique in Soviet historical writings and nothing short of sensational to a Soviet reader.

Also novel is Nekrich's treatment of the attitudes of Great Britain and the United States towards the Soviet Union. Unlike the more conventional communist historians, he does not accuse these countries of scheming to launch, in alliance with Hitler, a holy crusade against the motherland of socialism. He finds understandable Churchill's desire, in the spring of 1941, to see the Soviet Union embroiled with Nazi Germany and, again, unlike the others, he does not question the sincerity of Churchill's motives in his warnings to Moscow of the impending German attack.

But it is mainly in the last two chapters of his book that Nekrich becomes truly forceful in his criticism of the Soviet position. He does not say it in so many words, but the implication is strong that whatever excuses Stalin might have had for trusting Hitler earlier, his behavior after the Nazi campaign in the Balkans in April 1941 defied any and all rational explanation. The evidence Nekrich cites, mostly from Soviet sources little known in the West, of Moscow's exhaustive knowledge of the German preparations for the invasion, is overwhelming. He seems to be saying that even at this late hour a great deal could have been accomplished in organizing resistance to the invader, if only Stalin and those around him had been manly enough to recognize their errors in judgment and strong enough to make the necessary decisions. Nekrich implies what some Western observers have suggested all along, namely that after the German blitzkrieg in the Balkans Stalin did realize that the Soviet Union would be the next target but that he was paralyzed with fear and could think of nothing else but to search for ways of placating Hitler, vainly hoping that this would avert the catastrophe. Read along these lines, *June 22, 1941* represents the most powerful indictment of Stalin's leadership yet in the eyes of the Soviet people, containing a drama by far surpassing the experience of any other nation in the Second World War. Little wonder that Stalin's heirs reacted the way they did in suppressing the book and punishing its author.

JUNE 22, 1941

By A. M. Nekrich

Translated by
Vladimir Petrov

From the Author

We are rightfully proud of the great victory achieved by the Soviet people in the Great Patriotic War over Hitler's Germany. This victory was gained in cruel, bloody battles. The enemy was strong, experienced, and cunning. To destroy him our nation had to exert its whole strength, mobilize all its resources, and bear up under four years of difficult trials. The Soviet people carried on its shoulders the main burden of the struggle with the German fascist aggressor. The most cruel of wars ever waged by people on earth was won by us.

It is easier and simpler to speak of victories. To describe the flash of a solemn salute in honor of battles won is, of course, more pleasant than the bitter sorrow of defeats. To tell of the last day of the war is a more rewarding task than to tell of the first day. The war, that greatest of tragedies, not only had a brilliant ending but a difficult beginning as well. A historian who has taken on the task of studying the war is obliged to remember not only the way it ended but how it started. These events are inseparably connected; they cannot be separated. The reasons which led to the defeats of the initial period of the war must not be passed over quickly because such an approach not only damages historical truth, not only minimizes the heroism shown by Soviet soldiers in the initial period of the war and the grandeur of our victory in the war, which began under such extraordinarily unfavorable circumstances, but also objectively harms the interests of our state, leading to incorrect conclusions from the lessons taught us by history.

There is only one truth. And with grim straightforwardness the Communist Party of the Soviet Union told the Soviet people about this when it condemned, at the Twentieth and Twenty-second Party Congresses, the serious mistakes created by the cult of personality of Stalin.[1]

This book is concerned with the events on the eve of the Great Patriotic War. In preparing the manuscript, the author used not only materials published in our country and abroad but also valuable information derived by him from conversations with direct participants in these events.

The author expresses deep gratitude to Marshal of the Soviet Union F. I. Golikov, Professor N. N. Ivanov, Major General I. A. Susloparov, and Colonel G. P. Sechkin, who shared their recollections with the author.

Contents

June 22, 1941

Sunday   Noon   and suddenly:
*"ALL THE RADIO STATIONS OF THE SOVIET UNION
ARE SPEAKING. . . ."*

. . . The familiar world with its ordinary joys and sorrows suddenly fell apart. War tore in and caught millions of human lives in its whirlpool. Hitler's Germany perfidiously attacked the Soviet Union.

Part One—Preparation for Attack

"We Are Starting Where We Stopped Six Centuries Ago"

The noise of motors filled the streets of the little town of Bastogne, in the Ardennes. Raising clouds of dust, a column of cars painted in a dirty brownish-greenish camouflage color hurried by. The column halted on the square, which was full of soldiers. The submachine-gunners stood paralyzed in dead silence. Officers and generals, adjusting their uniforms on the run, rushed out of the doors of houses and froze in respectful salute. The Fuehrer himself, Adolf Hitler, had arrived at the headquarters of Colonel General von Rundstedt, the commander of the German Army Group "A." It was the seventh day of the German offensive on the Western Front.

On May 10, 1940, the German fascist armies had initiated their carefully prepared offensive in the West. In the course of the first week's fighting they were able to cut through Allied armies, force the Meuse, and emerge onto French territory in a broad front. Deprived of strategic leadership, losing communications and order, the French, Belgian, and British troops retreated. The roads were clogged with refugees. German dive bombers, with their screaming sirens turned on, swooped down to the earth, sowing terror and death.

In these days the fascist chieftain, drunk with the success of the German armies in Flanders and in France, returned once more to the idea of attacking the Soviet Union. Peace with England was supposed to make it possible to wage war on one front only, the Eastern Front. And it was about this that Hitler spoke on May 17, 1940, at Rundstedt's headquarters. Almost five years later, in February 1945, Hitler admitted to one of his closest assistants, Martin Bormann: "My goal was to try to reach an agreement with England to avoid the creation of an irreparable situation in the West. I always insisted that we must at all costs avoid a war on two fronts." [1] But in the summer of 1940 the military successes of Hitler's Germany seemed absolutely fantastic. Nobody, after all, had foreseen such a rapid and complete defeat of France and the other countries of Western Europe. This development was also unexpected for the highest political leaders: for Churchill in England, for Roosevelt in the United States. And it was not foreseen by J. V. Stalin either. The staggering successes of the fascist Wehrmacht were the base— not a solid one, it is true, as subsequent events showed—on which the fascist chieftains and their generals began to build new plans and calculations of conquest. It is no coincidence that the plan of attack on the Soviet Union was reborn in the fourth week in May, at a moment when the destruction of the French armies and the British expeditionary forces seemed foredoomed. Fate, in which the Nazi leaders so much believed, appeared to favor their plans. The fascist chieftains suspected least of all that fate would play the same evil joke on them as it did on Macbeth in his time. And here "Birnam wood be come to Dunsinane"!

Hitler and his closest collaborators, plotting war against the Soviet Union, began to seek out arguments which would justify the new, unprovoked German aggression in the eyes of the German people and world public opinion. After all, Germany had signed a nonaggression pact with the USSR in August 1939, and a treaty of friendship in September of the same year. It was essential to create a legend of "preventative war," as if Germany were being forced to attack the Soviet Union to prevent an

38

attack by the Soviet Union on Germany. Such a legend was necessary at least for the initial period; conquerors are not judged. Preventative war was the argument eagerly used by the Prussian militarists at the time of the Silesian wars, at the time of the Franco-Prussian War and the First World War, and in the attack on Poland in 1939. Why not use this tested remedy once again? Human memory is so imperfect, after all. It is striking that the myth of preventative war, created by Hitler, and resurrected by the German war criminals and their defenders at the Nuremberg trials and the subsequent trials of the German generals, is still alive in our time. More exactly, there are West German nationalists and some reactionary West German publicists and historians who are artificially maintaining this legend. Not so long ago, in 1961, Fabri's book on German-Soviet relations from 1939 through 1941 was published, in which he tries to make this lie believable. The political purpose of such speculations in our time is clear: it is to justify the arming of West Germany with modern weapons, above all nuclear ones, supposedly to counter the "threat from the East."

In the 1920's the German fascists had already taken into their arsenal the "theories" of the pan-Germanists, their plans of "Middle Europe," i.e., the absolute predominance of Germany, surrounded by satellite countries. The fascists also remembered the age-old dream of German militarists about a march against the East, "Drang nach Osten," which would furnish the German people with "living space" and would establish for centuries the mastery of the German race in Europe.

In the 1920's Adolf Hitler, serving time in the Landsberg prison for an unsuccessful attempt to seize power in Bavaria, recorded his political plans in a manuscript published in 1926 under the title of *Mein Kampf* (*My Battle*). The foreign policy of Imperial Germany and the policy of the Weimar Republic, wrote Hitler, must be rejected. The borders of 1914 could no longer satisfy Germany. Only the conquest of "living space" could ensure the flourishing of Germany. Only the Germans—the "highest race," or supermen—could be the "nation of masters." Only war could bring prosperity to the German people.

"We National Socialists," wrote Hitler, "are consciously turning away from the direction of foreign policy in the prewar period. We are starting where we stopped six centuries ago. We have finished with the eternal German striving toward the south and west of Europe and we are directing our gaze at the lands to the east. . . . But when we speak today of new lands in Europe, we can have in mind, first of all, Russia and its subordinate border states."

In this book, which after a few years became the bible of German imperialism, Hitler emphasized again and again that the future of Germany can be secured "wholly and in full only at Russia's expense." In giving a basis for the pretensions of German imperialism, Hitler insolently asserted that the only constructive element in Russian history was . . . Germans! "For centuries Russia lived precisely on account of the German core of the highest levels of its society," preached the mad racist.

In the first years after the publication of *Mein Kampf,* few people outside Germany proper were familiar with this misanthropic book. Even in Germany only a small circle of people—Hitler's followers—read it. But even those who at that time had become familiar with the contents of Hitler's book did not take it seriously and considered that the plans of world conquest expounded in its 750 pages were mere demagoguery.

A few years ago American historians found among captured German materials a manuscript discussing the foreign policy of Germany. After careful expert study it was established that the manuscript belonged to Hitler and was written by him in 1928, apparently with the help of his secretary at that time, Rudolf Hess. Published in 1961 under the title *Hitler's Second Book*, the manuscript contains a considerable number of "revelations" which prove that Hitler viewed as the principal task of German foreign policy the destruction of the USSR and the conquest of its territory. "One should search for the goal of German foreign policy," he wrote, "in the only place where it can exist: [the conquest] of territory in the East." In this book Hitler also shamelessly repeats the lie that everything positive which exists in Russia was created by foreigners, principally by Germans. By these declarations Hitler wanted to strengthen the German-fascist policy of aggression ideologically and to create, in the eyes of the German people, an idea of legality in regard to German claims to Soviet lands. These seemingly senseless assertions were not just the ravings of a maniac. They concealed a venom with which the Hitlerites were able, in succeeding years, to poison gradually the consciousness of hundreds of thousands, millions, of Germans and then lead them on the path to bloody crimes.

The Second Book appeared recently, but the "ideas" contained in it had been repeated thousands of times by fascist propagandists.

Not long after Hitler's seizure of power, some of his closest comrades-in-arms, such as, for instance, the chairman of the Danzig Senate, Hermann Rauschning, and Hitler's rival, Otto Strasser, who aspired to the role of leader of the fascists, men who had abandoned their Fuehrer at various times and for various reasons and fled abroad, came out with exposés. Rauschning and Strasser published articles and books which became widely known throughout the world and, it would seem, should have left no doubts that Hitler's plans consisted of establishing the world mastery of the German race and of the merciless destruction or enslavement of other peoples. One of his main goals was war against the USSR, the destruction of the Soviet state. "Soviet Russia," Hitler told Rauschning, "is, as a revolutionary socialist state, the enemy of the National Socialist order, but there is something more. As a great territorial formation, Russia is a constant threat to Europe. The principle of self-determination also applies to Russia. The Russian problem can be solved only in concord with European, that is German, ideas. Not only Russian border territories, but all of Russia must be dismembered to its component parts. These components are the natural imperial territory of Germany." [2] Thus spoke Hitler not long before coming to power. At that time the staff of the principal fascist "specialist" on agricultural questions, the future Minister of Agriculture, Darre, prepared a report about German policy in the East in which, with the insolence characteristic of German fascists, there was an enumeration of benefits awaiting the Third Reich after the "eastern territories" were joined to it. According to the plan presented by Darre, the Baltic states, the Ukraine, and the "Caucasian states" were to be part of Germany. On these lands the domination of the "German elite" was to be established. Darre's plan was discussed in a narrow circle of fascist leaders. Approving the plan, Hitler remarked: "Here, in the East, is our great field for experiments." About these "experiments" Darre's plan contained the following: "A country inhabited by an alien race must become a country of slaves, agricultural or industrial laborers." [3]

Thus, Hitler's plans for the enslavement of the peoples of the USSR, the dismemberment of the territory of the Soviet state and its merciless exploitation, were widely enough known.

In the years that followed, hatred for the Soviet Union and "anticommunism" became the distinctive feature of German policy and propaganda. In August 1939, trying to rid himself of the danger of a two-front war, Hitler proposed a nonaggression pact to the Soviet Union. But Hitler viewed the pact only as a deft diplomatic maneuver. In the eyes of the fascists, treaties were only "scraps of paper" and served Hitler's Germany as a camouflage for her aggressive plans. In one of his rather rare letters (the Fuehrer did not like to write letters), dated December 1932 and addressed to Colonel von Reichenau, one of the future leading commanders of the armies of the fascist Wehrmacht, Hitler wrote: "Treaties can be concluded only between partners who stand on one ideological platform. . . . The political cooperation of Germany with Russia provokes the whole world unpleasantly." [4]

These words are the key to an understanding of Hitler's political calculations after his coming to power. Anticommunism was the trump that Hitler would use to strengthen the foreign policy position of his regime. Anticommunism was the weapon which he employed against his political enemies within the country. Anticommunism was the lure with the help of which he hoped to ensure for himself the support of the ruling circles of England, France, and the United States. It should be admitted that, using anticommunism, Hitler achieved much in the field of foreign policy, forcing these powers to surrender to him, without battle, Austria and Czechoslovakia, and to give Germany the opportunity to arm openly, to prepare for the unleashing of a war of world domination. Skillfully playing on German dissatisfaction with the terms of the Versailles Peace Treaty, he achieved support within the country.

The war started. Poland fell. On October 18, 1939, the chief of the general staff of the German ground forces, Colonel General Halder, noted in his diary Hitler's words: "Poland is a region for future German operations." [5] Against whom?

43

Hitler's speech at the generals' conference on November 23, 1939, can serve as the answer to this question: "We can move against Russia only when we are free in the West."

Peace with England!

Let us return to the events of the summer of 1940. At that time the thing that worried the German fascist leadership most of all was the possibility of an agreement between England and the Soviet Union. The nightmare of a Soviet-British coalition had constantly pursued Hitler since the beginning of the campaign in the West. Manifestations of this concern could be detected in literally all of Hitler's appearances before the headquarters of Army Group "A" in May and June 1940. Colonel General Halder several times noted this worry of Hitler in his service diary. On June 2, 1940, Hitler was already stating categorically that "Now, that England is ready for peace, he would settle his accounts with the Bolsheviks." [6] Hitler's statements about his intentions to wage war against the Soviet Union were welcomed by the German generals. During June and July 1940, the decision to attack the USSR continued to mature. We learn from Halder's diary that England's unwillingness to discuss peace with Germany was viewed by the Nazi leadership as an expression of British hopes on the Soviet Union. At the end of June 1940, Colonel General Halder flew to Berlin to celebrate his birthday. There he met with his friend State Secretary of the German Ministry of Foreign Affairs Weizsaecker, an extremely well-informed diplomat. Weizsaecker gave Halder to understand that a decision to attack the Soviet Union was maturing in the highest German circles. On July 22, in a long speech at the headquarters of the commander of ground forces, von Brauchitsch, Hitler returned over and over again to the subject of Russia and England, and observed that both were disposed to gravitate towards each other.[7]

On the threshold of its attack on the USSR, Hitler's Germany was seeking methods by which it could achieve a complete political and diplomatic isolation of the Soviet Union. Getting England out of the war by any methods—military or nonmilitary—was the most important part of this plan.

Within the space of a year, from May 1940 until May 1941, Hitler's Germany did not lose hope of achieving the conclusion of a compromise peace with England. This hope was combined with military measures: preparations for the invasion of the British Isles and the accompanying aerial "Battle of Britain" were continued; operations in the Mediterranean Sea area and in Africa were actively carried out; attempts to blockade the British Isles, to cut England's sea communications, did not cease. The Nazis made wide use of all possible political and diplomatic channels. The fascist ruling group also hoped to gain the support of influential anti-Soviet circles in England and convince them, as was done at Munich in 1938, that war against the USSR was also in the basic interests of English capitalism. For this reason England should not interfere with Germany's implementation of a march to the East. Naturally, the Hitlerites masked in every way their intention of falling on England again, after the completion of the "Eastern Expedition," and forcing her into unconditional surrender. In working toward their purpose, the Hitlerites carefully collected information about the moods of the British ruling circles and used every opportunity for establishing contacts with England. There were many such attempts in 1940–41.

On June 11, 1940, at a moment when the defeat of France was no longer in doubt, Hitler granted an interview to the fascist journalist Karl von Wiegand to announce to the world that he, Hitler, had no intention of undertaking any hostile actions toward the Western Hemisphere, i.e., against the United States of America, that he did not desire the destruction of the British Empire but merely insisted on the removal of the "warmonger Churchill" from the post of British prime minister. This interview became sort of a program of activities for German diplomacy for the year following. A week later Hitler's minister of foreign affairs, Ribbentrop, confidentially informed the Italian minister of foreign affairs, Ciano, that England only had to recognize as an accomplished fact the establishment of German domination on the European continent and renounce certain of her colonial possessions. On these conditions, Ribbentrop emphasized, England could receive peace immediately; but if she refused the German offer, she would be destroyed.

The German proposals, as the Nazis had expected, were transmitted to London before the beginning of Franco-German peace talks. On June 22, 1940, in the Compiègne forest, in the same railroad coach in which Marshal Foch had once dictated armistice terms to a defeated Germany, defeated France signed a Franco-German armistice. Counting on achieving peace with England and persuading France to become an active collaborator of Germany in the "New Europe," Hitler decided not to lay down overly rough conditions: the colonies remained in French hands; the fleet was liable only to disarmament, and its personnel to demobilization.

The British answer turned out to be a completely unexpected one to the Nazi ruling group. On July 3, by order of Churchill, British forces attacked the French naval vessels in Oran, Alexandria, and Dakar. French ships in English ports were seized. England decided to ensure herself against the unpleasant and dangerous prospect of a seizure of the French fleet by the Germans, or its use in the war against England with the consent of Marshal Petain's defeatist French government.

The "answer" of the British threw Hitler into anger and confusion. However, the "peace offensive" continued. On July 19 Hitler delivered a long anti-British speech at a session of the Reichstag. But he finished it with an offer to England to conclude peace.[8] On the same day the founder and head of the Dutch aviation company KLM, Alfred Plesman, arrived in the capital of the fascist Reich. He came at the invitation of Reichsmarshal Goering. Although ostensibly the idea of such a meeting seemed to be Plesman's, its actual initiator was Hermann Goering. An experienced and crafty politician, even now, under wartime conditions, he tried to show himself off as a "man of peace" who was trying to obtain an agreement between Western powers. In spite of the fact that on July 22 the British minister of foreign affairs, Lord Halifax, had rejected Hitler's proposal in the name of his government, the discussion of "peace terms" between Plesman and Goering continued. At the conference of July 24 conditions were formulated by which, in Goering's opinion, England and Germany could come to an agreement. These conditions were summarized by Plesman in a confirming memorandum dated July 30: Germany insisted only on the return of its former colonies, lost as a result of the First World War. Germany "magnanimously" agreed not to demand the surrender of the British fleet. However, even these "peace terms" demanded from England the recognition of German hegemony in Europe, i.e., just what England did not recognize, did not want to, and could not recognize. The camouflage of the Nazis' real intentions looked clumsy: Poland and Czechoslovakia supposedly were not being deprived of "national development," but the rule remained in German hands and the intervention of other countries in other affairs was not allowed. Norway, Denmark, the Netherlands, Belgium, and France were supposedly free in the selection of their forms of government and administration, but this "choice" had to ensure their collaboration with Germany. In practice this meant the recognition of German domination in Europe. The British government did not allow Plesman to come to London. Plesman's proposals, delivered by him through the Dutch minister in Stockholm, were rejected after study by the British ministry of foreign affairs.

However, the German efforts to force England to capitulate (and a compromise peace under the conditions of German domination over Western Europe in practice meant capitulation for England) continued. At the same time the German air force stepped up its devastating air raids on the British Isles in order to crush the British will to resist, thus clearing the way for invasion.

"Plan Barbarossa"

The aerial bombardments of England and the already begun preparations for the invasion of the British Isles did not interfere with the Hitlerite military-political leadership's discussions concerning the possibility of attacking the Soviet Union.

From the end of May to the end of July 1940, there was a lively exchange of opinion in the highest German military circles about the timing and the means with which to start a war against the Soviet Union. The chiefs of the high command of the armed forces and the commanders of the basic branches of the armed forces—ground forces, navy, and air force—took part in these discussions. Nobody had any objections in principle to war against the USSR. The German militarists had long dreamed of destroying the socialist state. Now Germany was at the zenith of her military glory. It seemed that the most suitable moment had arrived. There were also considerations of a more practical character. The command of the naval forces agreed to the invasion of England with extreme reluctance, realizing that the navy was not in condition to ensure landings in force on the British shores and that the attempt in itself could lead to the total destruction of the German navy. For this reason the naval command, in the person of Admiral Raeder, was ready to support any operation which would not place the German navy in mortal danger. Two months passed in conferences and discussions of plans for invading England and preliminary drafts of the plan of attack on the USSR.

On July 3, 1940, Halder wrote in his diary: "The first order of business is the English problem, which must be worked out separately, and the Eastern problem. The basic contents of the latter are: how to deliver a decisive blow at Russia to force her to recognize the dominant role of Germany in Europe." [9]

On July 13, 1940, at a conference in Berghof, Hitler emphasized several times that "England still has hopes in regard to the Soviet Union and for this reason is not capitulating." He considered that England would have to be compelled by force to make peace. Yet Hitler approached this somewhat reluctantly. The reason: "If we smash England militarily, the whole British Empire will fall apart. However, Germany will gain nothing by this. The defeat of England will be achieved at the price of German blood, but the fruits will be gathered by Japan, America, and others." [10] Whether he really thought this way or was searching for arguments to explain his coming cancellation of the invasion of England, is hard to say. However in mid-July a group of German General Staff operations officers began to work out a war plan against the Soviet Union.

By order of the high command, intelligence work against the

USSR was intensified. About this there is a vague reference in Halder's diary in the entry of July 18, 1940: "Koestring [the German military attaché in Moscow—A.N.] has carried out the mission given to him in regard to Russia." [11]

On July 22 there was another conference in the headquarters of the high command of the German armed forces. Hitler's position was not clear.

On the one hand, he insisted that the "preparations for invasion must be carried out as fast as possible." On the other, the central theme of his speeches more and more often became the Soviet Union.

"England is trying, apparently with the help of Russia, to create disorders in the Balkans for the purpose of depriving us of sources of fuel, thereby paralyzing our aviation. The Russian question will be solved by an offensive. We must think through the plan of the coming operation." [12] And the generals were presenting this plan. What a contrast between the lying statements of Keitel and Jodl at the Nuremberg trials, that they had come out against the attack on the USSR, and that the planning for it had started only in the fall of 1940, and the information known to us from Halder's service diary!

At the conference of the high command, with Hitler participating, the commander-in-chief of the German ground forces, Brauchitsch, reported the practical calculations of the General Staff regarding war with the Soviet Union. The opinion of the high command of ground forces was extraordinarily optimistic. Germany would need only four to six weeks and not more than one hundred divisions to smash the fifty to seventy Russian divisions which were combat-ready, stated Brauchitsch.

The basic objectives of the attack are also named in Halder's record of the July 22 conference, namely: "To smash the Russian ground army or at least to occupy enough territory to protect Berlin and the Silesian industrial area against Russian air raids. It is desirable to penetrate Russia far enough so that our aviation could destroy the most important centers of Russia." At this same conference the most immediate political aims, providing for the dismemberment of the Soviet Union, were also mentioned. The record speaks of the creation of a "Ukrainian State," a union of the Baltic states, and mentions Byelorussia.

Brauchitsch thought that the war against the USSR could be started as early as 1940. Throughout July opinions about the possibility of an immediate attack on the Soviet Union were rather widespread in the highest German military circles.

The assistant chief of staff for operations of the high command, Jodl, declared at a special conference of the leading officials of Section "L": "Hitler has decided at the closest possible time, which means May 1941, 'once and for all' to rid the world of the threat of Bolshevism by a surprise attack on the Soviet Union." [13] The planning of the operation had to be started immediately. Such a change of plans was too unexpected for the officers of the operational branch, who were busy preparing the operation against England, and Warlimont even asked Jodl whether he had heard correctly. Questions were heard: What about the war against England? Aren't there good relations with the USSR? And won't all this lead to a two-front war? The answer was brief but expressive: "Gentlemen, this is not a subject for discussion, but a decision of the Fuehrer." [14]

One of the military arguments brought forth by Jodl was that Germany, in the present state of its armed forces (especially in naval power) was in no condition to overwhelm England. The defeat of the Soviet Union would deprive England of her last hope, and she would capitulate. Jodl also presented another

51

argument: after victory against England the mood of the people would be such that it would probably not be possible to venture on a new war—a war against the Soviet Union.

On July 26 Halder wrote in his diary: "Kinzel [chief of the section studying the armies of the East—A.N.] and the fourth chief quartermaster: report on the basic data about the enemy in operations against Russia. From this it is obvious that the most profitable decision is an attack on Moscow (keeping a connection with the Baltic Sea), after which a bypassing to the north of the Russian groupings in the Ukraine and the shores of the Black Sea would force them to fight with a reversed front." [15]

War against the USSR was in fact already decided; the announcement about this was made by Hitler at the Berghof conference of July 31, 1940. At this conference Hitler connected the question of victory over England and the whole further course of the war with the problem of relations between England and the Soviet Union. Above all he was afraid of an alliance between the two countries. In order to conquer England it was essential to smash the Soviet Union. "If Russia is beaten, England will be deprived of its last hope," Hitler stated in Berghof, "Then Germany will dominate Europe and the Balkans."

But England was not the only matter at hand. The defeat of the Soviet Union, Hitler declared, would decisively affect the position of the United States of America. "If hopes regarding Russia disappear, America will also fall away from England, since the consequence of Russia's defeat would be an unbelievable strengthening of Japan and Eastern Asia."

Thus Hitler was constantly dominated by the fear of the possible creation of an anti-German coalition between England, the Soviet Union, and the United States of America. In order to prevent this it was necessary first of all to knock out the most important of the potential participants, the Soviet Union. These were the main reasons why Germany had to attack the USSR. "Conclusion: on the basis of this reasoning Russia must be liquidated. Deadline—the spring of 1941." [16] And Halder underlines these words in his diary.

The rest of the operations of the German armed forces from then on became secondary, although some of them still had independent significance.

In the summer of 1940, the high command of the German armed forces initiated widespread activity to prepare troops designated for war against the USSR. The German command now intended to assemble 180 divisions. The railroad net was improved in order to transfer these divisions eastward. Old roads were repaired in Poland and new ones were put in; military constructions were erected, lines of communications established. Prisoner-of-war camps were also constructed.

During the height of the preliminary discussions of operational plans against the USSR, the transfer of German divisions to Poland had already been initiated.

To wage war against the USSR, the German command formed seventy-four new divisions, including ten armored and eight motorized divisions. [17]

In the winter of 1940–41 and the spring of 1941, officers of various ranks underwent special training, during which the experience of the past campaigns was studied. But this experience was not perceived critically. The idea of the superiority of German arms predominated everything else. The German generals carefully studied reports and memoirs about Napoleon's invasion of Russia. All information about the Red Army, the defensive capabilities of the USSR, and the attitudes of the population in various parts of the USSR was collected and analyzed.

The well-known American journalist Maurice Hindus relates:

53

"The Nazis always gathered information from anyone who had even the slightest personal contact with the country or the people . . . the subject which always interested them was the morale of the people and whether or not there would be an uprising in case of war." Hindus further writes about the enormous amount of information about the Soviet Union which was accumulated in Hitlerite Germany. The Nazis used information which they "gathered from unsuspecting persons who visited the Soviet Union, particularly from American correspondents." [18] Not a single event of any importance in the life of the Soviet Union escaped the attention of the Hitlerites.

However, the evaluation of intelligence information was not always correct. This is obvious from Halder's diary. The evaluation of the reorganization of the institution of war commissars (strengthening of single command) and the characteristics of the new types of Soviet fighters and long-range bombers was more or less correct; but, together with this information, Halder's diary reflects the German high command's incorrect view of the military capabilities of the Red Army. This underestimation of the Red Army was characteristic of the views of military circles in capitalist countries, including the German generals. The military attaché in Moscow, General Koestring, thought that the Red Army would need four years to complete its preparations for war.[19] Koestring's assistant Krebs went beyond his chief, insisting that "Russia would need twenty years before she would reach her former stature." [20]

Preparations for the attack on the USSR developed at full pace. The peculiarities of these preparations, in the words of the well-known Soviet military historian D. M. Proektor were: "The absence of any critical perception of their own previous experience; excessive self-praise; false concepts ('the superiority of the command,' 'the superiority of the German soldier') which somehow materialized and were considered an additional factor ensuring victory; the preparation on the operational level was carried out systematically, thoroughly, and from all aspects; the care, thought, and deliberation of these measured and 'scientific' preparations once again show that the German militarists did not fear an invasion from any side, and that the thesis of some bourgeois historians about the necessity of a 'preventative war' by Germany against the Soviet Union is only a bluff." [21]

The day after the Berghof conference, August 1, 1940, General E. Marx presented a variant of the plan of operations against the USSR to Halder. The plan provided for the creation of two large groupings of the German army—against Kiev and against Moscow. After acquainting himself with the plan, Halder emphasized that the main thrust must be aimed at Moscow.

On August 14 Goering instructed the chief of economics and armaments of the high command, General Thomas, to base military-economic preparations on the fact that the deliveries from the Soviet Union would be discontinued by the spring of 1941.

On August 26 two more German divisions, one of them motorized, were transferred to Poland. General Koestring, was told to inform the Soviet government that this had to do with replacing the older conscript age groups. Ten days later Jodl issued a directive on the necessity of observing strict disguise in the transfer of troops to the borders of the Soviet Union. The directive emphasized: "These troop movements must not create the impression in Russia that we are preparing an attack on the East." [22]

By December 1940 the preparation of the plan of attack on the Soviet Union was completed. Its basis was the principle of lightning-like war.

Hitler's opinion about the possibility of smashing the Soviet

Union in a lightning-like war was shared, supported, and substantiated by the German high command. Thus the plan of attack on the USSR, the initial idea for which had come from Hitler, which was natural in the conditions of a totalitarian regime, actually was the fruit of the intentions and thoughts, not only of the head of the Third Reich, but of the highest Nazi leaders and the German generals.

On December 5 at a conference with Hitler, the high command of ground forces (Brauchitsch and Halder) presented the plan of attack on the Soviet Union, encoded as "Plan Otto." The decision was: "Begin preparations at full speed according to the basis of the plan proposed by us. The guiding date for the start of the operation is the end of May [1941]." In connection with this, the plan of invading England ("Sea Lion") was put on ice; the operations in Libya were canceled. But the high command had not yet called off the invasion of Spain ("Plan Felix"), which it intended to implement within a month, and the invasion of Greece ("Plan Marita"), which was set for early March 1941. Soon, however, the necessity to conserve all forces and means for the attack on the USSR forced the high command to postpone the other plans of aggression, with the exception of "Plan Marita."

On December 18 Hitler signed Directive No. 21 regarding the attack on the USSR, worked out by the generals. The directive stated: "The German armed forces must be prepared to shatter Soviet Russia in a quick campaign ['Plan Barbarossa']." [23]

The following mission was put before the German-fascist armies: operating in two main directions, north and south of the Pripyat, to smash and destroy the main forces of the Red Army concentrated in the west; to emerge in the north to Moscow and capture it, and in the south to capture the Ukraine. As a result of the campaign, the Germans were to reach the Archangel-Volga line. And it was thus that the ancient dream of the German militarists, the march to the East and the capture of territories "up to the Urals," was to be achieved. The German fascists considered that the chief industrial centers in the eastern USSR, after the implementation of "Plan Barbarossa," would become accessible to German bombers. As far as the Asiatic part of the USSR was concerned, there Germany was counting on the intervention of her ally Japan.

The missions of the German armies in the war against the USSR were defined in greater detail in a directive of the high command of the German ground forces entitled "About the strategic deployment of forces," issued on January 31, 1941.

The transfer of German forces to Romania with the object of taking the Romanian oil wells under control began in December 1940, and the concentration of German armies in Poland started in February 1941. These measures reached their greatest intensity after the conquest of Greece and Yugoslavia in April and May 1941. Now the states of the fascist "Axis" had established their complete domination in the Balkans. "Plan Barbarossa," originally intended for the middle of May, was postponed because of the campaigns against Yugoslavia and Greece. The new date of attack on the USSR, June 22, was fixed on April 30, 1941. On June 17 this date was definitely confirmed by Hitler.

Hitler's headquarters was established in the Rastenburg area, in East Prussia. Here in the "Wolf's Lair" (how surprisingly accurately, if by chance, was the name of the headquarters encoded) Hitler made himself comfortable.

Military-Economic Preparations

Germany's military and economic preparations for attack on the USSR went through several stages: in the course of the first stage (1933–39) the general rearmament of Hitler's Germany was achieved, a modern army was created, the base for industry, food and raw-material production was enlarged, bridgeheads for the waging of aggressive war were established; in the second stage (1939–40) Germany, having smashed Poland and the Western European states, tested the combat capabilities of its armed forces and secured its rear for the conduct of war against the USSR; in the third stage (summer 1940 to summer 1941) the basic problem in military and economic preparations consisted of mobilization and use of the captured nations' resources for the necessities of the German military economy and in giving the economy itself a greater effectiveness.

At that time Germany completed its preparations of a theater of military operations; it mobilized military and economic resources not only in Germany itself, but in the whole of continental Europe, and implemented the essential military-political and diplomatic measures to create the best possible political and strategic conditions for the waging of war against the Soviet Union.

By the middle of 1941 Germany had established dominion over a wide territory from Narvik to the Bay of Biscay and from the estuary of the Danube to the English Channel. Beginning with 1938, when the German fascists accomplished their Anschluss—i.e., grabbed Austria—the peoples of Czechoslovakia, Albania, Poland, Norway, Denmark, Belgium, Holland, Luxemburg, France, Yugoslavia, and Greece had fallen under the yoke of the German and Italian aggressors.

Hitler cut up and reassembled the map of Europe. After the partition of Czechoslovakia, a "protectorate of Bohemia and Moravia" was created on the Czech lands, and Slovakia was, by orders from Berlin, declared "independent." The Sudeten province of Czechoslovakia and a number of border regions were incorporated into the Reich. After its defeat, Poland too was subjected to dismemberment. Important territories were torn from it and joined to the Reich, including Gdansk * and the Polish seacoast, the Poznan area, and upper Silesia. On the rest of the Polish lands Germany created the so-called Governor-Generalship, centered in Krakow. The territory of the fascist Reich was further enlarged by the annexation of the French provinces of Alsace and Lorraine, the Belgian departments of Eupen and Malmedy and the canton of Saint Vith. Luxemburg and some of the regions of Yugoslavia were completely incorporated into Germany.

The allies of Germany received their share of the loot: Italy annexed, through a personal union, Albania, which it had conquered in April 1939, a significant part of Yugoslavia's Dalmatian coast with its adjacent islands and Kotor on the Montenegrin coast; Hungary got the Transcarpathian Ukraine, Southern Slovakia, and Yugoslav Western Vojvodina. Bulgaria grabbed the Yugoslav and Greek parts of Macedonia, and also Western Thrace. Puppet vassal states were organized in Croatia, Serbia, and Montenegro. A government pleasing to the occupying powers was installed in Greece.

France was divided into two zones, occupied and unoccupied. The unoccupied zone was ruled by a government of collaborationists headed by Marshal Petain, which meekly fulfilled all Berlin's orders. Belgium, Holland, Denmark, and Norway were also under the occupation or control of Germany.

Hitler's Germany controlled a significant part of Europe. Germany, in fact, occupied a territory of 900,000 square kilometers with a population of up to 117 million people.

After the seizure of Czechoslovakia, the military-industrial base of Germany increased by almost 25 percent in the production of infantry and artillery equipment and ammunition and by

* Danzig—V.P.

approximately 20 percent in the production of aircraft, tanks, and prime movers.[24]

The economic consequences of Germany's victories in the West and in Southeastern Europe could not have been predicted by even the boldest estimates of the German military economy's leadership. Into the hands of Germany fell the highly developed industries of European countries such as France, Belgium, Holland, Luxemburg. This allowed Germany to utilize a significant part of her industry for consumer goods production and to maintain a rather high standard of living for the subjects of the Third Reich.

Germany took out of the occupied countries a large proportion of their raw materials and finished goods. Thus there was removed from France 29 percent of the coal produced there, 80 percent of the oil and fuel stores, 74 percent of the iron ore, 51 percent of the steel, rolled metal and pig-iron, 75 percent of the copper, 64 percent of the nickel, 76 percent of the platinum, 40 percent of the bauxite, 75 percent of the aluminum, etc. Of the finished products of French industry, Germany was taking 70 percent of the automobiles, 45 percent of the radio and electrical equipment, 75 percent of the building materials, 79 percent of the ships, 90 percent of the aviation industry's products, and was using 22 percent of the electric power.[25]

With the aid of the occupation authorities, German banks forced the entrepreneurs and banks of other countries to sell them stock at low prices, thus becoming the actual owners of enterprises. For instance, the Yugoslav boron mines were acquired by the Preussische Staatsbank as a result of crooked dealings.

The German monopolies were also imposing their control under the guise of mixed companies. The controlling votes in these belonged to the German stockholders. Thus the well-known

German concern I. G. Farbenindustrie became the owner of 51 percent of the stock of the French company Francolor. The Lorraine steel industry was divided among five German concerns: "Hermann Goering-Werke," Kloeckner, Rechling, Flick, and Stumm.[26]

The leading German banks, Deutsche Bank and Dresdener Bank, acquired control over an important part of Czechoslovakia's economy, directly or through subordinate banks.

Rich loot fell to the concern "Hermann Goering-Werke," which seized: in Austria, the metallurgical concern, Alpine Montangesellschaft; in Czechoslovakia, the arms plants of Skoda and Brno; in Poland, the whole of Silesian heavy industry; in Romania it established control over the factories of Rechitsa, which produced 80 percent of the country's steel, and in France over the iron ore of Lorraine and over many other industrial enterprises in European countries.

The situation with raw materials improved sharply. We will remind the reader that before the start of the war Germany possessed only seven strategic raw materials out of the thirty necessary for war industry. Its raw material reserves were insufficient to carry on a long war. Now, in addition to the large amount of raw materials seized in the occupied countries, the sources of these materials also fell into Germany's hands. Because of the shortness of the military campaigns, the expenditure of Germany's strategic raw materials had turned out to be less than expected. Germany received large supplies of food and liquid fuel. The fascist empire removed lead and zinc from Yugoslavia; bauxite from Hungary, Yugoslavia, and Norway; antimony from Yugoslavia; sulfur and pyrites from Italy and Norway; mercury from Spain; lumber from Poland, the Scandinavian countries, and Southeastern Europe; and oil from Rumania.

In the countries of Western Europe alone, the reserves of raw materials captured by Hitler's Germany (from the start of the war until 1941) amounted to: nonferrous metals, 365,400 tons; pig-iron, 272,000 tons; scrap iron, 1,860,000; rubber and its products, 12,200; chemical products, 164,000 tons, not counting huge stocks of leather and textile raw materials and finished products.[27]

As before, the German economy suffered from the lack of copper and raw rubber.

The conquest of Poland and then the victories in the West enabled the Hitlerite leadership to get hold of free labor. At first these were prisoners-of-war, sent to work in Germany's agriculture and industry, and later foreign workers, hundreds of thousands of whom were herded into slave labor in Germany. In German agriculture alone more than one million persons were used, mainly Polish war prisoners. In this way large numbers of Germans, whom the German army needed so badly, were made available for military service.

Germany became stronger by sequestering state and private property in the occupied countries. Thus, Germany confiscated the entire property of Poland. The occupied countries were subjected to merciless financial exploitation. Germany was receiving sixty billion marks in payments, fines, etc., alone. Germany received important benefits through the clearing system which allowed it to place the entire foreign trade of the occupied and dependent countries under German control by artificially changing the relationship between the Reichsmark and foreign currencies.

The goal of all of Germany's military and economic undertakings in enslaved Europe, i.e., the goal of the "New Order" proclaimed by Hitler, was to place the whole economy of Europe at the service of the greater German empire's needs. Inasmuch as the Germans were proclaimed to be the "Nation of Masters," all other peoples were from now on called upon to serve these new overlords. In addition to the establishment of a many-sided clearing system, the transformation of the captured countries into agrarian and raw-material producing appendages of the Reich was planned and partially accomplished. Industrial production was preserved there insofar as it was necessary for the conduct of the war, and mainly for wartime.

Special military and economic organizations were created for the most efficient exploitation of the riches of the captured nations. Attached to the high command of the armed forces there was a directorate of military economy and industry. As soon as German troops occupied a country, a military-economic agency in the shape of a headquarters, inspection, or *Kommandatura* was immediately created. These institutions exerted full control over the economy of the occupied country. The military-economic staff "Norway" was created on April 27, 1940; a month later a similar staff—"Denmark"—and in June of the same year, the military-industrial inspections "Holland" and "Belgium" came into being. In France, a similarly named military-economic staff had four inspections subordinated to it.[28] By the end of 1940 the "economic space" of Germany already consisted of four million square kilometers with a population of 333 million persons.

In preparing for its attack on the USSR, the German government adopted a number of measures for military and economic preparations. Leaning on the help of collaborationist circles in the occupied and satellite countries, Hitler's Germany forced an important part of the industries of these countries to work for it, with the help of punitive measures and threats of hunger.

In August 1940 the economies of the occupied and satellite countries began to be exploited systematically for the needs of the German economy, especially for the war. In anticipation of the attack on the Soviet Union, the German military planning agencies distributed their orders to the industries of the occupied countries. In Belgium alone the needs of the German armed forces were serviced by half the country's workers and employees, or by more than 900,000 persons. By the end of 1940 the German occupiers had been able to restore Polish industry to two-thirds of its productive capacity.[29]

On October 18, 1940, a decree concerning the second four-year plan was issued. The essence of the plan consisted of carrying out a full militarization of Germany, strengthening its raw material base, and ensuring a further growth of war industry. It happened that in connection with the easy victories in the West there had at first been a curtailment in Germany of some branches of industry, for instance in the production of ammunition, and the level of production continued to decline until the end of 1940. The object of the new four-year plan was to enlarge the scope of military production sharply. In order to realize the established objectives in the interests of large capital, many small enterprises were shut down by legislative means and their equipment and labor force transferred to the big corporations. Germany's economic indicators in the basic branches of industry began to grow at the end of 1940 and the beginning of 1941.

In the occupied countries Germany had seized a steel industry which by the summer of 1941 was producing sixteen million tons of steel. Thus, together with Germany's own industry, the yearly production of steel at the disposal of the Hitlerites reached forty-three million tons.[30]

The production of aluminum grew from 194,000 tons in 1939 to 324,000 tons in 1941, which made it possible to increase the production of airplanes significantly. In 1940–41 the production of airplanes in Germany had grown by 40 percent in comparison with 1938.[31]

The production of coal in Germany and the countries conquered by her grew to 404,000 tons in 1941. This enabled Germany not only to satisfy fully the demands of industry and the needs of the German population, but also to export coal to allied and neutral countries. The stockpiles of liquid fuel consisted of more than 2.5 million tons at the start of 1941.

Beginning with 1940, when the objective of preparing for war against the USSR was, in practice, laid down, military production in Germany grew sharply. In 1941 the average monthly production of artillery and infantry arms comprised (in millions of Reichsmarks) 74.3 (in 1940, 56.4); tanks—32 (in 1940, 14.3); airplanes—371 (in 1940, 345.1).[32] Having subordinated the economy of Europe to herself, fascist Germany had become one of the strongest powers on earth.

The "Twelve Commandments" of the German Fascists

Victory in the war against the USSR, according to the plans of the Hitlerites, was supposed to ensure them indivisible domination of the European continent and fully satisfy Germany's demands in food, raw materials, and labor. Plans for exploiting the territory of the USSR had been outlined in general form by the German fascists before their coming to power, in the 1920's. Their schemes were solidified during the preparations for the attack on the USSR and immediately after the start of the Soviet-German war.

On May 25, 1940, SS Reichsfuehrer Himmler presented to Hitler written considerations concerning the treatment of the local population in the eastern provinces. The "considerations" were approved by Hitler and confirmed by him in the form of a directive. This strictly secret document was shown to the narrowest circle of people immediately connected with the implementation of German policy in the occupied parts of Poland, and also to a few top personages of the Reich, including Hess, Darre, Lammers, and Bormann. As is obvious from other documents of a later period, the topic was a general plan of Germanization of the population of Poland and the Soviet Union, the so-called "Plan Ost." Although the text of the plan itself has not been discovered to this day, it is obvious from documents that have been found that it dealt with the deportation, in the course of thirty years, of thirty-one million people from Poland and the Soviet Union and the settlement of German colonists in their place. The Slavic population remaining on these lands was supposed to be Germanized or destroyed.[33]

At the end of 1940, the economic and armaments section of the high command of the armed forces, headed by General Thomas, started intensive work in the collection and analysis of information regarding the national economy of the Soviet nation. A special file was set up in which all of the most important Soviet enterprises were registered. In the beginning of 1941 the analysis of all possible data on the Soviet economy was undertaken by a "Staff Russia," specially created for this purpose.[34]

Beginning with April 1941, all activity in the field of creating enterprises to plunder the Soviet Union went on under the leadership of Goering. On April 29, 1941, at a special conference with representatives of the armed forces participating, it was decided, for the purpose of a more complete economic exploitation of captured Soviet territories, to establish an "Economic Staff of the East," with special economic inspections and commands in the largest cities of the European part of the Soviet Union. The personnel of these plunder commands were supposed to operate according to "twelve commandments" worked out for them. These "commandments" enjoined them to be cruel and merciless to Soviet people and to make use of all the resources of the country in a predatory way. One of these commandments read: "The more persistent you are, the more inventive can be your methods in achieving this objective. The choice of methods is up to each of you. . . ." [35]

"Only your will must be decisive, but this will can be directed toward the fulfillment of great aims. Only in this case will it be moral in its cruelty. Hold yourself far apart from Russians. They are not Germans, but Slavs," it was recorded in another "commandment."

As one of the Soviet prosecutors, L. P. Sheynin, stated at the Nuremberg trial, "Under the direct leadership of the defendant Goering, there was in advance conceived, prepared, trained, and drilled a whole army of plunderers of all ranks and specialties for the organized looting and plunder of the peoples' property of the USSR." [36]

In his capacity as plenipotentiary for the implementation of the fascist four-year plan, Goering put together a broad program of economic exploitation of the Soviet Union's territory and the peoples inhabiting it, which is recorded in the so-called "Green File" of Goering.

The "Green File" contained an exhaustive, detailed plan of exploitation and plunder of the people's economy of the USSR. Not a single branch of the Soviet economy evaded the Hitlerites' attention. Corresponding "recommendations" were made for each economic area. All of them were imbued with one general idea: plunder more, plunder more effectively, without considering anybody or anything. To take out to Germany as much food and oil as possible—that was the principal economic objective established by the Hitlerite leadership.

"The opinion is entirely out of place," it was stated in the document, "that the occupied areas must be put back in order as soon as possible and their economy re-established. On the contrary, the relationship to various parts of the country must be extraordinarily varied. The re-establishment of order must be carried out only in those areas where we can get important supplies of agricultural products and oil." [37]

In connection with Hitler's directive about doing the most possible damage particularly to Russia, measures were considered the goal of which was to wreck industry in the principal industrial regions of Russia, above all in Moscow and Leningrad, but also in the regions adjacent to them. Simultaneously it was planned to stop supplying the population of these districts with food and the most necessary goods, which meant starvation for tens of millions of people. It was pointed out cynically in the document: "Many tens of millions of people in this region will prove to be superfluous and will be forced to die or go to Siberia. All attempts to save the population from starving to death by importing surplus food products from the black-soil area would be at the expense of sending the food to Europe. Such a dispatch of food would lower the military power of Germany and undercut ability to resist the blockade in Europe and Germany." [38]

On 16 July 1941, Keitel issued an order to all units of the German army to carry out these directives unfailingly. By this alone the German army became a direct accomplice in the fascist crimes.

Later, in August 1942, at a conference of the Reich commissars of the occupied regions and representatives of the military command, Goering said with underscored cynicism: "Once this was called robbery. This corresponded to the formula of taking away what was conquered. Now the forms have become more humanitarian. Nevertheless, I intend to plunder and plunder effectively." [39]

Hitler placed the political problems of the future occupied territories of the Soviet Union in the hands of one of the theoreticians of National Socialism—Rosenberg. In 1933 the Baltic Baron Alfred Rosenberg had already published a book, "The Myth of the Twentieth Century," which became a most important textbook for the fascist racists. In this book Rosenberg, with pretensions at a scientific approach, investigated the characteristic peculiarities of various civilizations and cultures and came to the conclusion that only the Aryan race had preserved the ability for further development. The fascist "theoretician" preached: "A dictatorship of people of a higher order should be established over people of a lower order." To the former, the "Nordic race," the Germans belonged; to the latter all other peoples, above all the Slavs.

Like Hitler, Rosenberg kept saying that in Russia culture had been introduced by the Germans. "Within the Russians there always dozed an aspiration for a limitless expansion, an unbridled will for the destruction of all forms of life, which they merely perceived as naked restriction. The admixture of Mongol blood, even if strongly diluted, would boil up at any shock in Russian life and would carry people away to deeds which often were incomprehensible to the participant himself." These wild notions of the Russian people were hammered, day after day, by the fascist theoreticians into the heads of their colleagues in the movement. They were inoculated with the idea of the supposedly special predestination of the Germans "in this barbaric East." Rosenberg demanded the banishment of the Russian people

69

from Europe, forcing them out into Asia, because "there is no place for them in the West." It was this naked racist and hater of the Soviet people who was charged with the task of working out political plans in regard to the Soviet territories which Germany intended to conquer.

In one of the secret documents prepared by Rosenberg at the beginning of April 1941, he proposed the dismemberment of the Soviet Union into a series of regions. He considered that the harshest measures must be used against Russia—"Great Russia with Moscow as its center"—which he was preparing to weaken as much as possible and convert into an area of exile for undesirable elements, i.e., to create on this territory a gigantic concentration camp. He wanted to separate the Baltic republics— Latvia, Lithuania, and Estonia—from the USSR. They were supposed to be settled with representatives of the "Nordic race," Scandinavians, Dutch, and later, after the inevitable—in the Hitlerites' opinion—capitulation of England, with Englishmen too. An "independent" Ukraine, with the "Don oblast" and the Caucasus added to it, would form a "Black Sea Union," which was supposed to serve the Germans as "living space," from which the master race would draw its food and raw materials.[40] Actually all these projects, set forth by Rosenberg in his memorandum of April 2, 1941, were nothing but a more detailed repetition of the old delirious ideas of the German fascists back in the 1920's. But now all these plans had acquired an especially ominous ring.

On April 20 Rosenberg was commissioned to head the work of giving a more precise definition to German occupational policies in the East. In April and May 1941, from the depths of the departments subordinate to him, came a series of instructions for the Reich commissars of the future occupied lands of the East. It was obvious from all these instructions that Germany intended to dismember the Soviet Union, bleed it white, transform Soviet territories into German colonies, and enslave the population.

Three days before the attack on the USSR, Rosenberg announced to his closest colleagues: "The problem of feeding the German people stands first in the list of Germany's demands in the East. The southern [Russian] territories must serve to feed the German people. We see absolutely no obligation on our part to feed the Russian people as well, out of the produce of this additional territory. . . . The future has prepared very difficult years for the Russians." [41]

The program of enslaving the Soviet people began to be realized immediately after the attack on the USSR. On July 16, 1941, Hitler summoned the highest functionaries of the Third Reich to a conference, at which he announced a detailed program for the partition of the USSR. In the minutes of the meeting, put together by Martin Bormann, one of the most influential persons in the fascist state, it is recorded that Hitler announced as the war aim the seizure of USSR territory up to the Urals. The plan was to annex, i.e., to transform into provinces of the fascist empire, the Baltic states, the Crimea and adjacent areas, and the Volga regions. The Baku oblast was to become a German concession, a "military colony." The fate of being colonies of the German empire was prepared for the Ukraine, Byelorussia, and other regions of the Soviet Union, regardless of the various forms of administration which the German conquerors were going to give them.

The creation of a German protectorate headed by a Reich commissar was contemplated for the territories of Estonia, Latvia, Lithuania, and Byelorussia. A "Germanization of racially suitable elements, colonization by representatives of the German race, and destruction of undesirable elements" [42] was supposed to be carried out on these territories. Hence the Baltic peoples too were threatened with either Germanization or death. In the course of the war the German fascists followed this inhuman, misanthropic policy. The greatest centers of the country, first of all Leningrad, were condemned to destruction. In the minutes of the July 16 conference it was stated: "The Fuehrer wants to level Leningrad to the ground in order to give it to the Finns afterwards." [43]

Hitler did not conceal the fact that the objective of the Nazi leaders consisted of a permanent annexation of Soviet lands to Germany. "We ourselves," said Hitler at the conference of July 16, 1941, "must realize completely clearly that we will never leave these territories." [44] Hitler proposed to use the following principle as a guide: "No military power of any kind must ever be created west of the Urals, even if we have to carry on the war for a hundred years for this objective. Any successor to the Fuehrer must know that the Reich is secure only in the event that there are no foreign armies west of the Urals. Germany itself will defend these areas from anyone who may present a danger. Our ironclad principle consists and will consist of allowing no one, except Germans, to carry arms." [45]

On March 13, 1941, the high command of the German armed forces issued a secret order—a supplement to Directive No. 21 ("Plan Barbarossa")—concerning the measures which must be carried out in zones declared to be operational. Here the Reichs-fuehrer of the SS received special powers on his own responsi-bility to carry out measures to liquidate the political structure of these areas. But, the directive emphasized, the troop commander in each area (there were three: the Northern, i.e., the Baltic states; the Central, i.e., Byelorussia; the Southern, i.e., the Ukraine) was in supreme command and was to administer jus-tice in close cooperation with the appointed Reich commissars of the occupied Soviet regions.[46] Since this signified a close cooperation of the military command with the SS in the implementation of Germany's policy in the occupied Soviet territories, the German generals must carry full responsibility for the crimes committed.

"First of All, Destroy the Prisoners of War, and Then the Peaceful Inhabitants. . . ."

One of the component parts of the war plan against the USSR was the destruction of Soviet war prisoners. In March 1941, the high command summoned a secret conference of chiefs of military district prisoner-of-war affairs sections and officers of the high command. The chief of the directorate of prisoner-of-war affairs, Lieutenant General Reinecke, announced that, in connection with the preparations for war against the USSR, it was essential to look after the preparation of camps for the future prisoners. The camps were to be open spaces enclosed by barbed wire. The participants of the conference received a direct instruction about the treatment of Soviet war prisoners "stipulating shooting without any warning in case of an attempt to escape." [47]

On March 30 the high command assembled the senior officers who were to command the troops in the war against the USSR. This was a conference similar to those which Hitler had summoned on the eve of the war against Poland (August 22, 1939) and before the offensive on the western front (November 23, 1939). In a long speech, Hitler emphasized the special nature of the new war, which he had long dreamed of realizing—a war of two different *Weltanschauungen.* In this speech Hitler announced a special judicial system in the occupied areas, more correctly the liquidation of all justice, and the destruction of Soviet "commissars and functionaries." It was forbidden to consider Soviet party workers and political officers of the Red Army as prisoners-of-war. Having been captured, they were to be handed over immediately to special detachments of the SD and, if this was impossible, they were to be shot on the spot. Hitler justified in advance the violence and murder which German soldiers could commit in the occupied territories and insisted that courts-martial must not sentence soldiers to strict punishment in such cases. In practice this was a call for the murder of Soviet citizens. Hitler declared that in the war against the Soviet Union it was necessary to throw aside all soldierly ethics and laws for the conduct of war and be merciless, since the idea was not only to crush the Red Army, but to "root out Communism for all time." [48]

On May 12, 1941, the high command of the German ground forces issued a directive about the treatment of Soviet commissars and political workers captured by the Germans. It instructed prisoners of this category to be handed over to the security service and police for subsequent extermination.

Paragraph 3 of the directive stated: "Troop political officers are not considered to be prisoners and must be destroyed in the transit camps at the latest. They are not to be evacuated to the rear." [49] Jodl made the following addition to the draft of the directive: "We must consider the possibility of repressions against German aviators. Therefore it would be best to represent this measure as a retaliation." [50] This remark perfectly characterizes the perfidy and criminality of the German generals, who denied their participation in the crimes of the Hitlerites. But the directive of the high command of the ground forces was also operative in regard to war prisoners of other categories; in particular it pointed out that the use of weapons against Soviet war prisoners would be considered lawful and would free the guards from the "duty of formal inquiries." The guards were ordered to open fire without warning on prisoners trying to escape. This document, published before the beginning of the war, contained an almost open call for the killing of prisoners-of-war. The killers were relieved in advance of all responsibility. It should be stressed that the direct responsibility for this order was carried by the German high command, in the first instance by its leaders, Jodl, Keitel, and Heusinger.

At the Nuremberg trial, the Soviet prosecutor, General Rudenko, asked Keitel: "So you do not deny that already in May, more than a month before the war, a document about the destruction of Russian political and military workers had already been drafted. You don't deny this?"

Keitel: "No, I don't deny this; this was the result of orders which were communicated and worked out in writing by the generals in this document." [51]

Four weeks before the war with the USSR, the German fascists and their generals, with the pedantry characteristic of them, also made plans for the murder of peaceful inhabitants in the occupied territories, without trial or inquest. In the corresponding directive it was decreed that suspicious persons who were arrested must be taken immediately before an officer, who would decide on the spot whether they should be shot. A completely arbitrary rule by the military over the Soviet peaceful population was to be instituted.

The directives of the German military command, issued on the eve of the attack on the USSR, reflected the villainous plans which the Hitlerites had concocted. In the later course of the war, the German fascists and their satellites carried out a monstrous policy of genocide which led to the destruction of millions of people.

At the beginning of September 1940, the chief of the Abwehr (military intelligence), Admiral Canaris, received an order from Jodl to strengthen intelligence activity in connection with the operation being prepared against the USSR. Jodl warned that German preparations must not create the impression in the Soviet Union that Germany was preparing an offensive in the East. A similar order was communicated to all the other branches of service.

In the preceding years, the German intelligence service had not been able to create a sufficiently effective spy net over the territory of the Soviet Union. The vigilance of the Soviet people had wrecked more than one effort of German intelligence. A leading Abwehr operator, Leverkuehn, wrote after the end of World War II that the "dispatch of agents from Germany into Russia was possible only in very rare instances." [52] However, his statement must be approached with care. The information which was studied in Berlin consisted as a rule of agent reports, press articles, and the stories of correspondents, businessmen, and tourists returning from the Soviet Union or transiting across Soviet territory. An important source of information was that received from Germany's military-diplomatic representatives in the Soviet Union and its neighboring states. [53]

One of the supporting institutions of German intelligence was a special institute-library in which all the materials on Russia located in Germany were collected. Before the war the institute, which was located in Breslau, was occupied in collecting information on the Soviet economy, highways, and railroads; on relations among the peoples inhabiting the Soviet Union; on the political life of the country—in a word, on the entire complex of questions concerning the Soviet Union. Later the institute was transferred to Berlin and became known as the "Wannsee Institute," after the name of the Berlin suburb where it was located.[54]

Various German intelligence organizations tried to utilize, for espionage against the USSR, the documents of Polish intelligence, captured after the defeat of Poland, which had carried on an extensive espionage effort against the Soviet Union in the prewar years. The agents of the Polish intelligence services, and also officers and collaborators of the secret services of the Baltic states who had fled to Germany and Scandinavia, were partially uncovered and induced to collaborate. But still these attempts did not yield the desired effect. With greater success, the German secret service took advantage of the situation which had arisen after the defeat of Poland. The displacement of population from the west to the east and in the reverse direction, resulting from the defeat of Poland, had opened up for German intelligence new broad possibilities for espionage against the USSR on the territory of the western areas of the Ukraine and Byelorussia, and also in Lithuania, Latvia, and Estonia.

Although a large number of the German agents dispatched were rendered harmless at the Soviet-German border, some of them managed to penetrate Soviet territory in depth, and a few even reached such important centers as Leningrad and Kiev.[55] Thanks to the activities of their agents and to aerial reconnaissance, the German command possessed data about the location of military airfields and the deployment of Red Army units. Information about the armament and equipment of the Red Army, judging by General Halder's diaries, was far from accurate. German agents often confused the arms of the Red Army produced in the Soviet Union with Polish arms and equipment left behind in the territories of the Western Ukraine and Western Byelorussia, and drew incorrect conclusions from this. It is widely known how stunned Hitler was when he learned, after the war had started, of the existence of the Soviet tanks T-34 and KV, and with what mistrust he treated the information of German intelligence agencies afterwards.

But one cannot affirm with certainty that Germany did not possess substantive data of a strategic character about the armed forces and economy of the Soviet state. However, in evaluating intelligence information the high command made serious mistakes. Thus it underevaluated information about Soviet capabilities to evacuate industry eastward. It also did not trust intelligence data about the USSR's successes in the field of technology. The most important miscalculation was, of course, one made by German political, diplomatic, and intelligence circles in regard to the morale of the population of the USSR and the political stability of the country. Miscalculations fatal to the Hitlerites were also made in the evaluation of the productive capacities of Soviet industry in the eastern parts of the country. By way of important military data at the moment of the attack on the USSR, German intelligence possessed information on Soviet border fortifications and facts about some Soviet divisions deployed in the western regions of the Soviet Union.

According to Leverkuehn's statement, an important source of acquiring intelligence information was the White-guard emigration. The penetration of German agents into White émigré organizations where, it was considered, there were persons sympathetic to the Soviet Union, became especially intensive from the beginning of 1941. Special attention was directed at the Ukrainian nationalists, from the former Hetman Skoropadsky, to Bandera, Konovalets, and Melnik. All of them were supported by Hitler's intelligence. After the defeat of Poland, a section of German intelligence located in Krakow directly managed the Ukrainian nationalists. As early as 1938 the Abwehr had begun to prepare diversionist-terrorist groups of Ukrainian nationalists, training them in the techniques of terror and various forms of subversive activity. Some weakening of the connection with the Ukrainian nationalist anti-Soviet organizations resulted from the transfer of the Transcarpathian Ukraine to Hungary in 1939. There was no limit to the rage of the Ukrainian nationalist leaders, who had counted on the creation of a "Greater Ukraine" with the help of the Germans. To the aid of German intelligence came . . . Japanese intelligence, which took upon itself the running and subsidizing of the bands of Melnik and Bandera. However, as the time of attack on the USSR drew closer, the Hitlerites again established contact with the Ukrainian nationalists, who during the Soviet-German war served the Hitlerites with complete faithfulness in betraying the Ukrainian people. They became "glorified" as the most cruel executioners, committing monstrous crimes on the Soviet territory occupied by the German-fascist aggressors.

One of the important links in the German intelligence net surrounding the Soviet Union was an organization in Sofia created by a German intelligence officer working on the military attaché staff of the German embassy, Dr. Delius (real name Otto Wagner). Delius collected military and economic information about the Soviet Union and dispatched German agents into the Soviet Union from the Black Sea coast. The duties of Delius' co-workers also included the carrying on of espionage and subversive activities against other countries, particularly against the United States of America.[56]

The attention of the intelligence agencies was increasingly directed at the East. The chief of one of the branches of the main Reich directorate of security, Schellenberg, wrote in his memoirs: "The western sectors of our security net must be weakened to strengthen the eastern ones." [57]

The chiefs of the intelligence services, the military and the

Gestapo, periodically discussed the intelligence material received from the USSR. Their basic disagreements were in regard to the evaluation of Soviet military production. Schellenberg considered that Soviet heavy industry was at a rather high level. This particularly concerned the production of tanks. He was convinced that there were tank models in production better than the German ones. Canaris refused to believe this. Schellenberg had come to his conclusion in connection with an order of Hitler's to impress the Soviet Union with German power. For this purpose the Soviet military attaché was invited, in March 1941, to visit tank factories and schools for the training of tank crews. Noticing that the military attaché's attitude toward what he was shown was quite different from what he had expected, Schellenberg drew the conclusion that the USSR had more advanced types of tanks.[58] There were also disagreements in regard to the evaluation of the Soviet railroad net around Moscow, near the Urals, etc.

Schellenberg points out that if the material collected by the intelligence services did not fit in with the conceptions of the military-planning organs, the latter would simply ignore it.

"In spite of Canaris' tendency to underevaluate the technical progress achieved by Russia," writes Schellenberg, "in later chats with me he was dominated by fears that we would now be drawn into a two-front war with all its attendant dangers. But the opinion of the General Staff was that our superiority in troops, technical equipment, and military leadership was so great that a concentrated campaign against Russia could be concluded within ten weeks." [59]

Hitler and Himmler shared Heydrich's point of view that a military defeat would so weaken the Soviet state that with the help of Germany's political agents its complete downfall could be achieved. The chiefs of the intelligence services, Canaris and

Schellenberg, apparently were more cautious in their evaluations. Canaris, for instance, attempted to warn Keitel about underestimating the strength of the Soviet regime. However, Keitel disagreed with his conclusions, declaring that the measures undertaken by Hitler in the war against the USSR were so strong that "the Soviet system, no matter how solidly it may be organized, cannot stand up against them." [60]

The activities of German counterintelligence consisted first of all of attempts to penetrate the Soviet intelligence net in Germany in order to keep it under constant observation and misinform it. In particular it was decided to toss out to the Soviet intelligence people materials from which one could conclude that the German leadership had decided to revive "Plan Sea Lion" and carry on intensive operations against England.[61] But this venture did not succeed. Soviet intelligence possessed completely trustworthy information about the real intentions of Germany. According to Schellenberg's testimony, Hitler studied the materials of German intelligence extremely carefully, demanding that ever newer data about the condition of Soviet defenses and armed forces be presented to him.[62]

The chief of the Abwehr, Canaris showed nervousness in the last weeks before the attack on the USSR because he felt that the calculations of the high command on the prognosis of the course and duration of military operations against the Soviet Union were unrealistic, founded on incorrect evaluations, and were evidence of the self-satisfaction and overly high optimism of Brauchitsch, Keitel, Halder, and Jodl. This confirms once more the fact that the later declarations of the German generals, that they tried to restrain Hitler from attacking the USSR, do not correspond with reality. Keitel himself declared to Canaris: "Maybe you understand something about counterintelligence, but you are a seaman, and don't try to give us lessons in strategic and political planning." [63] Canaris' persistence was mainly explainable by his fear of the prospect of a two-front war.

Although in November 1940 Hitler was wholly engrossed in the study of information about the USSR, he worried about the position of the United States of America. The German intelligence agencies were ordered to clarify the position of the USA, the potential capabilities of its industry, particularly aircraft and ship construction. On this, it was thought in the highest military circles, would depend the amount of time Germany would have before a two-front war started. The chiefs of the intelligence services agreed that if the productive power of the USA were to support the military efforts of England, this would undoubtedly lead to an invasion on the continent. A powerful air offensive would precede a landing.

Diplomatic Preparation

The decision to attack the USSR had an immediate effect on German foreign policy, giving it a new impulse and direction. Soon after the conclusion of an armistice with France at Compiègne, a number of problems arose before the Reich's diplomacy. The most important of them were: the completion of the political consolidation of the principal fascist states; the accommodation of the foreign policy and economic resources of the other allies and satellites of Germany to the needs of the German military machine; the inducement of the conquered states to take part in the proposed war in some form; the implementation of a systematic political and diplomatic offensive on the positions of the Soviet Union which were of vital importance to its interests. All this was meant to lead to the creation of favorable strategic, political, and diplomatic conditions for the future war.

On September 27, 1940, the fascist aggressors—Germany, Italy, and Japan—signed a military-political agreement which recorded a preliminary division of the world among them. Germany received the "Euro-African space," Italy the Mediterranean region, Japan the "East-Asian space." By the time the Tripartite Pact was signed, Germany had greatly strengthened its position in Romania and Hungary, and also in Bulgaria. A month earlier, on August 30, 1940, Northern Transylvania was torn away from Romania and given to Hungary, by decision of Germany and Italy. Having committed this act, Germany strengthened its position in relation to these two countries and began to exercise an ever greater influence over their policies. In its own policy in regard to Romania, Germany was guided to a great degree by its interest in Romanian oil. The Romanian oil fields at Ploeşti were for Germany the only important source of natural petroleum. Romania served as an important agrarian and raw material appendage to the German economy. In addition, the territory of Romania formed a convenient springboard for attacking the USSR from the southwest.

On June 28, 1940, the Soviet Union had demanded from Romania the return of Bessarabia, illegally torn away from it in 1918. Bessarabia was returned to the Soviet state. At the same time, Northern Bukovina, whose people had taken a decision to reunite with the Soviet Ukraine as early as November 1918, became part of the USSR. These measures were of no little strategic significance to the USSR in case of an attack by Hitler's Germany.

After the second Vienna award, in September 1940, the Romanian King, Carol, decided to abdicate. Despised and hated by his compatriots, he left the country. The democratic forces in Romania were at that time disunited and too weak to take the fate of the country into their hands. Power was seized by General Ion Antonescu, a fascist by conviction and a partisan of orientation toward Germany.

A cruel dictatorship was instituted in the country. At Antonescu's invitation there arrived in Romania a German "military mission" so numerous that in fact it meant the occupation of the country by German troops. On November 23, soon after Antonescu's visits to Berlin and Rome, where his warlike plans in regard to the USSR found a sympathetic response, Romania joined the Tripartite Pact. Shortly thereafter, Antonescu signed several agreements of an economic nature with Germany, which even more firmly bound Romania to Hitler's Reich.

Germany's subsequent guarantee of Romania's integrity emphasized Romania's readiness to adhere fully to the course of foreign policy designed by Berlin. On March 5, 1941, the Romanian "Conducator" was summoned to Vienna to see Goering, who demanded a maximum increase in the production of oil and a significant curtailment of its export to other countries. Goering also made very transparent hints to Antonescu about the possibility of a German-Soviet war and advised the Romanian dictator to strengthen the antiaircraft defenses of the oil fields. Antonescu stated that thirty Romanian divisions were combat-ready. Antonescu did not conceal his hatred for the Soviet land, declaring, as aggressors always do in such cases, that the USSR was allegedly concentrating its troops in Bessarabia. The talk with Goering could not have left Antonescu with any doubts about the approaching war with the USSR.[64]

Three weeks later, at the beginning of April, in connection with the preparations for the attack on Yugoslavia under the pretext of "uncertainty" about the position of the USSR, Hitler asked Antonescu, through the high command of the Wehrmacht, to "increase defensive preparations on the Russian border, without arousing the suspicions of Russia by a general mobilization." Hitler expressed special worry about the defense of the oil wells. He demanded that all forces in Romania, German and Romanian, be grouped in such a way that they could be immediately directed to the Romanian eastern front.[65] But the Romanian dictator, and the monopolistic bourgeois and landowner circles supporting him, themselves nourished warlike intentions toward the USSR and their other neighbors. The Romanian ruling clique watched the war in Yugoslavia greedily, demanding part of the loot for Romania, namely Banat. On April 28, 1941, Antonescu tried to convince the German minister in Bucharest, Killinger, of the necessity to attack the Soviet Union as soon as possible. In particular the general explained to the German diplomat that it was essential to avert the "threat of a union of Slavs"; the historical mission of Romania, it turned out, had always consisted of serving as a barrier "against the Slavs and Turks." In connection with this, Antonescu suggested that Germany emerge to the Black Sea in two directions, through Lvov and through Romania, establish a condominium (joint rule) over large parts of Serbia and Greece, and he unfolded other plans for the enslavement of Slavic peoples. The first step in this direction was to be the attack on the USSR. Russia would be quickly crushed, assured Antonescu flatteringly. Then, he continued, the way would be open to the "oil of Baku and Iraq, and to India." Antonescu called for the Germans to begin the war against the USSR as soon as possible, so as to seize the harvest of Soviet fields. Guessing Germany's intentions and that Hitler was busy looking for arguments to justify the attack on the USSR, Antonescu provocatively assured Killinger that there existed, allegedly, a plan of cooperation between Yugoslavia, Greece,* Turkey, and the USSR, and the Anglo-American bloc.[66]

---

* This is strange, for by this time Yugoslavia and Greece had been conquered by the Axis.—V.P.

He of course knew full well that in actual fact no such plan existed. Although the Romanian ruling circles stood for the swiftest unleashing of war, the directive of the high command of the German armed forces "About the participation of foreign countries in 'Plan Barbarossa' " prescribed negotiations with Romania "as late as possible." The German command did not have high hopes on the restraint of its immoderately temperamental ally. The directive of the high command of the German armed forces established the priority of negotiations with its allies as follows: Finland, Hungary, Romania. As far as Italy was concerned, Hitler decided not to communicate anything to Mussolini until the very last day.[67] Antonescu's government could hardly contain its impatience, anticipating the war against the USSR. About this, in particular, the Romanian minister in Berlin asked the state secretary of the German ministry of foreign affairs, Wermann, in a slightly veiled form on May 30, 1941. But fearing that a premature disclosure could call forth undesirable political and military complications, the Hitlerites continued to hold the exact date of the attack in deep secrecy.[68] Finally, the Romanian dictator was summoned to Munich on June 11. There, in the presence of Keitel, Jodl, and other high German generals, Hitler told Antonescu of his intention to attack the USSR. The rapture of the Romanian dictator was boundless. He assured Hitler that Romania would actively participate in the war from the very first day. Antonescu's fervor was noted. He was appointed commander-in-chief on the Romanian section of the front.[69]

Four days before the attack on the Soviet Union (June 18, 1941) Hitler sent Antonescu a letter in which he stated that the German troops located in Romania and also the Romanian armed forces were charged with the safekeeping of Romanian territory. Special attention was directed to the necessity of ensuring the security of the oil regions, the harbor at Constantsa, and the bridges over the Danube, from air raids, parachutists, and saboteurs. The Romanian army was asked to create an illusion of a greater concentration of troops on the Romanian-Soviet frontier than existed in fact. In the future joint operations of Romanian and German troops on Soviet territory were contemplated.[70]

Horthy's Hungary, having received Northern Transylvania from the hands of Hitler's Germany, and before that the Transcarpathian Ukraine and Southern Slovakia, by this alone had become an accomplice of the German aggressor. The whole later history of Hungary right up to its entry into the war against the Soviet Union was to a significant degree predetermined by the second Vienna award. Horthy's government was thrown still another lure: in September 1940 Hitler gave out that in the future a complete fulfillment of all the territorial pretensions of Hungary would be possible, these including not only the whole of Transylvania but also Banat. The question of Transylvania was also used later by Germany to force Romania and Hungary to follow its policies. On November 20 Hungary joined the Tripartite Pact. In the diplomatic game which Germany was playing in the fall and winter of 1940 in the Balkans, trying to secure completely its rear in the region of the Balkan-Danube basin in the coming war against the USSR, a special role was reserved for Horthy's Hungary. It consisted of helping Germany neutralize Yugoslavia and, if that did not succeed, to help in the war for the destruction of the Yugoslav state.

In this connection Germany did not object to the conclusion, between Hungary and Yugoslavia, of a treaty of "eternal peace," which was signed in Belgrade on December 12, 1940. Some Hungarian and Yugoslav circles were counting on the use of the treaty in the future to counter the establishment of German mastery in the Balkans. The same thing was believed in Anglo-American circles. However, these hopes were not to be fulfilled. With special attention, Germany was seeing to it that the development of events was going in the direction necessary to her and was not allowing any deviation from the course she had charted for the Balkan states. This was all the easier to do because the other great powers either had retired from participation in Balkan affairs or did not have any real capabilities to resist the German thrust. Only the Soviet Union several times demonstrated its negative attitude toward the plans to establish German domination over the Balkans.

In the fall of 1940 and in the beginning of 1941, contacts along military lines were also strengthened between Germany and Hungary. In December 1940 the Hungarian war minister, Bartha, visited the headquarters of the high command of the Wehrmacht. As a result of the ensuing negotiations, Hungary agreed in principle to participate in a war against Yugoslavia and the USSR under certain circumstances and also declared its readiness to allow German troops to pass through the territory of Hungary.[71] Hungary also agreed to furnish fifteen large troop formations for the war against the USSR.

The attempts of some influential Hungarian circles, headed by Prime Minister Pal Teleki, to carry out a balancing policy between the German-Italian and Anglo-American blocs in order to realize annexationist demands without taking an active part in Hitlerite Germany's military aggression, ended with failure. On March 27, 1941, Hitler communicated to the Hungarian minister of foreign affairs, Sztójay, his "desire" that Hungary should take part in the projected attack on Yugoslavia. "In case of a conflict," Hitler stated, "Germany will not put limits on the revisionist demands of Hungary." [72]

The next day Sztójay handed Hitler the reply of the Hungarian dictator Horthy. The reply read: "I am wholly and fully with Germany." [73]

On April 6 Germany fell on Yugoslavia and five days later Hungary stabbed Yugoslavia in the back. For their betrayal the Hungarian ruling circles counted on getting a solid reward: the Yugoslav lands of Banat and Bačka, and in the future they counted on Germany's support for their claims to Fiume, which had been seized by Italy after World War I. As a result of the partition of Yugoslavia, Hungary received only Bačka. Having betrayed its neighbor Yugoslavia and occupied Yugoslav lands, Hungary had now been tied up hand and foot by Hitler's Germany.

After that Hitler had no further doubts that Hungary would take part in the war against the Soviet Union. The responsible military leaders of Hungary were also convinced of this. The chief of the Hungarian General Staff, General Werth, in a memorandum to the government dated May 6, 1941, proposed—in foreseeing an attack on the USSR—the conclusion of an immediate political alliance with Germany.[74] Talks began between the general staffs of Germany and Hungary to determine the concrete mission of Hungary in case of war against the USSR. But Hitler still concealed from Hungary, as he did from his other allies and satellites, the exact date of the invasion. However, in Europe at that time there was hardly anyone who doubted the German-Soviet war would soon begin.

On June 15 Ribbentrop informed the German minister in Hungary, Erdmannsdorff, that "at the very latest at the beginning of July" Hitler intended to "clarify German-Soviet relations," and demanded that Hungary carry out corresponding military measures on its borders.[75]

Four days later General Halder arrived in Budapest. He broke the news that war with the USSR was a question of the greatest immediacy and asked the Hungarian General Staff to attend to the strengthening of the Carpathian line. At the same time he recommended that they not undertake anything which might excite alarm on the Soviet side and thus interfere with the railroad shipments of German troops. Halder did not demand an immediate declaration of war from Hungary, although he made it understood that the participation of the Hungarian army in the war against the Soviet Union was not excluded. On June 21 Hitler directed a letter to Horthy in which he announced the beginning of the war against the USSR and thanked him for the measures taken on the Hungarian-Soviet border; they, in his opinion, had created security against flank attacks for the German army and pinned down Soviet forces. However, in the communication there was no direct invitation to enter the war. The immediate participation of Hungary in the war did not enter the plans of the German command. In addition, Hitler thought that for political reasons it would make sense to force the ruling circles of Hungary to "fight" for the privilege of making war against "Bolshevik Russia," and Germany in this case would not have to take upon herself obligations regarding future territorial compensations to Hungary. The psychological calculation was accurate: the Hungarian fascists were worried. Only on the second day of the war against the USSR, when the nervousness of the Hungarian ruling circles had reached a high pitch, was the Hungarian government "invited" to take part in the war against the USSR.

On June 27 Hungary declared war against the USSR.

From the point of view of the military and political leadership of Hitler's Germany, the most reliable ally in the coming war against the USSR was Finland. The Finnish government had already turned to Germany for help during the Soviet-Finnish conflict.

In spite of the peace treaty between the USSR and Finland,

signed on March 12, 1940, the Finnish fascist-leaning revanchist circles did not abandon their plans for war against the USSR. From the summer of 1940 on, a close collaboration was established between the military agencies of Germany and Finland on the basis of anti-Soviet policy.

In February 1941 the chief of the operational branch of the German air force, General Seidel, and the chief of staff of German forces in Norway, Colonel Buschenhagen, visited Finland. While Seidel's visit was mostly of a representational character, Buschenhagen conferred with the chief of the Finnish general staff, General A. Heinrichs, about the possibility of waging war against the Soviet Union. It became clear from the talks that the Finnish army would be prepared to cover a German troop concentration on Finnish territory in the Saal-Kandalakhti (Kandalaksha) area and was ready to take part in the war itself. Buschenhagen pretended that he was merely speculating, from which the Finns should not draw any conclusions. However, it was clear to the Finns, and even more to the Germans, that Finland was ready for military collaboration with Germany against the Soviet Union.[76]

At the beginning of April, the Finnish minister of foreign affairs, Witting, emphasized in a talk with the German minister, Bluecher, that Finland would from now on orient herself toward Germany. Because of this she was making every effort to ensure German interests in the Petsamo nickel mines to the disadvantage of England and the Soviet Union, and was also developing trade with Germany and meeting German desires to establish communications across Finnish territory with the German troops in Northern Norway. "In my personal opinion," Minister Bluecher concluded his dispatch, "the minister of foreign affairs would be glad to lead his country into the embrace of the Tripartite Pact." [77]

Soon after, in the name of the high command of the German

army, General Jodl told a prominent member of the German ministry of foreign affairs, Ambassador Ritter, that the moment had come to enter detailed military negotiations with Finland, particularly about the future movement of German troops into that country, about a joint plan of operations, the question of supreme command, etc. However, "Plan Barbarossa" was not to figure in the discussions. The high command of the German armed forces proposed inviting two officers of the Finnish general staff to Germany as soon as possible.[78]

By Hitler's order of May 22, Minister Schnurre went to Helsinki to confer with President Ryti and the Finnish government. Schnurre communicated Hitler's proposal to send Finnish military experts to Germany to discuss the situation which could arise from the sharp deterioration of German-Soviet relations. There was no room for doubt that this referred to the approaching German attack on the Soviet Union. The Finnish government, by testimony of Marshal Mannerheim, "unanimously decided to send a military delegation to Germany." The negotiations took place at Hitler's headquarters in Salzburg on May 25, 1941. Jodl, Colonel Buschenhagen, and others took part from the German side. The Finnish army was represented by a group of officers headed by General Heinrichs.

As opposed to the general conversations with Romania and Hungary, the German-Finnish military talks had a completely concrete character. The Finnish military delegation was informed about the main directions of the German blows against the USSR in the north, and told about the desirable specific participation of Finnish troops. The Finnish delegation showed by its position that Rangel's government was prepared to fight against the USSR with Germany. It was decided that, beginning with June 5, German troop transports would begin to arrive in Finland. The Finns demanded nine days to complete mobilization. The head of the Finnish delegation emphasized Finland's readiness to take part in the aggression against the USSR. "The presence of Finnish representatives demonstrates Finland's position, even though the authority to sign political obligations is still lacking." The Hitlerites were completely satisfied. Later, by order of Hitler, it was decided to limit the communications about the coming war to those already imparted to the Finns during the military negotiations.[79]

On June 4 Buschenhagen announced the "complete readiness" of Finland for military cooperation.[80] At the same time, in its negotiations with Germany, the Finnish side insisted on guarantees for the preservation of Finland's independence. The chief of the Finnish General Staff warned the Germans against attempts to impose some sort of Quisling government in Finland, which would immediately paralyze any further cooperation between Finland and Germany.[81] The Finnish government, it is apparent, had thoroughly studied the gangster habits of Hitler's Germany. But their misgivings were unfounded. Rangel's government suited Hitler well because it was ready to cooperate closely with Germany in the war against the USSR. The Finnish government's position was definite: it asked Germany, even in case the "military decision did not take place [i.e., if the attack on the USSR were postponed—A.N.], to guarantee the existence of Finland as an independent state, to guarantee its 1939 borders, rounded out if possible [i.e., padded with Soviet territory —A.N.], and to afford it economic aid." [82]

The report of the Finnish minister for foreign affairs, Witting, to the foreign affairs committee of the parliament about Finland's readiness to take part in the war against the USSR together with Germany was approved by an overwhelming majority of the members of the committee. In these prewar days, influential Finnish official and non-official personalities attempted to represent Finland's action of having started a mobilization on 10 June as defensive. The Finnish rulers tried with all their strength to deceive their people and impress on them that Finland was occupying a defensive posture, since she was threatened with attack from the Soviet Union.[83] But this was not the truth.

The best refutation to the version about the "defensive" war which Finland was allegedly forced to start in June 1941 consists of the following documented facts. On June 14 Jodl communicated to Ambassador Ritter an important fact: the Finnish General Staff had decided to proceed with a concealed mobilization and in this connection had asked for confirmation of previous German assurances of maintaining Finland's interests in case the attack on the USSR were postponed. Through Buschenhagen, Hitler told the Finns that "one could definitely count on the first alternative [i.e., on war—A.N.]." In a telegram to Buschenhagen, Keitel wrote: "You are authorized to declare that the demands and preliminary conditions put forth by Finland in regard to measures which must be undertaken should be regarded as fulfilled." [84]

The Finnish government, in trying to present the war against the USSR to its own people as a defensive one, did not stop short of outright forgery. Thus, in Hitler's announcement about war against the USSR, published in the Finnish press, the words "in alliance with Finnish divisions" was translated "side by side with Finnish divisions," which was meant to strengthen the Finnish government's assertion that Finland was waging a "separate" war against the USSR. It was also for this purpose that provocative German air raids on Finnish cities were organized, which were given out as operations of Soviet aircraft. Finland's attempt to place the responsibility for these raids on the USSR was categorically denied by the Soviet minister. At the same time, Finland, trying to gain time for completing her war preparations, avoided defining her position.[85] On June 25 Finland attacked the USSR.

Of no small importance to Germany was the position of Turkey. Formerly, Turkey, which had on October 19, 1939 signed a treaty of mutual aid with England and France, could be considered an ally of the anti-German group of states. In fact, Turkey's policy and her position were determined by the deployment of forces in the international arena at any given moment. Before the fall of France, Turkey had demonstrated her loyalty to the Anglo-French alliance and had helped England in carrying out her Balkan policies. After the defeat of the Allies in the West, Turkey strove to improve relations with Hitler's Germany without breaking, however, with England. In short, Turkey played both sides, trying to obtain the maximum advantage for herself. The change of situation in the Balkans—the defeat of England and the expulsion of her troops from the European continent, and the consolidation of German domination in Greece and Yugoslavia—exercised an enormous influence on Turkish policy. Turkey concluded a number of economic agreements extremely profitable for Germany, significantly increasing the delivery to Germany of strategic raw materials (chromium, copper) and, in addition, forbade the passage of English armed forces across Turkish territory. The Turkish government hoped that after the conclusion of the war in the Balkans, Germany would attack the Soviet Union. In this case Turkey was willing to assist Germany by any political means.

The day after Bulgaria joined the Tripartite Pact, March 2, 1941, Hitler sent a message to the President of Turkey, Ismet Inönü, in which he made assurances that Germany had no hostile intentions toward Turkey. In his answer, Inonu gave it to be understood that Turkey was ready to move in the direction of

German wishes. A month later, Turkey failed to answer England's proposal to break relations with Germany and Italy, and also failed in her obligations as a member of the Balkan Entente, according to which she should have given aid to Yugoslavia, which was being subjected to attack.* The position which Turkey took during the war in the Balkans encouraged the Nazi leaders to more decisive steps. In the middle of May the German ambassador in Ankara, von Papen, began secret negotiations with Inönü, and the minister of foreign affairs, Saracoglu, about the conclusion of a German-Turkish treaty of friendship and nonaggression. Germany, preparing for war against the USSR, was thus counting on covering its southern flank. Turkey informed England about her intention. England was only able to achieve the inclusion into the treaty of clauses about the preservation by Turkey of her previous obligations. An important stimulus that was pushing Turkey into concluding a treaty with Germany was the anti-Soviet position of the Turkish ruling circles, which considered that, in concluding a treaty with Germany, Turkey would be furthering the creation of a united anti-Soviet front of capitalist states. Saracoglu tried to convince Papen that, before beginning the war against the Soviet Union, it was essential for Germany to come to an amicable agreement with England and the United States of America. "First of all you must enter peace negotiations with the British, and then establish order in Russia, acting as the representatives of England and America and in agreement with them," he said in a talk with Papen on May 13, 1941.[86] It is quite probable that the Turkish political leaders thought that such negotiations were already taking place between Hess and the British government,

---

* This is not correct. Such help was required only if Yugoslavia were attacked by another Balkan state.—V.P.

and were hurrying to express their approval. Saracoglu's statement was also completely in harmony with the orientation of Papen himself, who was advocating an agreement with the Western powers and the creation of a united front against the Soviet Union. That is why in his reports to the German ministry of foreign affairs, Papen emphasized these particular arguments of Saracoglu. The Turkish statesman exhorted Germany to attack the Soviet Union as soon as possible, and promised that Turkey would be on Germany's side. The statements of the Turkish political leaders had such an obviously anti-Soviet character that they gave Hitler's foreign minister a basis to propose to Turkey a secret agreement, affording Germany the right of unlimited transit of arms and war materials, and also certain contingents of German troops, across Turkish territory. However, Turkey would not risk going so far, since she realized that such a step would in fact make her dependent on Germany and her freedom of maneuver would be lost. A considerable role in this decision was also played by the warning of the United States of America.

On June 18, 1941, four days before Germany's attack on the Soviet Union, the German-Turkish treaty of friendship was signed. This treaty was an important element in Germany's diplomatic preparation for war against the Soviet Union. On June 20 the *Manchester Guardian* wrote: "It may be that signing of the treaty at this moment is connected with the flood of rumors and counter-rumors, statements and denials, that day after day are raging over the Russo-German borders—what Hitler's plans are, what will Stalin's answer be? In this muddle only one thing is indisputable: from Finland to the Black Sea Hitler has concentrated forces stronger than those necessary for any defensive needs." [87]

The London *Times* stressed in an article on June 21: "It

97

seems definite that the conclusion of the new pact is connected with the German plans in regard to Russia." [88]

Hitler's confidence in the quick rout of the armed forces of the Soviet Union was so great that in February 1941 a branch of the high command of the German armed forces had already been given the problem of beginning preparatory work toward the development of plans for a campaign across Afghanistan into India. At the beginning of April, orders were issued that the possibility of an offensive on a broad front in North Africa must be borne in mind for the fall of 1941. After the completion of the war in the Balkans, the Hitlerites were already thinking of war against Turkey and Syria. As before, Hitler did not abandon his ideas of taking Gibraltar and occupying French Morocco.

The smashing of the Soviet Union had to lead to the complete fall of England, too, which territory would be subject to occupation by German troops. It was proposed that the extensive colonial possessions of the British Empire be divided among the partners of the fascist bloc. [89]

On June 11 the high command composed the draft of Directive No. 32, "Preparations for the period following the implementation of 'Plan Barbarossa.' " The directive itself, in a somewhat altered version, was signed by Warlimont on June 30.

The draft of the directive stated: "After the armed forces of Soviet Russia are overwhelmed, Germany and Italy will realize military domination over the European continent, at the present time with the exception of the Iberian Peninsula. There will no longer be any serious threat to the European region on land. For defense, and for the offensive operations still contemplated, a considerably smaller army than has existed up to the present will be required. The center of gravity in armaments will shift to the navy and the air forces." [90] The directive provided for operations against the British navy, and a pressure on Spain to force it to take part in the seizure of Gibraltar. Turkey and Iran would be compelled to take direct or indirect part in the war against England. The directive signed by Warlimont already speaks of the capture of Tobruk, North Africa, and an attack on the Suez Canal.

Part Two—The Soviet Union before the Attack by Hitlerite Germany

A State of a New Kind

Now that almost a quarter of a century has passed since the events described in this book, one falls to thinking over and over again about what, actually, Hitler's main miscalculation was in his evaluation of the condition of the Soviet state. One comes to the conclusion that Hitler repeated the same basic mistake the foreign interventionists had committed before him in the days of the Civil War. This mistake, or, more exactly, their fatal miscalculation, consisted of being unable to understand the nature of the state which had arisen as a result of the Great October Socialist Revolution; in ignoring the new character of relations between classes and social groups within the state, the absolute denial of the possibility of the creation of a new type of relationship, on the basis of social ownership, between the classes, nations, and peoples inhabiting the country, between the state and the individual; and the crying ignorance of the Hitlerites in the field of social relationships. For the twenty-year period of time which had passed between the end of the Civil War in the USSR and beginning of the Great Patriotic War of the Soviet people, the imperialists were unable to understand that the public ownership of the means of production established in the USSR—the workers' state—was the principal and determining factor in the life of our people. Having deprived private persons of the right to own enterprises, land, banks, and having declared former private property relationships null and void, the Communist Party, with full awareness of the great historical responsibility it had taken upon itself, roused the broadest masses of the people to the building of a new, socialist society. It was not easy, in two decades, to traverse the distance separating backwardness from progress.

This grandiose historical reconstruction took place in unfavorable circumstances. The first socialist state of workers and peasants in the world found itself surrounded by a hostile capitalistic world. The masters of this world did not hide their strivings, by one means or another, to achieve the liquidation of the socialist order in the Soviet Union. Russia was a multi-structured country. Most of the population of the country was composed of peasants, i.e., a class from which, as V. I. Lenin emphasized, every day, every hour, capitalism is born spontaneously.

Russia, possessing a gigantic potential, did not have a solid base of power and industry.

After the end of the Civil War, the Soviet people, led by the Communist Party, rebuilt the economy ruined by the Imperialist and Civil Wars in a very short period and, with enormous enthusiasm, applied itself to the building of socialism.

In the course of a historically extremely insignificant period of time—a bit more than one decade—the hands of Soviet people created all the branches of economy essential to a modern state, first and foremost electrical energy. V. I. Lenin's words, "Communism is the Soviet regime plus electrification of the whole country" [1] became part of life. From the Shatura and Kashira power stations, from the Volkhov hydroelectric station to the Dnieper hydroelectric station—what a gigantic jump in a few years! The output of electrical power stations in the Soviet land increased almost five-fold between 1929 and 1940 (from

101

2.3 million to 11.2 million kilowatts). Chemical, electrotechnical, aviation, tractor, machine-building, and many other branches of industry were created. The metallurgical industry was subjected to a decisive reconstruction. Gigantic metallurgical complexes arose in the Ukraine and the Urals—Dneprostal and Mangitogorsk. New blast furnaces, new mills, and metal, metal, metal, so essential to the needs of the country and above all for its defense. During the five-year plans, the question of transferring agriculture onto the rails of collectivization was decided, a question important in principle and one which was to play such an enormous role during the war with fascist Germany.

All this was done thanks to the gigantic organizational work of the Communist Party.

The Hitlerites, whose attitude towards the people was one of contempt, could not even imagine that the popular masses could be united and inspired by high ideals and, in the name of these ideals, would be ready for the most incredible sacrifices, suffering, and heroic feats. The goal of the Hitlerites, that reactionary party of German monopolies, consisted of establishing German domination over all other peoples and obtaining more and more riches for the German monopolies by means of plundering other countries and peoples. The ideology of the Hitlerites was, if this word can be applied at all to characterize the views of the German fascists, like the ideology of a band of robbers. Actually, some robbers would probably quite fairly consider themselves insulted by such a comparison.

The ideal of the communists, of Soviet people following the Communist Party, was the building of a society in which real equality and fraternity could be realized and exploitation of man by man fully banished, a society in which there was no ruling caste oppressing and exploiting the majority. In such a society labor was an honorable right and responsibility of each citizen. The people of the land of the Soviets were selflessly erecting the edifice of this society—a socialist, communist society.

In the years of the five-year plans, the heroism of labor was in truth that of the whole people, truly a mass heroism. All this could not be understood by the leaders of that reactionary party of warlike German chauvinists.

Another miscalculation of the Hitlerites consisted of the fact that they viewed the Soviet Union as an artificial conglomeration of nations, since they did not know of any other type of multi-national state and could not imagine one. And any conglomeration is maintained, as they well learned, by force, by state power. If this power is solid, then the peoples remain in obedience to the master nation. But let this power weaken, and the multi-national state falls apart. Had not it been this way with the empire of Alexander the Great, with the Roman Empire, with Byzantium, and finally with the Holy Roman Empire of the German nation? From this followed the conclusion: at the first misfortunes, the multi-national Soviet Union would begin to crumble to its component national parts—the Ukraine, the Baltic states, the Trans-Caucasian republics would fall away, and other non-Russian peoples would revolt.

But the greatest achievement of the Communist Party, of the Soviet state, was exactly the creation and then the strengthening of a free union of peoples, founded on the principles of self-determination, equality, friendship, proletarian internationalism, mutual brotherly aid. For the first time in the history of mankind, the Soviet regime succeeded in creating a free union of peoples, free from exploitation. If one takes into account the fact that many peoples inhabiting the Soviet Union had been at diverse stages of economic, social, and cultural development,

103

one can imagine the grandiose scale of national construction in the USSR. But the German fascists counted heavily on enmity and antagonism among the peoples inhabiting the Soviet Union.

Having no conception of the power of proletarian internationalism and fraternal friendship among the peoples of the USSR, the Hitlerites at the same time did not know, understand, or even try to understand, the deep patriotism of the peoples of the Soviet Union, and first and foremost that of the most numerous of the peoples, the Russian people. The hatred and contemptuous attitude toward the Slavic peoples in general, inherited by the Hitlerites from their ancestors, the Teutonic knights and the German aristocracy which found its way into the imperial house of Romanov, were an integral part of fascist ideology. German-fascist racism was strengthened by the ignorance of their chieftains.

The wild, fanatic escapades of the German fascists even before their coming to power, their persecution of progressive, democratic statesmen after January 1933, their massive killings of Communists and Social-Democrats, their racism in general and their anti-Semitism in particular, and their debauch of reaction—all this called forth among Soviet people a sharply hostile attitude toward the Hitlerites. In the course of several years, the Soviet people, similar to other peoples of the world, had been witnesses to Germany's feverish preparations for war. Every one of her aggressive acts, those against Austria, Czechoslovakia, Spain, called forth a decisive condemnation. The peoples of the Soviet Union regarded the fight against fascism as vital as the fight against the White-guard movement had been in the years of the Civil War.

The Communist Party of the Soviet Union, the Komsomol, the labor unions, and all mass and social organizations systematically carried on anti-fascist propaganda among the population.

The Soviet people proudly realized that their country alone was carrying on a tireless and persistent struggle against fascist aggression and for the organization of a collective security against it. In those years there were few who did not know of M. M. Litvinov's speeches in defense of peace and against fascism. A huge role in confirming the anti-fascist mood of Soviet people was played by the burning of the Reichstag in Berlin by the Hitlerites and the later trial in Leipzig of that glorious figure of the Bulgarian and international workers' movement, Georgi Dimitrov, whose acquittal and arrival in the Soviet Union were received as a triumph for the world proletariat. In 1935 the Seventh Congress of the Communist International took place in Moscow. Without even mentioning the remarkable decisions of the Congress, which have not lost their significance even up to the present day, one should recall that indelible impression that remained in the hearts of many people from their meetings with the delegates to the Congress, fighters for communism in their countries, underground workers, many of whom had come to Moscow at the risk of their lives.

But the spirit of proletarian internationalism attained its highest triumph in the Soviet land during the Spanish Civil War. The war in Spain was for two and a half years the chief subject of conversation, hot arguments, and enormous social activity. Spain, which the absolute majority of Soviet people had known only from books and works of art, became close, it seemed, to the Soviet Union. Thousands and thousands of meetings of solidarity with the Spanish people, protests against fascist intervention and the complicity of the English and French "appeasers," were held in those years. Tens of millions of rubles were collected for a fund to aid the Spanish people. All a Spaniard had to do was appear on the streets of Moscow and he was immediately surrounded by a huge crowd. Especially loved were the fighters of the International Brigade, that highest form of international class solidarity. Tales of the deeds of Soviet flyers and tank men taking part in the Spanish people's fight for freedom and independence were passed on from mouth to mouth. Newspapers with reports by Mikhail Koltsov and Ilya Ehrenburg sold out immediately. Thousands of young people, workers and students, collective farmers and military personnel, burned with the desire to start immediately for the battlefields of Spain. In those years the anti-fascist mood of the Soviet people reached a red-hot peak. Few had doubts that the war which was ripening —and its death-dealing breath was already reaching out from China, Ethiopia, and Spain—would be a war against fascism.

To be ready for the defense of the Motherland! This thought was so natural that it became a simple, everyday affair for millions of young men and girls. It was rare that anyone from the student and working youth did not belong to the military or sport sections of the Osoaviakhim (Society of Assistance to Air and Chemical Defense and Industry), the voluntary sporting societies, or did not train in the pilot clubs, the glider schools, or the medical nurses' schools. The Soviet state was in a capitalist encirclement. Fascist aggressors were threatening the world. That was clear and understandable to everyone. Tens of thousands of young people were preparing to be ready for the decisive battle against fascism, to be worthy of that great test. They were convinced that the coming war would end with the victory of socialism in the whole world. Few of them could actually imagine what the war would be like. It was well known that the Red Army would fight on enemy territory, with little bloodshed, and that in this war our allies would be the German workers and peasants, who would revolt against Hitler. The Soviet people were strict in differentiating between the workers and the capitalists. The German worker was for them a friend and brother.

Stretching out the hand of fraternal aid to the oppressed proletariat of the world, Soviet people naturally counted on proletarian solidarity. And hadn't that been the case in the past, during the Civil War, during the strain in Anglo-Soviet relations in 1927? Everything seemed clear and simple.

A Great Industrial Power

By the beginning of the Second World War the Soviet Union had turned into a powerful industrial state, the resources of which were actually only beginning to be developed.

Less than a decade and a half after the rehabilitation of the national economy, the Soviet nation had achieved colossal successes in its economic development. The policy of giving priority to the development of the production of means of production, worked out and adopted by the Communist Party, had secured the economic independence of the Soviet state. This economic independence, in its turn, ensured the development of the country's economy on a healthy basis. This was particularly obvious during the world economic depressions of 1929–33 and 1937–38, when the capitalist countries experienced serious economic and social shocks. But the Soviet nation, thanks to its planned economy, did not experience difficulties of this kind.

There is no need to compare in this book the economic indicators of pre-revolutionary Russia, i.e., 1913, and those of the Soviet Union before the beginning of the Great Patriotic War. Let us address ourselves merely to the comparative data of economic development in our country in the Soviet period. In comparison with 1928, the volume of gross output of all the industry of the Soviet Union had, by the beginning of the Great Patriotic War, increased seven times, and that of heavy industry eleven times. In 1940 capital investments had grown by 128 percent in comparison with 1928.[2] Industry developed especially rapidly between 1928 and 1937. At the end of that decade the Soviet Union occupied the first place in the world in the mining of manganese ore and the production of synthetic rubber, and the first place in Europe and the second in the world in the gross output of machine building, tractor production, and oil production; the second place in Europe and the third in the world in the production of electrical energy, cast iron, and steel; the third place in Europe and the fourth in the world in coal mining and cement production; the second place in Europe and the third in the world in the production of aluminum.[3] The Soviet Union's share of world industrial production amounted to about 10 percent in 1937.[4]

The most important characteristic of this period was the steady growth of the productivity of labor because in the long run this would decide who would win in the economic competition of the two systems. In comparison with 1928 (the indicators of which are taken as 100), labor productivity as computed for one worker amounted to 313 in industry, 247 in building, and 269 in transportation. The growth of labor productivity was responsible for 51 percent of the total increase in industrial production in the first five-year plan and 79 percent in the second.[5]

By the beginning of 1941 the decisive branch of heavy industry—ferrous metals—possessed a powerful industrial base, furnished in the majority of cases with modern equipment. Ninety-nine blast furnaces, 391 open-hearth furnaces, 245 electric furnaces, 73 adaptors, 227 rolling mills, 51 tube mills, 139 coke batteries—such are the figures about the development of the Soviet ferrous metals industry calculated by the Soviet researcher G. S. Kravchenko in his book, on the basis of statistical materials studied by him.[6]

The ferrous metal industry served as the fundamental military-industrial base of the country.

However, the geographical distribution of steel and iron industry plants did not correspond to the interests of defense. In spite of energetic measures to build ferrous metals enterprises in the eastern part of the country, undertaken in the years of the five-year plans, the main metallurgical base consisted, as before, of installations located near the Soviet western border, in the Ukraine. There, on the eve of war, was produced almost two-thirds of the cast-iron and more than two-thirds of coke firing.[7] The eastern regions of the country had about one-third of the production of ferrous metal. The situation was better with coal, which comprised a little less than two-thirds of the country's general fuel balance. The southwestern regions produced a little more than half of the coal. Aside from the Donbas, coal was produced in the regions near Moscow, in the Urals, in Siberia, Central Asia, the Transcaucasia, and in the far North. Although these regions' share of the coal industry was much lower than that of the Donbas, such a geographical distribution opened important opportunities, and these were used in the course of the Great Patriotic War.

The Soviet land had a powerful petroleum base and inexhaustible supplies of liquid fuel. At that time nobody was able to determine the oil reserves of the country accurately. Most of the oil was obtained in the Baku oil region, more than 70 percent of all oil production. In second place were the North Caucasian oil wells (Groznyi and Maikop) which yielded almost 15 percent; after them followed the oil deposits in the Urals and other parts of the country. The new oil deposits in the

109

Urals and the Volga region had a very rich potential which before the war had only started to be exploited. From a strategic point of view, the concentration of the oil industry in the south of the country, not far from the border, was unsatisfactory, since they were within range of air power based in neighboring states. It is known that during World War II the oil industries of Baku and the oil refining plants in Batumi were under direct threat of bombing.

Great were the accomplishments of the Soviet nation in the production of electrical energy, although it should be noted that the growth of industry demanded incessant increase in the amount of energy produced. The consumption of electrical energy by agriculture was insignificant, a fact which affected the level of agricultural development unfavorably.

The characteristic feature of the development of electric power production in the prewar days was the important increase in the number of electric power stations in the eastern regions, which produced more than one-fourth of all the electrical power in the country.

An especially important place in the military potential of the country was occupied by the nonferrous metals industry. It was one of the new branches of production. The basic nonferrous metals installations were erected in the years of the first and second five-year plans. At the same time a modernization and enlargement of the old ones took place. Similarly to the electric power stations, an ever greater number of nonferrous metal factories and plants were located in the eastern regions of the country. The Urals and Kazakhstan were a powerful arsenal of nonferrous metals, delivering a significant portion of the raw materials without which an uninterrupted development of the war industries would have been inconceivable.

Significant were the successes of the Soviet machine-tool production, also a new form of industry for our country.

An important positive factor for the Soviet war economy was the adequate number of specialists catering to the needs of a rapidly developing modern technology. Industrial engineers with higher education alone numbered 300,000 at the start of 1941, which was one-third of the total number of specialists with higher education working in the people's economy. Almost 1.5 million persons with secondary education, of which more than 320,000 were technicians, worked in the economy. The well-organized system for training qualified cadres permitted an uninterrupted improvement in the techniques and standards of industry.

In the years preceding the Great Patriotic War, in spite of the important changes in the ratio between the urban and rural population, most of the country's population continued to live in the rural areas.[8]

During the years of the five-year plans, agriculture was almost entirely collectivized. The lion's share of production for the market came from the collective farms (kolkhozes) and the rest was received mainly from the state farms (sovkhozes). In 1938–40, the average yearly gross grain harvest consisted of 4,756 poods.[9] Agriculture received a large quantity of machinery—tractors, combines, etc. At the same time, livestock raising lagged behind. By January 1, 1938, the number of cattle had shrunk to 50.9 million head, whereas there had been 58.2 million head on January 1, 1929. The situation improved a bit in 1938–40. As of January 1, 1941, cattle numbered 54.5 million head.[10]

The rates of growth of gross agricultural production were also uneven.

111

On the eve of war, the state, basing itself on the collective farm system, was able to create food reserves in case of extreme emergency. While noting the positive role of J. V. Stalin in leading the country and armed forces during the Great Patriotic War, it should be said that the cult of personality led to serious mistakes in the decision of a number of political and strategic questions on the eve of war and in the course of military operations against Hitler's Germany. The merits of J. V. Stalin and "the significance of his actions and pronouncements were exaggerated under the influence of the cult of personality, while at the same time the significance of the activities of the Central Committee of the Party as a whole were minimized." [11]

The economy of the Soviet state could have developed faster still and achieved an even higher level by the time the war started, if the situation in the country had not been adversely influenced by the cult of personality and, in connection with it, by the mass, baseless repressions conducted by J. V. Stalin against party and Soviet officials. For the "theoretical" justification of the punitive measures being carried out, J. V. Stalin, at the February–March 1937 plenum of the Central Committee of the All-Union Communist Party (Bolsheviks) put forth the erroneous thesis that class warfare would become sharper the nearer the country approached socialism. Stalin maintained that "contemporary wreckers" and "saboteurs, possessing party cards" had made their appearance. Making a report at the plenum, V. M. Molotov declared that practically all party organizations were littered with wreckers. The difficulties which the country was experiencing in connection with the rapid growth of industrial production and the revolutionary changes in the economy, often aggravated by the mistakes and miscalculations of J. V. Stalin himself, he tried to explain away as schemes of enemies of the people. The repressions came down on many party and

Soviet workers, including prominent persons active in the Soviet state.

After J. V. Stalin's death, the Central Committee took measures to end the arbitrariness of the period of the cult of personality. Unfairly convicted persons were freed. Their good names and all civil rights were returned to them. And those who had fallen as victims of arbitrary rule were posthumously rehabilitated. The Twentieth Congress of the CPSU re-established socialist legality in the country.

The repressions carried out on orders of J. V. Stalin made the country feverish, interfered with the development of production, introduced fear and uncertainty, fettered initiative. Managers of enterprises were replaced one after another. The new people coming into managerial positions in the economy often did not possess the necessary experience and knowledge. The atmosphere of spy-mania, artificially created by J. V. Stalin, strengthened suspicion and opened doors for ambitious men and lick-spittles, for unprincipled people and careerists, for self-seekers and slanderers. Under these conditions one needed a certain measure of courage to take responsibility for some industrial innovation or other, particularly if its advantages would not become apparent right away. Many enterprise managers avoided innovations for this reason, preferring to live quietly so as not to risk being accused of wrecking.

All this, together with reasons of an economic character, could not but affect the development of the economy negatively, particularly in the field of ferrous metals. After 1938 production fell leveled off. In 1938, 14,652,000 tons of cast-iron were produced; in 1939 production was 132,000 tons less. At the same time steel production (18,057,000 tons in 1938) was reduced by 493,000 tons, and rolled metal (13,258,000 tons in 1938) by 529,000 tons.

113

The situation in ferrous metals was discussed by the Central Committee of the party and the Sovnarkom (Council of People's Commissars) of the USSR; a resolution was adopted, the implementation of which permitted some correction of the situation. In 1940, in comparison with 1938, cast-iron production had increased by 250,000 tons, steel by 260,000 tons; the situation with rolled metal remained unsatisfactory in 1940 and began to straighten out only in the first half of 1941. In 1940, 240,000 tons more rolled metal was produced than in 1939, but 145,000 tons less than in 1938. The reduction in cast-iron, steel, and rolled metal production in its turn slowed down the development of machine building. For instance, the production of automobiles was reduced in 1940 by 28 percent in comparison with 1939, and tractor production by 25 percent.

Under the conditions of spreading war in Europe the most important factor in preparing for the repulsion of the aggressor if he should attack the Soviet Union was an efficiently organized industry. While giving encouragement in every way to shock workers, the foremost workers of industry, giving prizes to the best enterprises and the best workers, decorating them with orders and medals, the Soviet state was forced to take strict measures for the regulation of labor discipline.

In the summer of 1940 a decree was issued forbidding the quitting of work and the transfer from one enterprise to another without permission, and stipulating various penalties up to and including prosecution under law. At the same time an eight-hour day was introduced in place of the seven-hour day, and a six-day work week was established.

It should be noted that these measures were taken under extraordinary circumstances. War was already raging in Europe, and one had to be ready for all eventualities.

"Our first and most important obligation," M. I. Kalinin said in his report of November 6, 1940, "is the further strengthening of the economic and defensive power of the socialist motherland." [12]

The decisions to create state labor reserves for the needs of industry and transport, taken by the Communist Party and the Soviet government in the second half of 1940, had important significance for the strengthening of the country's military-economic potential. The labor reserves included a wide net of industrial trade schools and factory training schools. These training schools prepared cadres of young working men and women. During their training they were fully supported by the state. In 1940 about 750,000 young men and girls were undergoing training in the system of labor reserves.

Bringing a greater number of women workers into industry had important significance for the defense of the country. In 1940 eleven million women comprised one-third of the total labor force. In the years of the Patriotic War, when a great part of the male population was mobilized, this circumstance played no small part in the solution of the labor problem.

The objective process of development of Soviet society could not be stopped, even though it was held up by the negative influence of the cult of personality and the ugly phenomena accompanying it. Ever fresh thousands of people were being brought into the sphere of active productive and social work. As the general educational level grew, people's interests broadened, their needs as well as their aspirations to make their maximum contribution to the building of a socialist society increased. Manifestations of these aspirations were widespread socialist competition for the prescheduled fulfillment of the goals of the third five-year plan, economy in production, the increase in labor productivity, and the liquidation of absenteeism. The workers of many branches of industry, particularly in the field of defense, did not spare their efforts in strengthening the might of their country.

By 1941 the situation in industry had greatly improved. The Eighteenth party conference, which took place in mid-February 1941 took note of this fact and adopted an economic plan for 1941 in which much attention was paid to the development of heavy industry and particularly to the branches connected with defense.[13] During the first half of 1941, industrial production continued to grow rapidly throughout the country. But the clouds of war were already gathering on the horizon.

The Defense Industry

The Soviet state had always paid great attention to the defense industry. The creation of a powerful industrial and raw material base during the years of the first and second five-year plans had permitted military production essential to the defense of the state to be significantly increased.

Before the war more and more consideration was given to the development of an industrial base in the eastern regions and Central Asia, not dependent on the European regions of the country. Thus the third five-year plan provided for the creation of a new oil industry center beyond the Volga and coal-metallurgical bases in the Urals and the Far East; in Kazakhstan as well as in the Central Asian republics the nonferrous metal industry during the first five-year plan, was growing rapidly. The country was approaching the realization of a most important objective with an enormous defense significance: the construction of duplicate plants in the eastern regions. In the shortest time, airplane and tank factories, enterprises for the production of explosives, and factories for radio, optical, and other equipment were constructed.

116

The following factors exercised a great influence in determining the proportions of military industry to the total industry of the country, and in building the armed forces: the USSR was the only socialist state in a capitalist encirclement and, consequently, would have to depend exclusively on its own powers in the event of armed conflict. The deterioration of the international situation, the local wars which broke out in various parts of the world in the 1930's, the militarization of capitalist countries and particularly Germany after the fascists came to power there, all forced the Soviet Union to maintain its military might on an elevated and modern level, in order not to be caught unawares by some unexpected event. For this reason the funds earmarked for defense in the state budget, which amounted to only 5.4 percent of all expenses during the first five-year plan, increased to 12.6 percent in the second, and reached an average of 26.4 percent for the three years of the third five-year plan. In connection with the direct threat of war, the funds assigned to defense in 1941 comprised 43.4 percent of the state budget.[14]

The successes of the Soviet defense industry in the field of aircraft construction were significant. This was one of the newest branches of industry. The most talented scientific workers, designers, and engineers joined it, such as A. N. Tupolev, A. S. Yakovlev, S. V. Ilyushin, S. A. Lavochkin, A. I. Mikoyan, V. M. Petlyakov, N. N. Polikarpov, A. A. Arkhangelskiy, and many others.

Just as in our time, young men and girls dream of building space ships or becoming cosmonauts, the youth in the 1930's aspired to the professions of aviation engineers or pilots. The fantastic flights of V. P. Chkalov, M. M. Gromov, and their comrades, and the altitude records of V. K. Kokkinaki, attracted the whole world's attention for the unusual reason that all these flights were made in aircraft conceived by Soviet designers and workers. The Soviet heavy bombers designed by Tupolev and

117

the fighters designed by Yakovlev in the mid-1930's met the requirements of the level of aircraft development in that period. By the end of the 1930's, in connection with the unfolding armed conflicts, and particularly after the beginning of World War II, technical and flight performance requirements as to the speed, maneuverability, ceiling, equipment, and armament of aircraft had increased greatly. The war in Europe showed that fascist Germany had dive-bombers, medium bombers, and fighters of high quality. Fighter aviation developed rapidly in England. In a short time British fighters not only equaled the German ones in their military capabilities, but surpassed them. Aircraft production in the United States of America and Canada developed with gigantic strides.

Soviet designers labored tirelessly over the creation of new, more modern types of military aircraft. Soon after the beginning of World War II, the Soviet government adopted a number of urgent measures to assure the construction of new aircraft factories and the rebuilding of old ones. However, these decisions were not put through with sufficient speed or effectiveness, and their implementation greatly lagged behind the ever growing tempo of events developing in the world.

In 1939 the designer A. S. Yakovlev and his co-workers created the new fighter YAK-1. In 1940 the MIG-3 fighters were released according to the plans of the designers Mikoyan and Gurevich, and the fighter LAG-3 according to the designs of Lavochkin and his colleagues. These fighters were the most prominent achievement of the science of aviation of their time. For instance, the MIG-3 fighter developed a speed of up to 620 kilometers per hour, could climb to an altitude of 12,000 meters and had a range of 700 kilometers. Soviet aircraft builders also developed the magnificent low-flying attack plane, the IL-2 (designer Ilyushin), and the dive-bomber PE-2 (designer Petlyakov).

However, the mass production of the new planes was scarcely beginning to move. In 1940 only twenty MIG-3's, two PE-2's, and 64 YAK-1's were produced. In the first half of 1941, the production of new types of aircraft grew sharply but could not satisfy the demand of the armed forces, whose aircraft inventory had become largely obsolescent. One thousand nine hundred and forty-six of the new types of fighters, 458 PE-2 dive-bombers, and 249 IL-2 attack planes were produced.[15]

"By the middle of 1941," according to the *History of the Great Patriotic War*, "our aircraft industry was being rebuilt, and its production base was significantly increased and prepared for the serial output of new, high-quality military aircraft. New models of fighters, attack planes, and bombers were created, tested, and accepted as armament for the air forces." [16]

The tank industry had great possibilities. Here, too, there worked a galaxy of talented designers. Among them were N. V. Barykov, Professor V. L. Zaslavskiy (who became a victim of the repressions of the personality-cult period), V. M. Doroshenko, Zh. Ya. Kotin, N. A. Kukharenko, M. I. Tarshinov, and others. However, the war in Europe in 1939–40 showed that the tanks that were in serial production were outmoded. In 1939 and 1940 new types of tanks, the heavy KV and the medium T-34, were created. In their combat capabilities these tanks exceeded the known types of armored vehicles then being produced in the capitalist world. This was especially clearly confirmed during the course of the war with Hitler's Germany. However, before the beginning of the Great Patriotic War, the mass production of the new models was only just being organized. In 1940, 243 KV tanks and 115 T-34's were manufactured. In the first half of 1941 the tank industry had just begun to gather steam and produced 396 KV tanks and 1,110 T-34's.

The industry for the manufacture of artillery and infantry weapons produced an important quantity of various arms. The designing offices, under the leadership of V. G. Grabin, I. I. Ivanov, F. F. Petrov, B. I. Shavyrin, and others, worked out new types of weapons and perfected old ones. Important work in the improvement of infantry weapons was carried out by G. S. Shpagin, V. A. Degtyarev, and F. V. Tokarev. Many models of Soviet artillery weapons surpassed foreign ones in their specifications.

On the eve of war, A. G. Kostikov invented a rocket mortar which was already well-known by August 1941 and was nicknamed "Katyusha." However, there were serious deficiencies in the production of artillery which had come about as a result of outmoded conceptions about the qualities and forms of weapons demanded in modern war. In his memoirs, the late B. L. Vannikov, three times hero of Socialist Labor, who held the post of People's Commissar of Armaments, gives an example of the strikingly incompetent and frivolous attitude to questions of modern arms production held by some managerial personnel directly responsible for this activity. The chief of the Main Artillery Directorate, G. I. Kulik, proposed, on the eve of the Great Patriotic War, the removal from production of the 76 millimeter cannon and the quick design and production in its place of a new 107 tank cannon. Without advancing B. L. Vannikov's technical military arguments against this proposal, the main reason should be noted: "The 76 millimeter 'ZIS' cannon, only recently created and put into production, was the best contemporary cannon." [17] Because of Vannikov's objections, the matter was reported to J. V. Stalin. Here is how the affair then unfolded: "At the end of my explanations, A. A. Zhdanov came into the study. Stalin turned to him and said, 'Vannikov, here, doesn't want to make 107 millimeter guns for your Leningrad tanks. But those cannons are good ones, I know them from the Civil War. . . .' Stalin was speaking of a field gun of the First

World War period: aside from its caliber, it had nothing in common with the cannon which had to be created for modern tanks and modern battle conditions. Stalin's casual remark usually settled the matter. And so it was this time." In a meeting of the special commission studying this question, Vannikov declared to Zhdanov: "You are permitting the disarmament of the army before the war." Nevertheless, it was decided to cease production of the 45 and 76 millimeter cannons, the most necessary weapons for fighting the enemy's tanks. Not having looked into Kulik's completely baseless recommendations, Stalin approved this decision, which had such grave consequences for the army.[18]

The mass production of the excellent mortar designed by B. I. Shavyrin was delayed for a long time. It began to be manufactured only in 1940. Industry quickly assimilated the Shavyrin mortars, and 14,200 82-millimeter and 3,200 120-millimeter mortars were produced by the start of the war with Hitler's Germany. So, thanks to the efforts of the workers of the armaments industry, the matter was put right.[19]

It was characteristic of the conditions under the cult of personality that Beria's henchmen picked out, as the culprit for the interruption in mortar construction, none other than the designer B. I. Shavyrin, who was accused of wrecking activities. The People's Commissar for Armaments managed to prevent his arrest, but then at the beginning of June 1941, People's Commissar B. L. Vannikov himself was arrested.[20]

All was not well with the production of submachine guns either, through G. I. Kulik's fault. Because of his technical illiteracy and fear of responsibility, Kulik, not having a well-founded opinion of his own, in fact slowed down production of new models. It was because of this, in particular, that the production of antitank and antiaircraft weapons lagged behind.[21]

On the eve of war, antitank rifles were removed from production. The output of light and heavy machine-guns was reduced.

From 1939 to 1941, the Communist Party and the Soviet government adopted a number of energetic measures for getting rid of deficiencies in the work of the defense industry. Understanding the complexities of the international situation, so pregnant with every sort of unexpected occurrences for the Soviet Union, the designers, workers, and engineers of the defense industry toiled selflessly. The high conscientiousness of the scientists, the workers in the designing offices, and the laborers ensured the growth and strengthening of the country's defensive preparedness in spite of objective and subjective difficulties.

But military production was not keeping up with the headlong rush of events. Too little time remained.

N. A. Voznesenskiy, in his book about the Soviet war economy during the Patriotic War, published in 1948, stated that "The Patriotic War found the Soviet war industry in the process of developing new techniques, and a massive output of modern military equipment had not yet been organized." [22]

On the eve of war a mobilization plan for the second half of 1941, and for 1942, was adopted, providing for "the military rebuilding of industry in case of war," N. A. Voznesenskiy relates. With the start of war this plan turned into an operational problem.

Preparation of the Armed Forces to Repel Aggression

The Soviet Army is an army of the people. This short formula, which arose when the workers' and peasants' Red Army was first formed, could not be excelled as an expression of the purpose and problems of the armed forces of the Soviet state.

They were called to defend the achievements of the revolution against the encroachment of enemies. And the great moral strength of the Red Army consisted of this function of defending the socialist fatherland. Unlike the armies of the imperialist states, which were made ready for the waging of aggressive war, and in practice defended the interests of ruling classes—the bourgeosie, large landowners, monopolies—aggressive objectives were alien to the army of the Soviet state, because it defended the interests of the working class and peasantry who were vitally interested in supporting and preserving the peace.

Reared in the high ideals of communism, the Red Army enjoyed the great love of the people. Service in the ranks of the Red Army was an honor for every citizen of the Soviet state. The closeness of the army and the people was expressed in the first instance by the fact that the commanders came from the midst of the people. These were former workers, peasants, or people coming from the working intelligentsia. To whom could the people's aspirations have been closer and more accessible? The Red Army was an inseparable part of the Soviet people, its armed detachment. Just as the worker in industry, the peasant in the field, and the scientist in his laboratory worked to increase the might and well-being of their country, Soviet soldiers underwent their service, contributing their far from easy task to the common cause.

As of July 1940, the social origins of the officers of the Red Army were as follows: officers of working class origins, 37.9 percent; peasant origins, 19.1 percent; from the employee class, 38.2 percent. Officers originating from other social strata comprised 0.7 percent. More than half the officers (54.6 percent) were Communists and 22.1 percent were Komsomol members.[23]

The Communist Party and the Soviet government looked after their armed forces tirelessly, promoted the strengthening of their combat effectiveness, cultivated conscientious military discipline, raised the morale of the soldiers and officers, and did much to equip the army with the most up-to-date models of military hardware. An important role in maintaining the armed forces on the level of modern requirements was played by military science, which worked out an orderly system of views on the strategy and tactics of the armed forces of a socialist state. The troops were trained and the armed forces developed in accordance with the views and principles of military science.

The experience of the Civil War, and the local wars of the 1920's and 1930's, were studied and used creatively in the training of troops. In the 1930's Soviet military science was the source of advanced ideas in world military science. Thus, as early as 1932, the first mechanized corps in the world were formed by the Red Army, and in 1934 and 1935 armored and mechanized units were separated into a special branch of service. This was a bold, revolutionary decision, based on correct premises as to the growing role of this type of troops in the coming war. Unfortunately, in 1939, an incorrect conclusion was drawn from the experience of the use of tanks during the war in Spain. As a result the maintenance of large tank formations was considered inexpedient, and the mechanized corps were abolished.[24]

The Soviet Union was the birthplace of parachutism and of the airborne troops later created on this basis. The landing of airborne troops was successfully demonstrated at maneuvers of 1934 and 1935, attended by military delegations of several capitalist countries. In the opinion of foreign experts, the Red Army was one of the most advanced and modern armies in the mid-1930's. This conclusion played a far from unimportant role in the decision of the French, and later the Czechoslovak, governments to conclude mutual aid treaties with the Soviet Union.

Along with the quantitative and qualitative growth of armaments and military equipment, the organizational structure of the Red Army was also being perfected.

The development of military theory in our country was based on the teachings of Marxism-Leninism about war and the army, on the political and economic situation in the country, and on the experience of past wars. Soviet military theory resolved the basic questions connected with the characteristic peculiarities of the future war correctly, as the experience of the Great Patriotic War showed.

Soviet military science put enormous importance on the factor of morale, and this correct orientation completely justified itself during the war with Germany, particularly in its beginning phase. Soviet military science flowed from general Marxist-Leninist theses on the role of man in a socialist society. The discovery of the individual potentialities of each member of society, help in the development of his aptitudes in the collective for the benefit of the whole society—these theses, applied to military conditions, played a colossal part because, in teaching the soldier bravery, skill, and the ability to make independent decisions, they helped inculcate in him simultaneously a high, conscientious discipline, a feeling of responsibility for the fate of his comrades, his squad, his unit, his army, for the fate of the war and his country, for a feeling of mutual rescue, disdain for death, for heroism. It was thanks to these particular qualities that the Soviet soldier was able to hold out in the incredibly difficult circumstances of the initial period of the Patriotic War.

Soviet military doctrine proceeded from the probability of a new world war, which would take on a long, drawn-out character. In this war a coalition of imperialist powers could move against the Soviet Union. The war would strain all the resources of the state: economic, political, and moral. It was assumed that the war would be carried on on the enemy's territory, have the character of a war of destruction, and victory would be achieved with little bloodshed. Correct on the whole, these theses had substantial defects—they excluded the possibility of fighting the war on our own territory, and they mistakenly proceeded from a conjecture about insignificant losses. These defects were aggravated by the incorrect political assumption of indubitable armed support for the Red Army by the workers of the capitalist countries.

These incorrect views were widely circulated in the army and among the people. The works of some authors also spread mistaken views. For instance, before the war N. Shpanov's book *The First Blow* was published and quickly sold out. According to this book, there would already be a revolt against Hitler's regime on the second day of the war.

Checking the theory by the actual practice of war also showed that some questions were solved incorrectly, and that even the correct theses could not always be realized in practice. These occasional miscalculations by Soviet military specialists, together with the basic reason, insufficient preparedness to repel aggression, explain the tragic fact that a tactical surprise attack and the initial successes of the fascist army became possible.

Among the defects of Soviet military theory, one should name the insufficient elaboration of the character and contents of the initial period of the war under the conditions of surprise mass attack. As a result of this, the training of the troops did not always correspond to the type of military operations characteristic of the first period of the Second World War.

It is completely clear that the danger of war with Germany in 1941 was underestimated. Working out the war plan in case of Hitlerite aggression, our command considered that, at the beginning of the attack, military operations would be carried on by limited covering forces, and that after the mobilization and deployment of the main force, we could smash the aggressor in the frontier zone and pass on to a general offensive, transferring operations to the enemy's territory. The defense of the western borders was entrusted to the border military districts. The sizable forces belonging to the border districts were deployed at a great distance from the border and did not have sufficient means of transportation. Individual units only were located in direct proximity to the border.

Little attention was directed to the question of strategic defense. Regarding offense as the main means of battle, our theory did not sufficiently work out the organization and implementation of defense, which was considered subordinate in relation to offense. It was imagined that defense would have a local character and would be mounted only in limited areas, and not on the whole battlefront.

These and some other mistaken views on the basic questions of waging modern war had a negative influence on the preparation of the armed forces for war.

Many mistakes could have been avoided if some warning from Soviet military leaders had not been undeservedly forgotten. As early as 1936, the prominent Soviet military leader and theoretician of the art of war, Marshal M. N. Tukhachevskiy, publicly warned (in his appearance at the second session of the Central Executive Committee of the USSR) that Germany was preparing for a surprise attack, that the German army would be ready to attack without warning. Tukhachevskiy also thought that the Germans would be the first to start the war in order to ensure the surprise of the attack. However, as the well-known military specialist A. I. Todorskiy writes, Tukhachevskiy's considerations were not taken into account at the time.[25]

In addition to such local and specific military conflicts as the battles on the Khasan and at Halhaiin-Gol (against Japan in 1938–39), the military operations in Europe in 1939–40 and the Soviet-Finnish armed conflict had great meaning for the armed forces of the Soviet Union in their study of the experience and its practical application.

Soviet military specialists studied these battles exhaustively and hastened to derive lessons which could be used with the troops. However, there was very little time left for training the troops in the newest methods of waging war, and for re-equipping the Red Army, literally only a few weeks. And a great deal had to be done. A lot was done. At a conference of leading officers in December 1940 and January 1941, attention was directed to the necessity for training military cadets and officer students in methods and forms of modern warfare with the use of equipment employed in battle, such as tanks, artillery, etc.

In 1940 the People's Commissariat of Defense and the General Staff presented to the government their proposals on taking the necessary measures for strategic deployment. After the government had studied the considerations on strategic deployment for 1941, plans for screening action were worked out and a group of forces was created in the border areas.

In 1940, and also in the first half of 1941, the Soviet government adopted a number of resolutions in which attention was correctly directed to serious deficiencies in the training of troops, in technical equipment, and in the preparation of border defense positions. As a result the total number of infantry divisions grew significantly. Formation of artillery antitank brigades of the general headquarters artillery reserve was begun. Mechanized corps, and separate armored and mechanized divisions, were formed again. Great attention was paid to the numerical strengthening of airborne troops. In the first half of 1941, still before the beginning of the war, there was success in completing the formation of several airborne corps. The antiaircraft defense net (PVO) was enlarged and its organizational structure improved. A lot of work was undertaken in the navy and the air forces. New units of engineer troops, signal troops, and others were formed.

However, the re-equipment of the forces was delayed and had not been completed by the time of the attack by Hitler's Germany.

"On June 22, 1941," Colonel A. Nikitin writes, "new military aviation equipment in the border military districts comprised only 22 percent, old equipment 78 percent." [26]

There was a more or less analogous situation in the armored and mechanized units, which were only half supplied with new equipment by the start of the war. [27]

A serious mistake, which led to grave consequences at the beginning of the war, was made as a result of the decision to dismantle fortifications along the old (1939) border in connection with the construction of new defense positions. The disarmament of the old border was completed rapidly, while the building of new positions was delayed. It is sufficient to point out that the construction plans, approved in the summer of 1940, were calculated for several years! In his memoirs, Army General I. I. Fedyuninskiy, who commanded the Fifteenth Infantry Corps of the Kiev special military district, beginning in April 1941, relates that the construction of fortifications was far from complete. [28]

The former commander of engineer troops of the Leningrad Front, Lieutenant General B. Bychevskiy, writes that the construction of fortifications in the Leningrad military district area was still going on as of June 21, 1941, and was not complete. Bychevskiy also cites the statement of the chief of the engineer directorate of the Baltic Military District, Major General V. F.

Zotov, that "the sapper units of that district, just as in our own, were engaged in constructing pill-boxes, and there were no ready fortifications." [29]

The centers of defense with completed fortifications in many cases lacked the prescribed armaments. Garrisons needed to be brought up to strength. The chief of the Main Political Directorate of the Red Army, Army Commissar A. N. Zaporozhets, reported to the People's Commissar of Defense, Marshal S. K. Timoshenko, on April 15, 1941: "The fortified regions of our western borders are, for the most part, not combat ready."

If the old border had not been disarmed, the Red Army in its retreat could have, even without the completion of the new defense centers, made a stand at the old fortifications and gained precious time for regrouping units and delivering a counterblow.

A sad picture also exists in the story of the reconstruction of old airfields and the construction of new ones near the western border. In light of the military command's warning, simultaneous work was started on most of the airfields near the border. And many of them were being built dangerously close to the border. The construction had not been completed by the beginning of the war, and the air force found itself in very unfavorable circumstances because of the great density and the limitations in maneuver and deception.

Since, in case of war, the idea was to parry the enemy's blow and then transfer military operations to his territory, the basic supply dumps and mobilization stores were located not far from the old border, in Byelorussia, in the Ukraine, and near Smolensk. In 1940, when the government was reviewing the question of the location of mobilization supplies, the representatives of the central supply directorates and the General Staff proposed to move them beyond the Volga. However, J. V. Stalin rejected these proposals and ordered the mobilization stores to be concentrated on the territory of the border military districts. Later this mistake had to be paid for dearly, military specialists write.[30]

In 1940 numerous measures were taken to strengthen individual commands. The institution of military commissars, introduced in 1937, was abolished. In its place the position of deputy to the commander for political affairs was established.

The armed conflict with Finland and study of the condition of the armed forces showed serious deficiencies in the training of the officer corps. This was especially true in the infantry, which was understaffed in officer personnel by one-fifth as of May 1, 1940. It was established that the yearly number of military school graduates was not sufficient to ensure the creation of essential reserves. The quality of training was low. It appeared that 68 percent of the platoon and company commanders had only the benefit of a short junior lieutenant's five-month course of instruction.

The repressions which J. V. Stalin loosed on the Red Army officer corps made the situation still worse in the command cadres. One of the first victims was the Soviet Union's military attaché in London, V. Putna, falsely accused of clandestine counterrevolutionary Trotskyite activities. At an open trial of the "anti-Soviet Trotskyite center" in January 1937, the name of Marshal of the Soviet Union M. N. Tukhachevskiy was mentioned. And although it was declared there that Tukhachevskiy had nothing to do with the affair and was not being accused of anything, a shadow was cast on his name. This was, apparently, the objective of the state prosecutor at the trial, Vyshinskiy, who named the marshal at least ten times in his questions directed to the accused.

Marshal Tukhachevskiy continued to occupy his post, but his

fate was in fact decided at that time. In the rush to compromise Tukhachevskiy and others among the more talented leadership of the Red Army, they were accused of a plot against the Soviet Union.

Several versions of this story exist. They are based on materials produced by the former adjutant of Kaltenbrunner, the assistant chief of the Gestapo, Hoettl, who in 1950 published the book *Secret Front* under the pseudonym W. Hagen. Later Hoettl republished the book under his own name. In this book Hoettl tells of the Gestapo's provocative espionage activities, including the story of how, in the depths of the German intelligence and counter-intelligence agencies, documents were concocted for the purpose of compromising the Soviet high command. This material corroborates the account of events contained in the posthumously published memoirs of the chief of one of the branches of the Reich security service, W. Schellenberg. There are other materials on this affair, mentions of it in the memoirs of statesmen in Western countries, etc.

The repressions against party and Soviet cadres, dedicated to the communist cause, called forth malicious joy among the enemies of the Soviet nation. There was particular joy in Berlin, where the fascists had long been considering plans to weaken the Red Army and the Soviet state. These efforts increased after the Soviet Union, France, and Czechoslovakia concluded pacts of mutual aid, which served as a barrier to fascist aggression in Europe. Considerations of an internal political nature also moved the Hitlerites. These calculations consisted of completely subordinating the German army to fascist influence, forcing the German generals to abandon once and for all any attempts to carry out any independent policy. This was all the more important, in the opinion of the Hitlerites, because rearmament and enlargement of the German armed forces, already under way, demanded the complete subjection of the commanders to fascist influence. For this reason attempts did not cease to compromise the more "stubborn" generals by any and all means. The German generals could be accused of having entered into criminal collusion with the Soviet generals . . . Documents could be fabricated to prove this . . . Finally, a way could be found to send these documents to Moscow to compromise the Soviet generals as well.

At the beginning of 1937, Heydrich, Schellenberg's direct superior, ordered him to prepare a survey of the mutual relations between the Reichswehr and the Red Army in the past years.

As is known, in the 1920's, after the signing of a treaty in Rapallo between Germany and the USSR, Soviet-German relations developed normally: trade and contact along scientific and technical lines were arranged. Germany and the USSR also exchanged military delegations.* Some military leaders of the Red Army studied at the German military academy. One of the students was, for instance, Army Commander I. E. Yakir, who graduated from this academy with high honors. By request of the Reichswehr leaders, Yakir gave a course of lectures on military operations during the Civil War for the German officers. On all these and other questions there was the usual official correspondence between Soviet and German agencies. Among this correspondence there were papers signed by chiefs of Soviet agencies, including military ones. The German archives contained facsimiles of the signatures of Tukhachevskiy and other prominent Soviet military leaders. This circumstance played an important role in the preparation for their doom.

Schellenberg quickly produced the demanded survey. Hey-

---

* Their military cooperation was, of course, much more extensive than that.—V.P.

drich informed Schellenberg that he had information that the Soviet generals, headed by Tukhachevskiy, were preparing to carry out a revolt directed against Stalin, with the help of German generals. This idea had been "served up" to Heydrich by the Russian White-émigré general Skoblin.* Heydrich, according to Schellenberg, immediately understood how to make use of this thought. "If one went about it the right way, one could deal such a blow to the leadership of the Red Army that it wouldn't recover for many years," Schellenberg writes. The plan was reported to Hitler and received his approval. The Gestapo, which did not have, one may be sure, any documents on this subject, began to fabricate them with speed.[31]

Leaving aside the manifold details of this monstrous provocation, we will point out that the forged documents accusing the high command of the Red Army of a plot were prepared by April 1937. A German agent in Prague established contact with a person in the confidence of the president of Czechoslovakia, E. Beneš, and reported to him that he had documents concerning a plot among the high command of the Red Army. Beneš immediately informed Stalin. Soon a special plenipotentiary of Yezhov arrived in Prague. In April and May 1937, the arrests of the highest officers of the Red Army took place. Among them was Marshal M. N. Tukhachevskiy. I. E. Yakir, I. P. Uborevich, A. I. Kork, R. P. Eideman, and B. M. Feldman were also arrested, and, before them, V. M. Primakov and V. I. Putna. Those who gave the orders for their arrests and their trials must have known that the accusations were baseless and the documents forged. On June 12, 1937, Tukhachevskiy and his comrades were shot.[32] The chief of the Main Political Directorate, Ya. B. Gamarnik, committed suicide. The arrests and destruction of

---

* Skoblin, by the way, was a double agent and worked for the Soviets as well.—V.P.

military cadres also continued after the end of 1937. Thus, through false accusations, perished Marshal V. K. Bluecher, a hero of the Civil War who for many years had commanded the army in the Far East; the former chief of General Staff and first deputy People's Commissar, Marshal A. I. Yegorov; Army Commander G. M. Stern, hero of battles in Spain and the Far East; and many others. In the *History of the Great Patriotic War* it is recorded that "subjected to repressions were nearly half of all the regimental commanders, almost all the brigade and division commanders, all corps commanders and troop commanders of military districts, members of military councils and chiefs of the political directorates of the districts, the majority of the political workers of corps, divisions, and brigades, about a third of the regimental commissars, many lecturers at higher and intermediate educational institutions." [33] Marshal of the Soviet Union I. Kh. Bagramyan, in an interview with a *Literaturnaya gazeta* correspondent on April 17, 1965, stated that the destruction of prominent Soviet military leaders as "enemies of the people" on the eve of war was actually one of the reasons for the great failures in the first period of the war. [34]

The repressions which fell upon the Soviet military cadres also had very unfavorable consequences for the USSR's foreign policy. President Beneš also informed the French Premier, Léon Blum, about the alleged plot just at the time that the French government was discussing the question of concluding a Franco-Soviet military convention, providing practical steps for the realization of a mutual aid treaty. In his letter, delivered through Blum's son, Beneš recommended that extraordinary care be shown in dealing with the Soviet General Staff, since its chiefs were in a plot with Germany. Blum later insisted that it was this communication which frustrated the conclusion of the Franco-Soviet military convention. French political circles inimical to the Soviet Union began to insist that it was impossible to sign military agreements with the USSR, since there was a plot there; if the plot was a fabricated one and the repressions continued, this would be evidence of the instability of the USSR's internal situation. Consequently, they concluded, the Soviet Union could not be counted on in a war against Germany.[35]

In Germany the news of the massacre of the Red Army commanders evoked rejoicing.

The Red Army lost its best commanders exactly at the moment when the clouds of war were gathering ever more thickly on the horizon.

It was not so simple to prepare, in a short time, new commanders for regiments, brigades, divisions, and corps. Unit commanders promoted to these posts often lacked knowledge and experience which could not be replaced by mere aptitude and devotion to duty. At the beginning of the war, only 7 percent of the officers had higher military education, and 37 percent had not completed their intermediate military education. By the summer of 1941, about 75 percent of the commanders and 70 percent of the political workers had not been in their jobs for more than a year.[36] It was only in the course of the war that the talents of the commanders manifested themselves, and their skill at commanding troops developed in all its splendor.

The International Situation of the USSR

The highest goal of the foreign policy of a socialist state consists of ensuring favorable conditions for its peaceful development. To maintain peace, not to permit war and armed conflicts, to let the people of the country work and develop under

136

conditions of peace, to support the struggle against imperialist aggression and for peace for other peoples—these aspirations are completely natural and in harmony with the governmental, national, and international interests of the Soviet nation.

When war erupted in Europe, the Soviet Union was able to stay out of it, although the fires of war raged at its very borders. It was able to avoid a simultaneous war on two fronts: in Europe with Hitlerite Germany, in Asia with militaristic Japan. To stay out of war as long as it was possible was the main goal of Soviet foreign policy from the beginning of the Second World War to the perfidious attack of fascist Germany on the Soviet Union. M. I. Kalinin declared this in a forthright manner in his report at a solemn meeting at the Bolshoi Theater of November 6, 1940: "When almost the whole world is enveloped by such a war, to be outside of it is a great happiness." Our country tried to use those twenty-two months to increase its capabilities for defense, and to improve its position in case the Soviet Union was subjected to an attack from outside.

In this rather short period of time one can tentatively distinguish three phases of Soviet foreign policy: the first, from September 1939 to the defeat of France in June 1940; the second, until the Soviet-German negotiations in Berlin in November 1940; and the third, until Germany's attack on the Soviet Union.

At the first stage, the foreign policy position of the Soviet Union was at its most solid and stable. In the West there existed, in the form of England and France, which were in a state of war with Germany, a counterbalance to Germany's aggressive aspirations. As long as the war continued in the West, the threat of invasion to the Soviet Union from that side was not very likely, although it was necessary to reckon with the attempts of certain imperialist circles in France and England, during the period of the so-called "strange war," to create military bridgeheads as

137

close as possible to the borders of the USSR, for instance in Scandinavia and Turkey. In the Far East, after Japan's defeat at Halhaiin-Gol and the conclusion of a nonaggression pact between the Soviet Union and Japan's ally, Germany, the danger of an immediate Japanese attack on the Soviet Union practically did not exist.

The most important element in the foreign policy of the Soviet Union from August 23, 1939, until June 22, 1941, remained its relations with Germany.

Germany knew that the Soviet Union was a peaceloving state and was not about to attack anybody. But could this be said about such an aggressive state as fascist Germany?

Soviet-German relations were regulated by the Nonaggression Pact of August 23, 1939, and the Treaty on Friendship and Borders, signed September 28, 1939. Between Germany and the Soviet Union there was established a dividing line of national interests, which was recognized as final by the treaty of September 28.

In concluding the friendship and borders treaty it was stipulated that economic relations and trade in commodities of every kind would be developed between the Soviet Union and Germany, and that an economic program would be created for this purpose. The USSR obligated itself to supply raw materials to Germany; Germany was to supply the USSR with industrial equipment and machines.[37] Later economic agreements were concluded between Germany and the Soviet Union, on February 11, 1940, and January 10, 1941. The last agreement was meant to regulate the exchange of commodities between the USSR and Germany until August 1, 1942. The USSR delivered to Germany industrial raw materials, petroleum products, and food produce, particularly grain derivatives; Germany delivered industrial equipment to the Soviet Union.[38]

The Soviet Union carried out the political and economical agreements concluded with Germany with strict honesty.

Under the complicated conditions of spreading world war and a rapidly changing international situation, the Soviet Union undertook a number of measures to strengthen its own security. The reunion of the Western Ukraine and Western Byelorussia with the Ukrainian and Byelorussian Soviet Socialist Republics, which followed in September 1939, served this purpose in particular. As a result of this step of the Soviet government, the frontier was moved two hundred to three hundred kilometers to the west of the old national border, and more than twelve million inhabitants of these regions were saved from the danger of fascist enslavement.

Measures to strengthen the security of the Soviet state were also undertaken by the government in the northwest. The efforts in 1938–39, to reach an agreement with Finland about concluding a treaty of mutual aid were not crowned with success. Relations became progressively more tense, until they led to the armed Soviet-Finnish conflict in the late fall of 1939. After fighting which was heavy and bloody for both sides, the conflict was settled by the conclusion of a peace treaty on March 12, 1940. The Soviet Union presented very moderate demands, which did not go beyond the security considerations dictated by the ever spreading war in Europe. In particular, the Karelian Isthmus, with Vyborg, went to the USSR. The border on the northwest was moved out somewhat. The Soviet Union received the Hangö Peninsula in lease, for a naval base.

The Soviet-Finnish conflict was a sad episode in the mutual relations between the two neighboring states, particularly since Finland had obtained its independence thanks to the Great October Socialist Revolution.

The Soviet-Finnish peace treaty also played a positive role for

Sweden, which had furthered its signing. Actually the liquidation of the conflict, which the Western powers was preparing to use for the creation of a new theater of war in Scandinavia, corresponded to Sweden's vital interests. Less than three weeks later all doubts on this score disappeared. On April 9 Hitler's Germany invaded Denmark and Norway. On April 13 the Soviet government summoned the German ambassador to Moscow, Schulenburg, and told him that the Soviet Union was interested in preserving Swedish neutrality. Germany could not ignore the USSR's warning. On April 17 the Soviet ambassador in Stockholm, A. M. Kollontai, informed the Swedish minister of foreign affairs, Guenther, of the USSR's position and the German reply; Guenther thanked the Soviet government and declared that "the action on the part of the Soviet Union will strengthen the cabinet's line and the firm will of Sweden to observe neutrality." [39]

Measures were taken not to allow the fires of war to start up in the Baltic area. The Baltic states—Estonia, Latvia, and Lithuania—had for two decades served as centers for the anti-Soviet intrigues of the imperialist countries and the White-émigré organizations supported by them. After the start of World War II, the influence of Hitler's Germany on the Baltic states became stronger. Hitler's emissaries, such as Colonel General Halder and the prominent German intelligence chiefs Pickenbroek and Bentevigni, visited the Baltic countries and made agreements with the local responsible military leaders about using the territories, resources, and armed forces of these states in the interests of Germany. This threatened to transform the territories of the Baltic states into an anti-Soviet bridgehead. The peoples of the Baltic states opposed this policy.

German intelligence possessed a very widespread net in the Baltic area. It supported financially, in particular, such highly placed persons as the chief of the second (intelligence) branch of the Estonian General Staff, Colonel P. Maasing, Colonels L. Jakobsen, I. Soodla, and others.

Relying on the support of the Baltic peoples, the Soviet Union was able to sign with the governments of the Baltic states treaties of mutual aid which afforded the Soviet Union military and naval bases on the territories of these states. The Soviet-Estonian treaty was signed on September 28, 1939, and the similar treaties with Latvia and Lithuania on October 5 and 10 of the same year. The more farsighted statesmen of the Western powers understood the strategic indispensability of these measures. As early as the spring of 1939, Winston Churchill stated in the House of Commons: "For Russia it is of vital interest that these states [Lithuania, Latvia, and Estonia—A.N.] not fall into the hands of Nazi Germany." [40] However, the British government, then headed by Chamberlain, did not share this opinion in the least.

At that time relations between the USSR and France, and the USSR and England, were strained. In the prewar years the Soviet Union had persistently striven to create a system of collective security, the most important role in which was to be played by the USSR, England, France, and their allies, bound among themselves by obligations of mutual aid in case of unprovoked aggression on the part of Germany. However, the attempts of England's ruling circles to promote a clash between Germany and the USSR, and the ambiguous and inconsistent position of France, which concluded, on the one hand, a mutual aid pact with the USSR and, on the other, carried out the Munich policy, directed against the USSR—these were important reasons for the frustration, on the eve of World War II, of the plan to form an anti-fascist coalition. This circumstance affected the relations of the Soviet Union with the Western states in the most baneful way. In fact, after the beginning of the war in Europe, intercourse was limited simply to maintaining diplomatic relations. Toward the end of the first stage, Anglo-Soviet and Franco-Soviet relations deteriorated sharply in connection with the loudly expressed hostile position of England and France during the Soviet-Finnish armed conflict. At that time the Anglo-French staffs, by order of their governments, were working out plans for direct military aid to Finland by sending an expeditionary corps and shifting the war's center of gravity from the west to the north and northwest. However, for various reasons, the British government wavered somewhat, in spite of the energetic pressure of the French government and its attempts, with the aid of American diplomacy, to hinder the peace talks which had begun in Moscow. The March 12 treaty between Finland and the Soviet Union finally frustrated the British and French anti-Soviet plans of that period and forced the British government to undertake a more realistic policy toward the USSR. Evidence of this, in particular, was the British government's March 18, 1940, proposal to renew the trade talks which had been cut short in the fall of 1939. However, the trade talks soon came to another dead end, since the British government insisted that the Soviet Union support the economic blockade of Germany, carried on by England, which the Soviet Union could not do without harming its position as a neutral state and its relations with Germany.[41]

Soviet-French relations in these months had a strained character. From the first days of the war, an unbridled anti-Soviet campaign had begun in France, reaching its apogee during the Finnish conflict. Together with England, France succeeded in excluding the USSR from the League of Nations in December 1939. Daladier's French government, under the pretext of aid to Finland, made every effort to drag the Soviet Union into the world war in one way or another. Simultaneously with the plan of attack against the USSR in the northwest, the French General

Staff was working out plans for attacking the USSR from the south, which were to be implemented as follows: from the air, by bombing the centers of oil production and refining in Baku and Batumi; from the sea, by the dispatch of an Anglo-French squadron into the Black Sea to bombard the Black Sea coast of the Soviet Union. For this purpose France was able to obtain the agreement in principle of Turkey. Preparing for a break in relations with the USSR, the French police made a raid (February 5, 1940) on the offices of the Soviet trade delegation in Paris, the Intourist office, and the former Soviet school in Paris. Safes containing official documents were opened. Searches were made in the quarters of the employees of Soviet organizations in Paris. Some of the documents were removed. This police provocation made relations still worse. There is no doubt that the French authorities were busy searching for excuses which would later make it easier to explain the break in relations with the USSR.[42]

Franco-Soviet relations became worse still at the time when the French government was intensively working on anti-Soviet military plans. The conclusion of the Soviet-Finnish treaty led, on March 20, to the fall of the government of Daladier, who had made anti-Soviet policy the main direction of his course of action in these months. Daladier's last act as premier was to demand, on March 19, the recall of the Soviet ambassador in France, Ya. Z. Surits, for sending a congratulatory telegram to the Soviet government on the occasion of the conclusion of a peace treaty with Finland.[43]

The new French government of P. Reynaud tried to continue the policy of aggravating Franco-Soviet relations and, on March 25, it sent the British government a memorandum in which it continued to insist on implementing the former bankrupt policy in regard to the USSR. The British government treated the memorandum with reserve. Meanwhile Germany invaded Norway and Denmark, and on May 10 began an offensive on the western front. The military catastrophe which followed significantly altered the situation. After the capitulation of France the whole western part of the European continent found itself under the domination of Hitler's Germany. Of all the Western European countries participating in the war, England alone survived. But her position remained extremely grave.

The quick rout of France was a complete surprise. Germany had become the only military power on the Western European continent. There was nobody left to oppose her there. The balance of power had altered significantly. The international position of the Soviet Union had deteriorated greatly. Nobody could predict in which direction Germany's next aggression would unfold. The authors of the multi-volume Japanese publication *The History of the War in the Pacific* point to the fact that Hitler, in his speech after the defeat of France, in which he proposed peace with England, did not say anything which could have testified to his benevolent attitude toward the USSR.[44] The Nonagression Pact between the Soviet Union and Germany could not in itself serve as a sufficiently reliable guarantee against attack under the conditions of the rapid growth of Germany's economic might and the incredible self-satisfaction of the German fascists. Taking these circumstances into account, and striving to ease England's serious position, the new British War Cabinet, formed in mid-May by Winston Churchill, decided to try to mend relations with the USSR. On June 12, 1940, the newly appointed British ambassador, a well-known active figure in the Labor Party, Stafford Cripps, arrived in Moscow. On June 25, 1940, Churchill directed a letter to J. V. Stalin. In the letter Churchill expressed the hope that neither the distance dividing the two countries, nor the difference in systems, nor ideological divergences, should prevent the two countries from maintaining mutually advantageous relations. Thus recognizing the fairness of the Soviet foreign policy principle of peaceful co-existence, Churchill emphasized that the Soviet Union itself must judge whether or not the German claims to domination in Europe threatened its interests. For his part, the head of the British government made assurances of his readiness to discuss with the Soviet government "any of the vast problems created by Germany's present attempt to pursue in Europe a methodical process by successive stages of conquest and absorption." [45]

On July 3, Churchill received the Soviet ambassador in London, I. M. Mayskiy, and had a frank chat with him. However, the situation was extraordinarily complicated. In practice England could not give any immediate help to the Soviet Union in case Germany attacked it. Even without taking into account the anti-Soviet prejudices still widespread in the British ruling circles, the situation of England itself was extremely grave. From day to day a German invasion of the British Isles had to be expected. The situation was correctly characterized at the time by the Laborite Cox in a speech in Parliament: "In these circumstances we are not in a position to defend the Soviet Union to any perceptible degree. For this reason any hope that we can at the present time attract Russia to our side is futile. At the same time Russia does not wish for German victory. . . . We must cultivate the most friendly possible relations with Russia. . . ." [46]

A very alarming time had arrived for the Soviet state. The situation at the Soviet borders was not stable enough. In the Baltic area, under the impact of German victories and the Soviet-Finnish conflict, the ruling circles secretly began to scrape together a military alliance between Estonia, Latvia, and Lithuania, directed at the USSR. On the Soviet southwestern border, in connection with the heightened tendency toward a Romanian-German rapprochement and the aspiration of frankly fascist elements in Romania itself to take power, a dangerous complication had arisen. In the political circles of many capitalist states, there were persistent rumors that Germany would try to achieve the complete economic and political subjugation of the countries of Southeastern Europe and above all the Balkans. This meant that a new threat to the Soviet Union would arise there in a short time.

The workers of the Baltic area, worried by the strengthening of Germany, demanded the transfer of power to genuine people's representatives. In June 1940, people's governments came to power in Estonia, Lithuania, and Latvia.

At the end of June, Bessarabia and Northern Bukovina, and in August 1940, Estonia, Latvia, and Lithuania became part of the Soviet Union. The Baltic states became union republics. Bessarabia was united with the Moldavian Autonomous Republic. These two parts, joined together, composed the Union Republic of Moldavia. The USSR's borders were moved westward. However, there was a very little time left for their fortification. This should have been obvious after the signing of the aggressive Tripartite Pact by Germany, Japan, and Italy on September 27, 1940.

Although the Soviet government was informed by Germany about the imminent signing of the Tripartite Pact before it was made public, it was not misled as to the true character of the pact. A lead article in the newspaper *Pravda* of September 30, 1940, on the Tripartite Pact emphasized that its signing meant a "further intensification of the war and a broadening of its scope." At the same time the Soviet press directed attention to the reservation that the Tripartite Pact did not affect the′ relations of its participants with the USSR, and explained that this reservation had to be understood "as a confirmation of the force and meaning of the Nonaggression Pact between the USSR and Germany and the Nonaggression Pact between the USSR and Italy." [47]

The fact that the tone of the Soviet press in regard to England became friendlier is evidence that the significance of the Tripartite Pact as a pact for the preliminary division of the world was not doubted in the USSR. For instance, on October 5, 1940, *Pravda* printed a very detailed and sympathetic story from London about the visit of a TASS correspondent to one of the London antiaircraft batteries. From this article the reader could easily come to the conclusion that England was putting up a serious fight and her strength was growing. [48]

The Soviet government continued to carry out scrupulously the agreements it had concluded with Hitler's Germany, not giving her the slightest excuse to worsen relations. Germany, on her part, tried to take advantage of the situation to pressure the Soviet Union and force it to conduct its foreign policy exclusively in the German interest. For this purpose the chairman of the Council of People's Commissars of the USSR and the People's Commissar for Foreign Affairs, V. M. Molotov, was invited to Berlin in November 1940. In the course of the conversations which took place between him, on the one hand, and Hitler and Ribbentrop on the other, an offer was made to the Soviet Union to join the Tripartite Pact and take part in the remaking of spheres of influence in the world. The Soviet government turned down the German proposals.* The Berlin conversations left no doubt that Germany's aggressiveness had grown, and she was attempting to achieve world domination in the shortest time.

The final stage in the development of German-Soviet relations

---

* This is factually not true.—V.P.

ran from the unsuccessful November conversations to Germany's attack on June 22, 1941. The Soviet Union, as before, made every effort to prevent war. From Germany's side everything was done to put the Soviet Union in the least advantageous political, diplomatic, and military situation at the moment of attack.

After the November conversations there could no longer be the slightest doubt about Germany's true intentions. The events which exploded in the Balkans should also have led to this conclusion.

In the summer and fall of 1940, Hitler's Germany, making skillful use of the Romanian-Hungarian differences over Transylvania, forced both states, first of all Romania, to follow in the channel of German policy. In September 1940, a German military mission was sent to Romania, meaning in practice the occupation of Romania by German-fascist troops. With such measures, Germany counted on taking the Romanian oil wells and refining plants in Ploeşti under full control, and also on using the Romanian military base for the future war with the USSR. In the person of the Romanian dictator, Antonescu, Hitler found a ruler ready to throw himself headlong into any anti-Soviet adventure. The conquests of fascist Germany, particularly her inroads into the Balkans, which Italy had long considered as the sphere of her own interests, provoked the indignation of the Italian "Duce," Mussolini. Without warning her German ally, Italy attacked Greece on October 28, 1940.

Not long before the attack, Mussolini said to his minister of foreign affairs, Ciano: "Hitler always faces me with an accomplished fact. Now I will pay him back in his own coin. He will find out from the papers that I have occupied Greece. In this way the balance will be restored." [49]

However, the Italian invaders stumbled onto the brave defense of the Greek people and were forced not only to take up defensive positions, but also to evacuate some of the captured territory. Italy found herself threatened by a military catastrophe. Hitler's Germany came to the aid of her ally.

The decision to invade Greece showed that Germany was trying to subordinate wholly the countries of Southeastern and Southern Europe to her policies in the shortest period of time. In connection with this, the pressure increased on Yugoslavia, which was asked to join the Tripartite Pact. At that time Romania and Hungary had already done this. Pressure increased on Bulgaria as well. Thus an obvious threat to the Soviet Union was created in the Balkans, since Germany's seizure of the Balkans inevitably meant the approach of the German threat to the borders of the Soviet Union. Logic dictated that if Germany managed to take care of the Balkan situation and deprive the British of their last beachhead on the continent, the threat to the USSR would grow a hundredfold.

Meanwhile the relations between the Soviet Union and its potential allies, England and the United States of America, still remained unchanged in this period. England and the United States, as before, "did not recognize" the entry of the Baltic states into the Soviet Union. The funds of these states, deposited in British and American banks, remained frozen. Anglo-Soviet trade was practically halted, and Soviet-American trade came up against great difficulties as a result of the discriminatory measures of the United States government. Nevertheless, in both England and the United States, another tendency was gradually making itself felt—a tendency to improve relations with the Soviet Union, recognizing the historical necessity for all three powers to unite against the presence of the fascist bloc's threat. Many statesmen in England and America did not hide their regrets that the projected creation of an anti-

Hitler coalition in the summer of 1939 had been stopped. In their speeches British members of Parliament insisted more and more often that, in connection with the active German military and political advances in the Balkans which threatened British interests not only there but also in the Near and Middle East, England should enter without delay into discussion with the Soviet Union, for which the establishment of German domination in the Balkans concealed enormous danger. In the late fall of 1940, the British ambassador, Stafford Cripps, tried by instruction of his government, to carry on negotiations in Moscow on political subjects, but they did not lead to any results. In the summer and autumn of 1940, and the first months of 1941, American-Soviet relations began to improve a little. On August 6, 1940, the Soviet-American trade agreement was renewed.[50]

The most important result of the Soviet-American negotiations was the lifting of the "moral embargo," i.e., the United States government's recommendation to American firms to refrain from trade with the USSR made at the height of the Finnish conflict in December 1939. Although the lifting of the "moral embargo" at the end of January 1941 did not have any practical economic meaning because the American government as before exercised strict control over exports to the Soviet Union, the political effect of this step must not be underestimated. "This was," writes the Soviet researcher, L. V. Pozdeyeva, "in its way a conciliatory gesture of the United States government toward the USSR."[51] The USSR's position on the whole, as Secretary of State Hull emphasized in his talks with the British Ambassador in Washington, Halifax, was directed against many of the plans of Germany and Japan.

The movement on the part of the United States of America to grow closer to the USSR found a certain reflection in the rejection by the United States Congress, in March 1941, of an amendment to the Lend-Lease draft bill which proposed to exclude the Soviet Union from the aid program envisioned by it. During the debate, some congressmen expressed their hope that the USSR might possibly come out "shoulder to shoulder" with the Western powers.[52]

However, unfortunately, affairs did not reach a state of genuine rapprochement with England and the USA, or even a serious improvement in relations with them. The Soviet Union's efforts to oppose German aggression in the Balkans were undertaken unilaterally.*

Beginning with the end of 1939, there was some improvement in Bulgarian-Soviet relations. Economic and cultural agreements were concluded, which helped establish more solid contacts between the USSR and Bulgaria. The traditional sympathies of the Bulgarian people for the Russian people, which had in the past helped in the former's struggle against Turkish domination, and the widespread idea of Slav solidarity, were cemented by the Bulgarians' enormous interest toward the land of socialism, and by the socialist traditions of the Bulgarian workers' movement. All this taken together also influenced the foreign policy of Bulgaria. In addition, the significant strengthening of Germany in the Balkans as a result of her victory in the West caused considerable worry in Bulgaria. Fears of attack by Turkey also played a role. The Soviet Union was the only country which could realistically withstand the schemes of the German fascists in the Balkans, including Bulgaria. During the Soviet-Bulgarian talks in the fall of 1939, the Soviet government proposed the signing of a treaty of friendship and mutual aid. However, the royal Bulgarian government rejected this proposal. Later, under the influence of events in Western Europe

---

* This is factually false in view of the British efforts in Greece, Yugoslavia, and Turkey.—V.P.

and the fear of strengthened Soviet influence and the spreading of the ideas of socialism, the Bulgarian government leaned more and more toward the bloc of fascist aggressors. After the November negotiations in Berlin, the Soviet government, on November 19, 1940, proposed a treaty of friendship and mutual aid to Bulgaria. A week later, the Secretary-General of the People's Commissariat for Foreign Affairs, A. A. Sobolev, arrived in Sofia to confirm this proposal. The Soviet Union announced its readiness to give aid to Bulgaria, including military aid, in case of attack by a third power or group of powers. The USSR expressed its readiness to give Bulgaria financial and economic aid as well. And in this connection the Soviet Union declared that the pact would in no way touch on the existing regime, or on the independence and sovereignty of Bulgaria.[53] On the same day, November 25, the Soviet proposal was discussed at a meeting of the Bulgarian cabinet with Tsar Boris, and rejected. The German minister in Sofia was informed about this Soviet proposal.[54]

Although the Bulgarian government rejected the proposal of the USSR, the latter still played a certain positive role in delaying Bulgaria's shift to the camp of the fascist aggressors. The Bulgarian minister in Stockholm reported to his government in the middle of December 1940: "Here they are noting with interest the recently displayed Russian intercessions in favor of Bulgaria and Sweden in order to keep these two countries not only out of the war, but out of a combination with Germany against England."[55]

In January 1941, in connection with reports circulating that German troops were being sent to Bulgaria with the consent of the USSR, the Soviet government officially stated that if this fact was actually true, "it had taken place and was taking place without the knowledge and agreement of the USSR."[56]

Four days later the Soviet government informed the German

Ambassador in Moscow, Schulenburg, that it viewed the territory of the eastern Balkans as a USSR security zone and could not remain inactive in regard to events threatening this security. This was repeated on January 17, 1941 by the Soviet ambassador in Berlin to the state secretary of the German ministry of foreign affairs, Weizsaecker. However, on March 1, the Bulgarian government joined the Tripartite Pact, opening its territory for the passage of German troops for military operations against Greece, and then against Yugoslavia.

In a special declaration the Soviet Union condemned this step of the Bulgarian government, pointing out that its position "leads not to the strengthening of peace, but to the broadening of the sphere of war and to dragging Bulgaria into it." [57] On March 3 the German ambassador in Moscow was informed that Germany could not count on the Soviet Union's support of her actions in Bulgaria. [58]

The failure with Bulgaria showed that Germany had already commenced hostile military-political steps against the USSR. The collision in Bulgaria was, in fact, a test of the solidarity of Soviet-German relations. From the results of this experience, appropriate conclusions had to be drawn.

Serious apprehensions arose in the Soviet Union because of the position of Turkey during the "strange war," and also because the Turkish government continued to maneuver between the warring sides, leaning to one side or the other, depending on the power relationships at any given moment. However, the movement of German troops into Bulgaria frightened the Turkish government. As a result of the exchange of opinions between the Soviet and Turkish governments in March 1941, mutual assurances were given that in the case of attack on one of the sides, the other could "count on full understanding and neutrality. . . ." [59]

The events in the Balkans showed that relations between Germany and the USSR were developing in a dangerous direction. The German-Soviet conflicts of interest, which were of an irreconcilable nature because of the Hitlerites' aspiration for world domination, and which had merely been softened by the agreements of 1939, now made themselves felt with new strength. Germany continued to prepare armed bases near the borders of the USSR. Having come up against the resistance of the Soviet Union in regard to German aggression in the Balkans, the Hitlerites tried to frighten the Soviet Union with their military might. On February 22, 1941, a responsible official of the German ministry of foreign affairs, Ambassador Ritter, by order of his superiors, informed Ambassador Schulenburg in Moscow, in a top secret coded telegram, that the time had come to make public the facts about the number of German troops in Romania in order to impress Soviet circles. The 680,000-man German army in Romania was in full combat readiness. It was technically well equipped and numbered motorized units within its forces. This army was supported by "inexhaustible reserves." Ritter asked all the members of the German mission to begin the dissemination of this information about German strength, by themselves and through persons of confidence. This power should be presented in an impressive manner, Ritter wrote, emphasizing that it was more than enough to meet any eventuality in the Balkans from whatever side it might come.[60] This information was to be spread not only in government circles, but among interested foreign representatives accredited to Moscow.

Along with this intimidation, the Hitlerites tried to mask the military preparations being carried on along the Soviet-German border. On January 10, 1941, a treaty on the Soviet-German border from the Igorka River to the Baltic Sea was signed between Germany and the Soviet Union.[61] * After the conclusion

---

* Never published in the USSR, this treaty resolved several vexing problems in Nazi-Soviet relations.—V.P.

of the treaty, a demarcation of the border defined by the treaty was to be carried out by commissioners from both sides. Discussions about the commission's work began on February 17. The German side dragged them out. By demand of the high command of ground forces, Schulenburg was ordered to delay the discussion in every possible way, in order not to let the Soviet commission work on the border. The Germans were afraid that their military preparations would otherwise be discovered.[62]

The Hitlerites strengthened their aerial reconnaissance of the Soviet border areas. Simultaneously they began to insist, for the purposes of camouflage, that the rumors about the invasion of the Soviet Union being planned by Germany were being spread especially by "English warmongers." Precisely at that time, the Soviet Union received a warning, through diplomatic channels, of a German plan to attack the USSR.

A new complication in the relations between the USSR and Germany then arose because of Yugoslavia. On March 27, 1941, the government of Cvetković, which had signed the agreement to join the Tripartite Pact, was overthrown in Yugoslavia. The Yugoslav people were full of determination to show armed resistance to the German aggressor. "The latest events in Yugoslavia," wrote *Pravda*, "have shown with all clarity that the peoples of Yugoslavia are striving for peace and do not want war, or their country to be sucked into the whirlpool of war. By means of numerous demonstrations and meetings, the various strata of the Yugoslav population have expressed their protest against the foreign policy of Cvetković's government, which threatened to drag Yugoslavia into the orbit of war. . . ."[63] On 5 April a Treaty of Friendship and Nonaggression was signed between Yugoslavia. The Soviet Union publicaly condemned this act of the sides were subjected to an attack, the other was obligated to observe "a policy of friendly relations to it." On the day the treaty was made public, April 6, Hitler's Germany attacked

Yugoslavia. The Soviet Union publicly condemned this act of aggression in a communication of the People's Commissariat for Foreign Affairs, dated April 13, 1941, on the attitude of the Soviet government toward Hungary's attack on Yugoslavia. Although Hungary was accused in the communication, the initiator of the aggression, Hitler's Germany, was also indirectly accused.[64]

Yugoslav events showed that the relations between Germany and the USSR were approaching a denouement.

In a situation of growing tension, the Soviet Union was able to achieve an important success in its affairs with its other potential enemy, Japan.

The prospect of an improvement, though perhaps a temporary one, in Soviet-Japanese relations had gradually begun to appear by the end of 1939. After Halhaiin-Gol a certain sobering-up process began in Japanese military circles. Attempts to put pressure on the Soviet Union by military means had ended in failure. War against the Soviet Union appeared to be an extremely complicated and dangerous affair. The conclusion of the Soviet-German nonaggression pact of August 23, 1939, which resulted in a cooling off in relations between the partners of the Axis, also exercised a definite influence on Japan's policy. The ruling circles of Japan realized that in these conditions Japan's chances of carrying on a victorious war against the USSR had significantly diminished. In spite of the anti-Soviet campaign started in Japan during the Soviet-Finnish conflict, supported and kindled by pro-British and pro-American circles, the matter did not go beyond anti-Soviet statements in the press. A number of Japanese businessmen and financiers interested in developing economic relations with the USSR, and especially those in the fishing industry, put pressure on the government, demanding improvement in relations with the USSR and the signing of a new fishing convention, the last one having expired in 1939. Articles appeared in the Japanese press demanding a nonaggression pact with the USSR. This was the situation at the moment of the fall of France. That event significantly strengthened the Japanese circles which supported expansion in the direction of the South Seas. They also found support in Germany, which at that time considered her main mission to be the waging of war against England, and therefore came out for the regularization of Soviet-Japanese relations, "in order to free Tokyo's hands for expansion to the south. This would have to attract the attention of England and the USA to the Pacific Ocean, weakening their position in Europe." [65]

At the beginning of June, the question of the borderline between Manchu-kuo and the Mongolian People's Republic in the area of the 1939 conflict was regularized. A month later, the Japanese ambassador in Moscow, Togo, proposed the signing of a Soviet-Japanese treaty for a five-year period. The essence of such a treaty, which would have been based on the Soviet-Japanese treaty of 1925, consisted of preserving neutrality in case one of the sides were subjected to the attack of a third party. The Soviet Union agreed to the Japanese proposal, but, as a condition, refused to use the treaty of 1925 as a basis for the new agreement since the convention of 1925 was for the most part seriously outdated. In connection with the change of cabinet in Japan in July 1940, negotiations were broken off, and Ambassador Togo was recalled to Tokyo. However, the tendency for the regularization of relations with the USSR continued to become stronger as advantageous perspectives appeared for the intensification of Japanese aggression in Southeast Asia as a result of the weakening of England and the defeat of France and Holland. This tendency was briefly formularized at the end of September 1940 in the Japanese newspaper *Hopi:* "If Japan wants

157

to move forward in the south, she must be free from fear in the north." [66] A new ambassador was appointed to Moscow, Tatekawa, who, in the words of Minister of Foreign Affairs Matsuoka, was entrusted with "turning a new page in the relations between Japan and the Soviet Union." [67]

Under those conditions, the conclusion of the Tripartite Pact of September 27, 1940, meant the strengthening of the Japanese circles which favored aggression toward the south, i.e., against the British possessions in Asia. At the same time, it had to be taken into account that, if the international situation should change, for instance in the case of an attack on the Soviet Union by Germany, Japan might give support to the latter. This point was often emphasized by responsible leaders of the Japanese government at secret meetings.

In the fall of 1940 and the beginning of 1941, Soviet-Japanese negotiations were continued. The USSR put out a proposal to sign a neutrality treaty on the condition of liquidating the Japanese oil and coal concessions on Northern Sakhalin. In that case the USSR obligated itself to compensate the concessionaires and supply Japan with Sakhalin oil for five years under the usual commercial conditions. The Japanese government agreed to discuss the draft of the treaty, but refused the proposal to liquidate the concessions. [68]

However, in spite of all difficulties, Soviet-Japanese relations were already emerging into a period of temporary regularization. The prospects improved after the signing, in the second half of January 1941, of a protocol on the prolongation of the fishing convention until the end of 1941. The unsuccessful beginning of Japanese-American negotiations also had a definite effect on Japan's position.

Soon after the signing of the Tripartite Pact, the Japanese government made a proposal to the government of the USSR to conclude a nonaggression pact. At the same time Japan asked Germany to assist in the conclusion of the pact.

The plan proposed by Ribbentrop was rejected by the Soviet government in November 1940.* Meanwhile, those who favored Japanese aggression's being directed toward the south exerted increasing influence on Japanese foreign policy and demanded, for this purpose, the securing of the Japanese rear in the north, i.e., in the northeastern regions of China bordering on the Soviet Union, and the Mongolian People's Republic. The fact that the lessons of Halhaiin-Gol had not yet been forgotten by the Japanese warlords played a considerable role. The prospect of war against the USSR seemed far more dangerous than an attack on the British possessions in Southeast Asia, since England was in a very difficult situation. On February 3, 1941, at a joint meeting of the government and representatives of military circles, the "principles of carrying on negotiations with Germany, Italy, and the Soviet Union" were approved. On March 12 the Japanese minister of foreign affairs, Matsuoka, departed for Europe. During a stop in Moscow Matsuoka proposed the conclusion of a nonaggression pact to the Soviet government. Let us recall that in the 1930's the Soviet Union had more than once directed such a suggestion to Japan, but it had always been rejected by Japan. In the new situation, the Soviet Union did not consider the conclusion of a mere nonaggression pact as being sufficient. It was important to ensure the neutrality of Japan in case of complications with Germany. For this reason the Soviet Union made a counterproposal: to include a treaty of neutrality. On March 26 Matsuoka went off to Berlin with this proposal.

After issuing directive "Barbarossa," Hitler's Germany be-

---

* This statement is a considerable distortion. The Soviet government did not reject the Ribbentrop plan but made counterproposals that Germany did not accept. See Appendix.—V.P.

gan to pressure Japan to force her to take a position which would be advantageous to the German plans. In the meeting with Mussolini in Berghof in the second half of January 1941, Hitler said of Japan that "her freedom of action is limited by Russia, just as is that of Germany, which must keep eighty divisions on the Soviet border in constant readiness in case of action against Russia." Evaluating Japan as an important factor in the struggle against England and the United States, Hitler stressed, quite deliberately, that a part of the Japanese forces was tied down by the Soviet Union.[69]

Hitler, in receiving on February 3, 1941, Japanese Ambassador Kurusu, who was paying him a farewell visit, made transparent hints to the ambassador about the possible development of German-Soviet relations. "Our mutual enemies," he said, "are two countries—England and America. The other country —Russia—is not an enemy at the moment, but represents a danger to both states [i.e., to Germany and Japan—A.N.]. At the moment relations with Russia are in order. Germany trusts that country, but the 185 divisions which Germany has under her control ensure her security better than treaties do." "In this way," Hitler concluded, "the interests of Germany and Japan are absolutely parallel in three directions." [70]

To attempt to draw Japan into the war as soon as possible— such was the task laid down in Directive No. 24 of the supreme command of the armed forces, dated March 5, 1941, regarding cooperation with Japan. In this document it was frankly pointed out that the aim of German policy consisted of "drawing Japan into active operations in the Far East as soon as possible." "Plan Barbarossa," it further stated, "creates especially advantageous political and military conditions for this." [71] From this directive it was clear that the matter concerned Japan's attack on the British possessions while Germany, attacking the Soviet Union,

160

would free the Japanese troops pinned down in the Far East.*

During the stay of the Japanese foreign minister in Berlin, this arrangement was the theme of all the talks Hitler and Ribbentrop held with him. Emphasizing the fact that England had already suffered defeat and that it would be profitable for Japan to move out against her immediately, the head of the German fascist state also directed the Japanese minister's attention to the fact that England's hope was American help, and the Soviet Union. In mentioning the Soviet Union in this connection, Hitler wanted to prevent Japan from signing any political agreements in Moscow. Ribbentrop also tried to suggest to Matsuoka the idea of a quick defeat of England and the liquidation of the British Empire; accordingly, Japan should hurry, attacking, say, Singapore. Ribbentrop gave his interlocutor to understand in every way that a war between Germany and the USSR was inevitable.[72] From this Matsuoka himself was supposed to draw the conclusion that there was no sense in entering into a political agreement with the Soviet Union. Its ally, Germany, after all, was taking everything upon herself. Ribbentrop explained to Matsuoka: "The German armies in the East were prepared at any time. Should Russia one day take a stand that could be interpreted as a threat to Germany, the Fuehrer will crush Russia. Germany was certain that a campaign against Russia would end in the absolute victory of German arms and the total crushing of the Russian army and the Russian state. . . . The Fuehrer is convinced that in case of action against the Soviet Union, in a few months there would be no more a Great Power of Russia. . . . It must also not be overlooked that the Soviet Union, in spite of protestations to the contrary, was still carrying on communistic propaganda abroad. . . . Further, there was the fact

---

* Which suggests again that Hitler's principal enemy was England and not Russia.—V.P.

161

Germany had to be protected in the rear for her final battle against England. . . . The German army had practically no opponents left on the continent with the possible exception of Russia." [73] *

In the conversation of March 29, 1941, Ribbentrop assured Matsuoka in his usual provocative manner: "If Russia ever attacks Japan, Germany will strike immediately." Accordingly, Japan's security in the north was assured.[74]

The pressure on Matsuoka went on with unabated persistence during the entire stay of the Japanese minister in Berlin. On April 4, Matsuoka talked with Hitler again, and on April 5 with Ribbentrop. Over and over again the German ministers assured Matsuoka that England would collapse any minute, and peace would be achieved at the price of her full capitulation. Japan must hurry. Matsuoka understandingly said yes, pretending that he agreed with everything, and asked for arms aid for Japan, particularly the equipment for submarines.[75] Matsuoka promised his partners to support in Tokyo the plan of an attack on Singapore, although during his stay in Berlin he had received a warning from the Japanese high command about the undesirability of undertaking any military obligations, such as an attack on Singapore. Matsuoka himself proceeded from the premise that war against England would not necessarily also mean war against the United States of America. In spite of Ribbentrop's assurances that Germany would ensure the security of Japan in the north, Matsuoka, acting in the spirit of the directives he received from Tokyo, decided to strive for a straight Japanese-Soviet agreement.[76] On February 2 a document entitled: "About the acceleration of the policy of moving forward in a southerly direction" had already been approved in Tokyo.

---

* A comparison of Nekrich's quotations with the full text of the record shows how clever deletions can distort the meaning.—V.P.

The negotiations on the conclusion of a Soviet-Japanese pact were renewed on April 8, after Matsuoka's return to Moscow. They took place in an atmosphere of continuing disagreement about the character of the treaty. The Japanese minister of foreign affairs insisted on the conclusion of a nonaggression pact. The Soviet side agreed with this on condition of the liquidation of the Japanese concessions in Northern Sakhalin. After long arguments it was decided to sign a treaty of neutrality, which was done on April 13, 1941.[77] Simultaneously, Matsuoka made a written obligation to decide the question of concessions on Northern Sakhalin in the course of a few months. Later, in connection with the start of the German-Soviet war, neither side returned to the problem of the concessions.

The Soviet-Japanese neutrality pact was approved in Tokyo, since at that moment the partisans of expansion in the south had the greatest weight. This was expressed by the fact that a decision was taken, on June 12, to activate Japan's operations in the south, not stopping short of war with England and the United States of America. The final decision was taken, ten days after Germany's attack on the Soviet Union, at the imperial conference of July 2, 1941.[78] *

* Nekrich fails to mention that this attack took the Japanese by such surprise that Matsuoka lost face and resigned.—V.P.

Part Three—Warnings That Were Disregarded

"It Is Reported from the Border. . . ."

It is doubtful that clearer proof is needed of Hitlerite Germany's disregard of the Soviet Union's interests than the attack on Yugoslavia on the very day the Soviet-Yugoslav treaty was concluded. At the same time, the signing of the treaty with Yugoslavia, and, a week later, the neutrality pact with Japan, served to show that the Soviet Union did not intend to close its eyes to hostile German acts.

From various sides and from varied sources came warnings about the attack in preparation by Germany against the USSR. They flowed together in Moscow in the form of reports from military districts, information from the border guard service, materials from foreign press and radio, and finally from intelligence and diplomatic channels.

On the Soviet-German border, in spite of the Soviet-German agreements, the situation remained tense. A secret, and sometimes open, war went on. Enemy scouts, saboteurs, and armed bands "felt out" the border day by day. Enemy losses from military clashes on the border amounted to about thirteen hundred men in killed and wounded alone. Armed groups would try to penetrate Soviet territory on one part of the border; on another, enemy agents with radio transmitters would be discovered in the immediate rear. From 1939 to 1941 all possible types of border violations numbered, without exaggeration, in the thousands. For espionage and sabotage against the Soviet Union, the Hitlerites made wide use of Ukrainian and Polish nationalists,

164

members of various White-guard groups, and fascist and semi-fascist organizations. According to data cited in *The History of the Great Patriotic War*, border troops in the territories of the western military districts detained about five thousand enemy agents and destroyed a considerable number of armed bands. On the territory of Poland alone, according to intelligence reports from the Soviet border troops, ninety-five German agent recruitment and dispatch points were discovered. The information which the border guard service obtained by various means left no doubt that on the territory of the so-called "General-Gouvernement," the Hitlerites were carrying out intensive military preparations directed at the USSR, and that troops were being transferred there from Western Europe and the Balkans. This information was absolutely trustworthy and in many cases contained specific troop unit designations, facts on the numbers of arriving troop trains, on military equipment in these units, on the construction of airfields, roads, and railroad spurs.

Another reliable indicator of the growing war danger was the sharp increase in the number of enemy agents trying to cross the Soviet border. The number of enemy agents caught or destroyed in 1941 increased fifteen to twenty times in comparison with January–March 1940, and twenty-five to thirty times in April–June 1941 compared to April–June 1940! [1]

All this information, passing through service channels beginning at frontier posts, went to the appropriate section of the Main Directorate of Border Troops (GUPV) which immediately informed the general staff of the People's Commissariat of Defense, and the government.

The closer matters got to war, the more brazen the Hitlerites became in sending armed groups onto the territory of the USSR. In the *History of the Great Patriotic War* an example is given of a group of sixteen armed German soldiers crossing the Soviet border in the uniform of Red Army engineer troops. Eleven of the Hitlerites were killed in a fight with the border guards, and five were taken prisoner.[2]

At that time a huge number of people occupied with the construction of border fortifications were concentrated in the border regions.

Enemy agents mingled with the construction workers and penetrated undetected into Soviet territory. In April and May 1941, the fascist intelligence service began to send highly skilled agents into the Soviet Union. Most of them had gone through special intelligence schools in Stettin, Koenigsberg, Berlin, and Vienna. Many were caught, but many others got through to the rear and made their presences known on the day of June 22 by sabotage, attacks on people, and murder. Commanders of Red Army units deployed near the border did not always have a clear picture of the cases of penetration by enemy saboteurs and, generally, about the situation on the border because at that time there existed no orderly system of information flow between border guard units and infantry divisions. Exchange of information existed only between the border guard district and the military district. In a number of cases this information went directly to the main directorate in Moscow and only there was passed to the People's Commissariat of Defense which, in turn, would decide whether or not to inform the troops in the field. Such was the complicated path along which information valuable to a given division at a given moment often had to travel.

And what was the situation in the air? In spite of the fact that German aircraft, even after border agreements, continued to violate the Soviet frontier and carry on intensive reconnaissance, orders were issued not to fire on them. This order was given in April 1940 on the insistence of the People's Commissar of Internal Affairs at that time, the later-exposed traitor Beriya.

166

Beginning in April 1940, not only the border troops but also the Red Army units were forbidden to open fire on violators of Soviet air space. Judging by German documents, Hitler's government was officially informed of this.

Chief Marshal of Artillery N. N. Voronov confirms the fact that the antiaircraft defense had "categorical orders not to open antiaircraft fire on German planes; fighter aircraft were also forbidden to shoot them down. Upon meeting German planes, the fighters were supposed to invite them to land at one of our airfields. However, such invitations were not, of course, accepted by the Germans, and they calmly returned to their own territory." [3]

Marshal of the Soviet Union I. Kh. Bagramyan relates that the commander of the Kiev Special Military District, Colonel General M. P. Kirponos, requested "Moscow to permit the operations of the fascist aircraft to be hindered at least with warning fire. But he was put in his place: 'What are you trying to do—provoke a war?' "

It is true that the Soviet border guard air service sometimes forced German airplanes to land. In a few cases film was discovered on the crews of the German planes which left no doubts about the premeditated character of their "accidental" penetration of Soviet air space. But even in these cases unheard-of generosity was shown: the flyers were sent back to Germany and the aircraft were returned to the German authorities. Saddest of all was the fact that while the investigation was being carried on, the German flight personnel often remained at the military airfields where they had been forced to land and, taking advantage of their relative freedom, could carry on observations and undoubtedly did so. This information was very valuable for the command of the German air forces, which was pinpointing bombing targets on Soviet territory for the first days of the war.

167

The violations of Soviet border air space took on greater scope with every passing month. The Soviet government repeatedly made protests to the German government. From January 1941 until the beginning of the war, German planes violated the Soviet border 152 times.[4]

Between March 27 and April 18, 1941, there were eighty cases of violation of Soviet air space by German aircraft. On April 15 a German plane landed at Rovno; a camera with exposed film of part of the topography of the USSR was found in it; all this undeniably testified to the fact that the plane was carrying out a spy mission. According to a communication from the German chargé d'affaires in the Soviet Union, Tippelskirch, the People's Commissariat of Foreign Affairs gave him a verbal note on this subject. The German counselor was reminded that the border troops had been ordered not to open fire on German aircraft flying over Soviet territory until these flights became frequent. Tippelskirch informed his superiors in Berlin: "Serious incidents must be expected if German aircraft continue their crossings of the Soviet border." [5]

Additional Information

Information arriving in Moscow through diplomatic and intelligence channels also should not have left the slightest shadow of doubt as to the active preparations being carried out by Hitler's Germany for an attack on the Soviet Union.

Soviet diplomatic and military-diplomatic representatives, from the summer of 1940 on, systematically informed Moscow of the intensive military preparations of the Germans. Thus, the Soviet military attaché in France, Major General I. A. Susloparov, has told the author that in July 1940 he received the official report of the French General Staff on the reasons for the defeat of France. In July 1940, during a visit to Moscow, the Soviet military attaché reported this in detail, as well as the location of German troops on the Soviet-German border and in the other countries of Europe.[6]

The cooling off of German-Soviet relations was quickly felt by Soviet diplomatic personnel in France as early as January 1941. The German authorities created obstacles for the movement of Soviet personnel, including the military attaché, on French territory. Susloparov also relates that the issue of exit visas for the USSR to Soviet citizens was stopped. The Germans demanded that the Soviet assistant military attaché, Major Vlasiuk, leave Paris. At the beginning of February all the personnel of the Soviet embassy, including the military attaché staff, with their families, left for Vichy. Only the Soviet consulate remained in Paris.

In April the Soviet military attaché sent a report to Moscow, pointing out that Germany's attack on the USSR was being planned between May 20 and 31. But at the same time it became known that "in connection with the late spring" the Germans were postponing the start of the offensive for a month.*

At the end of April and the beginning of May, Susloparov was thoroughly informed from various types of sources about the German attack in preparation. "By that time," Susloparov relates, "I already possessed facts about the attack on the USSR, received by me from the Yugoslav, Chinese, American, Turkish, and Bulgarian military attachés, with whom I had formed rather good relations at that time. From all the information which I

---

* This supports the view of those military analysts who have taken issue with a more common contention that the fatal postponement of Operation Barbarossa was caused by Hitler's campaign in Yugoslavia and Greece.— V.P.

169

had, it followed inexorably that Germany was completing preparations for an attack on the Soviet Union." [7]

In the middle of May, Susloparov sent a dispatch on his findings to Moscow.

Reports received through intelligence channels also were becoming alarming. The Soviet intelligence agencies possessed broad and completely authentic information on the position of Germany and her intentions. The hatred of Hitlerism felt by the broadest segments of the European population materially eased the problems of Soviet intelligence.

Under the conditions of the fascist terror which held sway in Germany herself and in the territories occupied by her, Soviet intelligence men carried on heroic and necessary work. At that time Europe was a gigantic concentration camp. The German fascists mercilessly plundered the occupied countries. The invaders dealt cruelly with discontented and nonconformist elements. The fear induced by the seemingly irresistible might of Germany gradually began to dissipate, however. Here and there antifascist groups and organizations arose. Their make-up was extremely varied: here there were workers, and peasants, and intellectuals, and military personnel, and priests, people of various political views and religious convictions. The best organized and most purposeful were the antifascist organizations headed by the communists.* The antifascist underground carried on a tireless war against the occupiers. At the first stage of the resistance which had arisen in Europe, its most widespread forms were sabotage, the undermining of the Hitlerites' military efforts, armed attacks on the most hated individual representatives of the occupation authorities, and the destruction of traitors. Gradually the struggle began to take on a wider and more

---

* This is factually false. During the years of the Nazi-Soviet partnership, the communists remained largely inactive—or collaborated with "fascists."—V.P.

organized character. The antifascist organizations which sprang up in Europe united patriots around themselves and at the same time searched for support wherever they could get it. Some oriented themselves toward help from England, others toward help from the Soviet Union.

Many of the organizations, particularly those of a rightist or conservative trend who were connected with England, furnished her with strategic and political information. The leftist antifascist organizations, as a rule, oriented themselves above all on their own people, realizing that they themselves would have to make the principal contribution toward the liberation of their country. The German antifascists, and antifascists of other European countries, foremost among them the communists, viewed their international duty as being toward the first socialist state in the world, the USSR, and their national duty as being toward their own people, in furthering the weakening and final destruction of Hitler's Reich by all means available to them. Risking their lives, the antifascists of Europe, above all in Germany herself, gathered information about Hitlerite plans, the condition of the German armed forces, information of a military and economic type, any facts with which they could help themselves and also aid those who were carrying on the war against Germany or could become the object of a sudden attack by the Hitlerite bandits. Those who obtained this information were doing so out of the strength of their convictions and were not motivated, as a rule, by any other considerations. Such a dangerous and complicated struggle, under the conditions of wartime, occupation, and treachery, could successfully be carried on only by sincere antifascists. Faith in freedom, in liberation, in the downfall of the hated fascist new order, moved these people, over whom constantly hung the threat of arrest, torture in Gestapo dungeons, and death.

Information confirming Germany's preparations to attack the

USSR was received from the other end of the earth, from Tokyo. There the talented Soviet intelligence man Richard Sorge operated. More than one book has been devoted to the biography of Sorge, and no matter what the attitude of the authors toward Sorge, no matter what their political convictions, they all, from the American General Willoughby, who published a book about Sorge in 1952, to Allen Dulles, the former head of American intelligence, cannot write of him without admiration.

Sorge was born in 1895 in Baku. His father, a German, was a petroleum technician by profession. His grandfather was a relative of Karl Marx's associate Adolf Sorge. His mother was Russian. As a youth he left Russia with his parents. In Germany he interested himself deeply in the personality of his grandfather, and this gave rise to his interest in socialist doctrine. The experiences of the First World War, in which he was a participant, strengthened the decision to which he inevitably had to arrive. In the years of the Weimar Republic, Sorge became a communist. Thanks to his unusual capabilities, after graduating from the University of Kiel, he began to work for popular European newspapers, first of all the *Frankfurter Zeitung*, widely circulated in Germany. For several years Sorge lived in the USSR. He was convinced that he would best be able to serve the cause of socialism in the field of intelligence. For this he had all the qualifications. Sorge left for Shanghai, and later Tokyo, as a correspondent for the *Frankfurter Zeitung*, traveled, and visited the United States of America. Not long before his arrival in Tokyo, he had joined Hitler's party and had soon become accepted in circles close to the professor of geopolitics, General Karl Haushofer, who was developing his theory of "living space." At that time Haushofer was at the head of the political intelligence organization.

In Tokyo, Sorge rapidly obtained the confidence of the Ger-

172

man military attaché and then that of the German ambassador, Ott, who made him the unofficial deputy to the chief of the embassy's information office, but, in fact, his own adviser. At the end of 1935 Sorge created an intelligence organization which also contained the German Max Klausen, a highly qualified radio man in the service of Soviet intelligence; the Serb Branko Bukelić; Odzaki Hotsumi, a brilliant Japanese political journalist and a person in the confidence of the Japanese prime minister, Prince Konoye; and Yotoko, a painter and actor. For six years information was constantly transmitted from Tokyo to Moscow. In 1939 alone there were sixty reports totaling 23,139 words, and in 1940 almost 30,000 words were transmitted. This was completely unique information. Sorge had people in various Japanese government agencies supplying him with important data. But the most valuable worker was, of course, Odzaki Hotsumi, who had access to the most secret government papers, which Prince Konoye gave him personally. The microfilms of these documents were sent by special couriers to Shanghai, Hong Kong, or Manila, and thence on to their destination.

From time to time Sorge reported that Japan, in spite of all its hostility toward the Soviet Union, would not attack the USSR and in the end would turn against the United States of America.

On May 1, 1941, Hitler, in a talk with the Japanese ambassador in Berlin, Oshima, told him of his intention to attack the Soviet Union on June 22. It would be fine, Hitler tried to persuade the Japanese ambassador, if Japan would attack the Soviet Union at the same time.* This became known to Odzaki immediately. The information was passed to Sorge.

On May 12 Sorge and Klausen transmitted a report to Mos-

---

* No source is given. It also contradicts what Nekrich said on pp. 161–62.—V.P.

cow that 150 German divisions were concentrated along the Soviet border for an attack along the entire front on June 20. The main direction—Moscow.

In another report, on May 15, Sorge made the date more precise—June 22. In an article published in *Pravda* on September 4, 1964, the Soviet journalist V. Mayevskiy wrote that, in addition to this, Sorge in his reports "gave the general scheme of military operations which the Hitlerites would follow." [8]

In addition to this most important communication, Sorge also reported to Moscow in October 1941, regarding the intentions of the Japanese government to start a war in Southeast Asia against the colonial holdings of England and the Netherlands. For a long time Japanese counterintelligence was unable to come upon the traces of Sorge's organization, but finally it succeeded.

On October 18 Sorge was arrested and, three years later, on November 7, 1944, he was hanged in a Japanese jail. Thus the life of the fearless Soviet intelligence man, the communist Richard Sorge, was cut short. On November 5, 1964, Richard Sorge was posthumously awarded the title of Hero of the Soviet Union. Sorge's associates, Klausen and his wife, who were liberated from a Tokyo prison after the capitulation of Japan and who now live in the German Democratic Republic, were also decorated with Soviet medals.

Thus, from Berlin, Berne, and Tokyo, to Moscow, through intelligence channels, came the alarming information: Germany will attack the Soviet Union on June 22.

The United States and England Give Warning

Since 1934, Sam Edison Woods had served in the embassy of the United States of America in Berlin as a commercial attaché.

At the moment of the events to be described, he was forty-eight years old. He was simultaneously an engineer, businessman, and diplomat. Woods had wide connections in higher German circles and operated so slyly and quietly that it never occurred to German counterintelligence to suspect him of forbidden activities. Woods had a friend, a German, who belonged to the anti-Hitler opposition, but, of course, had concealed this carefully. The German belonged to high society and not only enjoyed confidence at the ministry of economic affairs and the Reichsbank—institutions headed at various times by Hjalmar Schacht, who trusted him—but also had influential connections in the high command of the Wehrmacht.

In August 1940, Woods's friend sent him a theater ticket. When the lights went off in the hall, he placed a folded piece of paper in the attaché's jacket pocket. After the end of the show they separated, not revealing by a single gesture that they were acquainted. At home Woods took the note out of his pocket. In it was written: "There have been conferences in Hitler's headquarters about preparations for war against Russia." Woods immediately transmitted the information to the State Department of the United States of America. There, however, according to the late Secretary of State of the USA, Cordell Hull, Woods's information was received with distrust.[9] In the USA they were convinced as before that Hitler intended to invade the British Isles. And in August 1940 it actually was not so simple to imagine that Hitler would decide to turn toward the east, starting a two-front war.

In spite of the State Department's doubts, Woods was ordered to undertake a careful study of Hitler's new plans. Woods's friend assured him that the information had been received by him from a person deserving of confidence. This person belonged to a narrow circle of especially trusted officers in the high command of the German armed forces. He told Woods that

Hitler was preparing for a surprise attack on the Soviet Union under the cover of the devastating air raids on England.

A study of events shows that Hitler would have tried to carry out an invasion of England if that were feasible. The fact that the planning of the invasion of England continued in the headquarters of the high command, along with the initial work of the General Staff officers in planning the attack on the Soviet Union, also bears witness to this. Woods's informant soon told him that economic plans for the exploitation of Soviet territory were also being worked on intensively, and the printing of Russian currency had begun.[10]

After Hitler had confirmed Directive No. 21 ("Plan Barbarossa") all the details of this plan were immediately communicated to Woods. In January 1941, Woods's informant gave him a copy of the directive and communicated the details of the three main directional thrusts of the German armies. All the preparations for war against the USSR had to be completed by the spring of 1941, Woods's German friend emphasized.

By this time the United States State Department had been able to check Woods's information and had received confirmation of the correctness of his reports. In January 1941, Hull reported Woods's information to President Roosevelt. After a number of conferences, it was decided to inform the Soviet ambassador in Washington about Hitler's plans. On March 1 Under Secretary of State Sumner Welles acquainted K. Oumansky with the material sent by Woods. Hull later wrote in his memoirs that the ambassador, having heard Welles's message, turned pale. After a short pause, Oumansky, himself again, warmly thanked the American government and said that he fully realized the importance of the information received by him and would immediately inform the Soviet government.[11] On March 20 Welles confirmed the March 1 communication to the Soviet ambassador and added a number of further items of information.[12]

This was the first warning from foreign diplomatic channels, and not the "very first warning the USSR had received," as Farago claims, because the first warning had already been received in 1940 through intelligence channels. But actually all the warnings were overtaken by the same fate: J. V. Stalin simply ignored them.

Although the British prime minister, Winston Churchill, was given Woods's information, his attitude toward it was skeptical until March 1941. Meanwhile, the British intelligence service on the continent continued to send in reports about suspicious movements of German troops. It is true that these reports, apparently, still did not add up to a clear picture because British intelligence was interested in Germany's intentions only from the point of view of the invasion of the British Isles and because preparations for operation "Sea Lion" seemingly were proceeding as usual on the shores of the English Channel and the Straits of Calais; training for amphibious landings was being carried on, etc.

On one of the last days of March, Churchill, reading a regular intelligence summary, directed his attention to a report from British agents in the Balkans. They reported that at the same time as the Yugoslav ministers arrived in Vienna for the signing of the protocols about Yugoslavia's entry into the Tripartite Pact, three out of the five German armored divisions which had recently moved into Romanian territory in the direction of Yugoslavia and Greece, had been stopped and turned back in the direction of Krakow. From this Churchill drew a conclusion: the Germans, apparently, were in fact preparing for an attack against the USSR. And although a few days later these divisions

177

were again thrown against Yugoslavia, the British prime minister merely made a correction in his conclusions—the attack on the USSR would begin in June instead of May. At the beginning of April, the joint intelligence committee stated in a report to Churchill that Germany was concentrating large forces in the east, and sooner or later there would be war. However, the committee did not consider war likely within a short time. Moreover, on May 23 the committee reported that rumors about Germany's attack on the USSR had died out. However, even before he received this report, Churchill no longer doubted that after Yugoslavia and Greece would come the turn of the Soviet Union.

In a letter to Eden, who was then in Athens, dated March 28, 1941, Churchill asked his minister of foreign affairs to concentrate his efforts on making an alliance between Yugoslavia, Greece, and Turkey (one of the many ideas of the British prime minister that turned out to be stillborn). Churchill wrote: "If a united front were formed on the Balkan Peninsula, might not Germany consider it beneficial to abandon its attack on Russia? We have had many reports of heavy concentrations of [German —A.N.] troops in Poland and intrigues in Sweden and Finland." [13] *

The British prime minister not only was not grieved by this turn in the war, he was delighted. A German attack on the Soviet Union would save England from the danger of invasion, would relieve her most grave military and political situation, and would afford a breathing spell for her to gather her strength. For

---

* The author appears to have mistranslated Churchill, whose original statement reads as follows: "Is it not possible that if a united front were formed on the Balkan Peninsular, *Germany might think it better business to take it out of Russia*, observing that we had many reports of heavy concentrations in Poland and intrigues in Sweden and Finland?" (Italics mine.)—V.P.

this reason he considered that a warning should be sent to Stalin. It was necessary for the German attack not to catch the Russians by surprise and for the struggle in the east to continue as long as possible.

On March 31 information confirming the earlier reports came to London from Belgrade: supposedly Hitler, in a talk with the Yugoslav Prince Regent, Paul, had told him that the attack on the Soviet Union was scheduled for June 30. The same information was received by the British ambassador in Washington from Under Secretary of State Welles on the evening of April 2. The following day Churchill made a final decision. Stafford Cripps, the British ambassador in Moscow, was sent a message from the prime minister for personal transmission to Stalin. On April 5 Cripps informed London that there was no possibility of handing the message to J. V. Stalin personally. There followed an instruction to pass the message to V. M. Molotov, but Cripps was not able to arrange to be received by Molotov either. The infuriated ambassador, at his own risk, then sent a personal letter to the deputy People's Commissar for Foreign Affairs, in which, without saying a word about the prime minister's message, he went over the whole complex of Anglo-Soviet relations. The Foreign Office, for its part, also began to doubt the expediency of delivering the message. But Churchill insisted on the immediate execution of his instruction.

On April 19, two weeks after Churchill's message was received, it finally was delivered, but not to J. V. Stalin, and not to Molotov, since they absolutely refused to meet with the British ambassador, but to the People's Commissariat for Foreign Affairs. Two priceless weeks were lost: Churchill in his message warned of the attack being prepared against the USSR. Yet two months still remained until the outbreak of war.[14]

On April 22 the English ambassador was notified that the

message of the British prime minister had been delivered to J. V. Stalin.

But Churchill's message, too, evoked the same reaction: J. V. Stalin was convinced that this was an intrigue of the British government, the purpose of which was to cause a quarrel between the Soviet Union and Germany. Not long before, the German military attaché in the USSR, General Koestring, had received an instruction to inform the General Staff of the Red Army that the transfer of German soldiers from west to east was being done to replace the older age groups with the younger ones, in order to use the former in industry. In addition, the conditions for the training of young soldiers in the east were more advantageous, since there was no danger of air raids.[15]

Information about the attack being prepared against the USSR was reported to J. V. Stalin continually. On April 10 the aforementioned talk of Hitler with Prince Regent Paul was reported to him. On May 5 new information about the preparation of an attack on the USSR was given to J. V. Stalin. In the same month the information received from Sorge was reported. On June 6, Stalin received data on the concentration of enemy forces numbering about four million men on the Soviet frontier. On June 11 J. V. Stalin was informed that Berlin had ordered the German embassy to prepare itself for evacuation within seven days, and that they had already started burning documents there on June 9.[16]

Marshal of the Soviet Union F. I. Golikov was the chief of the Intelligence Directorate of the General Staff precisely in the period of Germany's preparations for the attack on the USSR, from the middle of July 1940.

In a talk with the author of this book, the marshal answered a number of questions about events preceding the war.

"*Question:* A lot is written abroad about warnings which the

Soviet Union received through various channels about the attack being prepared. The impression is created that the first warning came in March 1941. [The message of United States Under Secretary of State S. Welles to Soviet Ambassador K. Oumansky —A.N.] Is that so?

"Answer: No, that is not so. The first warnings came from Soviet military intelligence much earlier than March 1941. The Intelligence Directorate carried out enormous work in the collection and analysis of information, through various channels, about the intentions of Hitler's Germany, particularly, and in the first place against the Soviet state. Along with the collection and analysis of extensive agent data, the Intelligence Directorate exhaustively studied international information, the foreign press, the comments of public opinion, the military-political and military-technical literature of Germany and other countries, etc. Soviet military intelligence had trustworthy and tested sources for obtaining secret information in a whole series of countries, including Germany itself. For this reason, the American communication was not, and in any case could not have been, news for the political and military leadership of our country, beginning with J. V. Stalin." [17]

Marshal of the Soviet Union I. Kh. Bagramyan also believes that there was enough information "to evaluate sensibly the attack being planned on the Soviet Union." [18]

And so, all witnesses testify that Soviet intelligence carried out its duty with honor before the people on the eve of war. Soviet intelligence men did everything in their power. But their warnings were disregarded.

Part Four—On the Eve

The Last Months

The negotiations in Berlin in November 1940, and events in the Balkans that followed, testified to the development of Hitlerite Germany's aggressive plans.

Hopes that the war in the Balkans would drag on, and the Germans would be forced to abandon their attack on the USSR in 1941 because of the advancing autumn, if they really had such an intention, did not materialize. The fact that J. V. Stalin hoped for such a development of events is testified to by the statements of the Yugoslav ambassador in Moscow, Milan Gavrilović, after his arrival in Ankara in May 1941. But Yugoslavia was smashed in a swift campaign. Now J. V. Stalin tried not to give Germany any excuse to attack the USSR. In the face of facts, J. V. Stalin was convinced that Hitler's Germany would not dare to violate the Nonaggression Pact and attack the Soviet Union. Such an evaluation led to an underestimation of the aggressive essence of Hitler's Germany. The international situation changed quickly and became more complicated. The course of events broke up the unrealistic concept of international relations created by J. V. Stalin. But he continued to cling to it stubbornly. He considered as before that England was only looking for an opportunity to provoke a Soviet-German conflict.

In actual fact no political agreement was any longer possible between England and Germany. A compromise peace was impossible because under the conditions of German domination of Western Europe, with the British defeat in the Balkans and the

Middle East, the conclusion of any peace would mean for England the end of the British Empire, and her virtual capitulation. England, of course, could not agree to this. In England herself, and also in the United States of America, the struggle between two tendencies kept growing: the old, Munich one, and the new one—a policy for drawing closer to the Soviet Union and creating an anti-German coalition together with it. The second tendency found the most influential partisan in the person of Winston Churchill. Under the new conditions, the hostility between England and Germany had reached such a degree of tension that the conflict could be settled only by a total defeat of one of the rivals. Finally, political changes also were taking place in the USA, where the partisans of military intervention in favor of England were acquiring greater preponderance. In all the proposals of a political character which the British government made, J. V. Stalin saw only one side—an attempt to provoke an armed conflict between the Soviet Union and Germany. He viewed the reports pouring in from various channels about the impending German attack against the Soviet Union in exactly the same way.

Chief Marshal of Artillery N. N. Voronov states that J. V. Stalin thought that "war between fascist Germany and the Soviet Union could occur only as a result of provocations on the part of the fascist militarists, and he feared these provocations most of all." This is a very interesting remark. If Voronov did not use the expression "fascist militarists" by accident, this cannot be otherwise understood than as a confirmation that J. V. Stalin continued to put his hopes in the nonaggression agreement, that is, he believed Hitler but did not trust the German generals, intoxicated with their military victories. This also would explain the later orders to Red Army units not to fall for fascist provocations.

J. V. Stalin regarded with special suspicion all communications coming from British or American sources, merely seeing in them confirmation of his own analysis of the Soviet policy of "noninterference": the Western powers wanted to drag the Soviet Union and Germany into a war with each other, and then they themselves would warm their hands at the fire. The version, spread by the Hitlerites, about the provocative nature of the rumors and reports regarding the attack being prepared on the USSR, perfectly fitted his own judgments. Curiously enough, it appears that, at the beginning of April, the rumors about the imminent German-Soviet war were being spread mainly by German citizens. This is stated in particular in a report to the German ministry of foreign affairs by the latter's representative at the high command of ground forces (OKH) on April 3, 1941: "OKH has received the information according to which travelers coming from Germany are spreading rumors among German citizens living in Russia that a German-Soviet clash is inevitable. It is said likewise that foreign diplomats in Moscow are also alarmed by these rumors." In connection with this, the OKH made a request to the ministry of foreign affairs that Germans traveling across the territory of the USSR be strictly ordered not only not to spread such rumors, but to deny them.[1]

However, the rumors became more alarming with every day. To ignore them completely, to pretend that everything was in order, was impossible. Wishing apparently to emphasize their disbelief in such rumors and confirm their desire to adhere strictly to the agreements made with Germany, Stalin and Molotov unexpectedly appeared on the platform at the railroad station during the departure of Japanese minister of foreign affairs Matsuoka. In a dispatch to the ministry of foreign affairs, the German ambassador in Moscow, Schulenburg, wrote: "Matsuoka's departure was delayed for an hour, and then there took place an unusual ceremony. Unexpected, apparently, to Japanese and Russians alike, Stalin and Molotov appeared and greeted Matsuoka and the Japanese who were present in an emphatically friendly manner, and wished them a pleasant journey. Then Stalin loudly asked about me, and when he found me, came up to me and embraced me around the shoulders and said: 'We must remain friends, and you must do everything you can for this!' A little later Stalin turned to the acting German military attaché, Colonel Krebs, and, after first convincing himself that he was a German, said to him: 'We will remain friends with you under all circumstances.' Undoubtedly Stalin greeted Colonel Krebs and me in this way deliberately and in so doing consciously attracted the attention of the numerous public which was present here." [2]

Soon afterwards, Schulenburg was summoned to Berlin for consultations. By the testimony of the counselor of the German embassy in Moscow, Gustav Hilger, Schulenburg brought to Berlin a memorandum composed by him jointly with the military attaché, General Koestring. The memorandum was transmitted through channels to Hitler, but the latter was in no hurry to converse with the ambassador. Schulenburg waited for two weeks for an audience.

His protracted stay in Germany again gave birth to numerous rumors. This was reported, in particular, by the Romanian ambassador in Moscow, Gafencu. According to the German minister in Bucharest, Gafencu supposedly wrote that: "A grave impression in this connection was created in Soviet circles by rumors that preparations for the departure of children and valuables from the German embassy were under way." [3]

On April 28 Schulenburg was, finally, invited to see Hitler. The whole character and the tone of the talk left the ambassador with no doubts that the decision to attack the USSR had been taken, and Hitler was now busy searching for arguments to explain or justify the attack. This theme rings out with particular clarity in the memorandum of record composed by Schulenburg after the conversation. In particular, Hitler insisted that the Soviet-Yugoslav treaty of April 5 had been concluded in order to frighten Germany. "I denied this," writes Schulenburg, "and repeated that the Russians only intended to underscore their interest, but nevertheless showed correctness in informing us of their intentions."

Hitler insisted that the Soviet command was carrying out a strategic concentration of troops. Schulenburg denied this: "I cannot believe that Russia would ever attack Germany." Schulenburg's reaction, apparently, made Hitler cautious; in dismissing the ambassador, he said to him: "Oh, another thing, I don't intend to wage war against Russia." [4] But on returning to Moscow on April 30, Schulenburg drew aside Counselor Hilger, who was meeting him at the airport, and whispered to him: "The die is cast. War with Russia is decided." He said also that Hitler had lied to him. [5]

Hitler did not forgive Schulenburg his negative attitude toward the war against the USSR. Having taken part in the plot against Hitler, Schulenburg was executed in 1944.

Five days after the return of the German ambassador to Moscow, Colonel Krebs, who had been acting military attaché in the absence of General Koestring, arrived in Berlin from Moscow. Krebs told Halder: "Russia will do everything to avoid war." [6]

Meanwhile rumors about the inevitable German-Soviet war were ever more persistently circulating among Moscow's diplomatic circles. The German naval attaché in Moscow, Captain Norbert Baumbach, informed the naval command about this, with a reference to the travelers coming through Germany. He also stated that, according to the counselor of the Italian embassy, the British ambassador in Moscow (i.e., Stafford Cripps —A.N.) "predicted June 22 as the date the war would start." Other diplomats named May 20. Baumbach stated that he was denying these rumors.[7]

In the month of May the rumors about imminent war not only did not weaken, but continued to become stronger. The London *Times*, for instance, reported in its May 1 issue that in many European capitals German officers and propagandists were announcing to anyone who would listen that the German army was on the eve of an attack on the Soviet Union. Lithuanian émigrés were being encouraged by Berlin. The Ukrainian nationalists significantly widened their activities, particularly after they had received rights equal to those of the *Volksdeutsche* in Poland. In Bucharest there was talk about annexing Bessarabia to Romania. In Turkey, German propagandists spread a whisper campaign about an attack by the USSR on Turkey, supposedly in preparation.[8]

On the third day after his return to Moscow, Schulenburg wrote to the ministry of foreign affairs with badly concealed irritation: "I and all the higher officials of my embassy have always combated rumors of an imminent German-Russian military showdown since it is obvious that these rumors constitute a great hazard for the continued peaceful development of German-Soviet relations. Please bear in mind, however, that attempts to counteract these rumors here in Moscow must necessarily remain ineffectual if such rumors incessantly reach here from Germany, and if every traveler who comes to Moscow or travels through Moscow not only brings these rumors along but can even confirm them by citing facts." [9]

In answer an order came from Berlin: deny these rumors by citing the fact that they are nothing but a renewal of England's efforts to poison German-Soviet relations. Schulenburg was also required to spread provocative rumors about a significant concentration of Soviet troops supposedly going on at the frontier, while Germany was keeping near the Soviet borders only those forces absolutely essential for covering her rear in the Balkan operation. The ambassador was also asked to seed rumors about a transfer of German troops from east to west, which had supposedly commenced.[10]

J. V. Stalin's actions in this period had an extremely contradictory character: On the one hand, they pointed to his striving to cling to discredited dogma as before, and on the other, they witnessed his fear of war and his uncertainty. On May 5, at a reception for the graduates of military academies in the Kremlin, Stalin gave a forty-minute speech, in which he demanded improvement in military skills and readiness to repel aggression. But from whom could an attack be expected at that time? Clearly only from Germany. The next day, a communiqué about the appointment of Stalin as chairman of the Council of People's Commissars was published in the newspapers. Molotov remained People's Commissar for Foreign Affairs. This appointment emphasized that Stalin was taking upon himself the full power and the whole responsibility for Soviet policy.

J. V. Stalin's assumption of the post of chairman of the Council of People's Commissars was interpreted abroad as a gesture of invitation to Germany to open negotiations, which he would be ready to carry on personally.

But Germany did not react.

The well-known English historian John Erickson writes that on the day that J. V. Stalin assumed the post of chairman of the Council of People's Commissars, the Soviet military attaché in Berlin reported that the Germans would attack the USSR on May 14 from the direction of Finland and the Baltic states. On

May 22 the assistant military attaché in Berlin reported that the German attack would take place on June 15, or maybe in the beginning of July.[11] *

The lack of reaction on Germany's part to J. V. Stalin's new appointment also should have called for caution. It was impossible, after all, to limit oneself to the supposition that Hitler was indulging in extortion and wanted to "drive up his price" before proposing negotiations. But, apparently, this was exactly what J. V. Stalin assumed. His scarcely explicable conduct apparently had its deepest roots in his simplistic understanding of the outside world, about which he could really judge only on the basis of the information which he received, and, most importantly, which he wished to receive. Not once up to that time had he been outside the limits of the Soviet Union. Actually even in his own country he traveled very little. From his statement, speeches, and appearance, it is clear that he considered England to be the main enemy of the Soviet state in the prewar years. In 1941 this feeling must have been even stronger in him, since at the head of the British government stood the old foe of the Soviet regime, the experienced and crafty politician Winston Churchill. There is no doubt that the sudden flight to England of Hitler's deputy in the Nazi Party, Rudolf Hess, strengthened J. V. Stalin's suspicions regarding the intrigues of "perfidious Albion."

This happened on May 10, 1941.

Enough has been written about Hess's mission. There is no necessity to stop and examine this episode in detail. In our opinion, its significance has been exaggerated. But it is such a tempting subject!

Familiarization with documents, materials, memoirs, and studies at the disposal of historians gives serious reason to

---

* Note that Nekrich must rely on foreign sources for this information.

believe that Hess undertook his flight to England on his own responsibility and risk, on his own initiative. During the Nuremberg trial, Hess admitted to the American psychiatrist Kelly that one of his astrologers (Hess was addicted to mysticism and surrounded himself with stargazers, as did others among the "supermen") had predicted to him that the stars pointed to the fact that he, Hess, had to undertake something to conclude peace.[12] Hess was under the strong influence of a professor of geopolitics, Karl Haushofer, who had for many years advocated an agreement between Germany and England against the Soviet Union. Hess, knowing that there was to be an attack on the Soviet Union, decided to try to explain to the British personally how they should act in connection with this event. Successfully landing in Scotland, Hess was then interned by the British authorities. The conversations carried on with him by British ministers, among them Lords Simon and Beaverbrook, and the former British chargé d'affaires in Berlin, Kirkpatrick, showed that Germany was on the eve of attacking the Soviet Union, and Hess's flight had not been inspired by some sort of "humane motive," as Hess's attorney at the Nuremberg trial tried to present it, but by a desire to spare Germany the danger of war on two fronts, to achieve at least the neutralization of England during the coming war. It was exactly this, as Hess well knew, that Hitler was dreaming of. Hess proposed the division of Europe into spheres of influence: Soviet territory up to the Urals must go to Germany. In a talk with Beaverbrook, Hess insisted on the necessity of concluding an Anglo-German alliance against the USSR.[13]

For the British War Cabinet, Hess's "proposals" were mainly valuable in that they confirmed the intention of Hitler's Germany to attack the Soviet Union, and that among the Nazi leaders there was an agonizing fear that Germany might be forced to fight on two fronts. What would England's position be at the moment when Germany began the war against the Bolsheviks? For England the German "expedition to the East," and this was never concealed by British statesmen, was a life-saving breathing spell. In their opinion, the longer a German-Soviet war went on, the better for British interests. This is why the decision was taken in London: first, to hold Hess as a prisoner-of-war, and secondly, to notify the Soviet Union about the continuing transfer of German troops to Poland, closer to the Soviet border.

In Western countries, Hess's flight was received as an expression of the uncertainty of the Hitlerite leadership and its wish for a compromise peace. The American isolationists especially insisted on this. Thus, according to a London *Times* report, one of the isolationist leaders, Senator Wheeler, tried to convince President Roosevelt to propose peace negotiations. Hess's flight proved, Wheeler insisted, that Germany's morale was undermined and this was the very time to start peace negotiations.[14]

Hitler, for his part, was infuriated by Hess's escapade and gave orders to remove him from office.

Hess's flight made a big impression on J. V. Stalin who, as his later talks on the subject with Churchill and Beaverbrook showed, was convinced that England was instigating Germany to attack the USSR and that secret negotiations were in progress in London on the basis of Hess's proposals. Without taking this circumstance into account, it would be very difficult to understand that inner hostility with which Stalin received, in the last prewar month, every new report on Germany's imminent attack on the Soviet Union; he considered such reports to be British provocations. From April to June 1941, J. V. Stalin continued to do everything to convince Germany of his intention to continue and strictly observe the concluded agreements, in the political as well as economic spheres. All this occurred at a time when Germany was bringing her troops up to the Soviet borders and violating economic agreements, delaying deliveries of equipment to the Soviet Union, and, in particular, gun turrets for cruisers.

In Western historical literature there is an account according to which the German ambassador in Moscow, Schulenburg, and the counselor of the embassy, Hilger, tried to warn the USSR's foreign ministry of Hitler's decision to attack the USSR. This attempt was undertaken at the end of May or the beginning of June 1941. In his memoirs Hilger relates that he proposed that Schulenburg make use of the arrival in Moscow of the Soviet ambassador to Berlin, Dekanozov, to tell him of Germany's intentions. As is known, Dekanozov was one of the persons closest to Beriya. (In 1953 Dekanozov was found guilty of complicity in Beriya's crimes by a Soviet court.) Schulenburg vacillated. Hilger writes: "It was extremely difficult to persuade him. He said, quite correctly, that the German government would try him and me for treason if it leaked out that we were about to warn the Russians. I argued, however, that too much was at stake and that we could not let any concern about our own existence deter us from such a desperate step."

The secret meeting took place in Schulenburg's residence. According to Hilger's statement, in spite of the fact that Schulenburg and he from the very beginning made it known to Dekanozov that they were acting on their own initiative, the latter stubbornly tried to learn whether they were authorized by their government. If not, he could not transmit our statements to the Soviet government. Apparently he could not imagine that we were conscientiously subjecting ourselves to the highest danger because of a last hope to save the peace. The German diplomats' advice was that the USSR should show initiative and first start negotiations with Hitler; then, having been drawn into negotiations, Hitler could no longer attack the USSR. Hilger admits that such a proposal could, logically, have been considered a provocation.[15] And one can agree with this. However, to disregard this new, unexpected warning was impossible. No matter how Schulenburg's step was evaluated, it was essential to strengthen military measures to counter an invasion.

In the first days of June, Ambassador Cripps was recalled to London from Moscow for consultation. On June 10, 1941, the Soviet ambassador in London, I. M. Mayskiy, was invited to visit the British permanent assistant minister of foreign affairs, Cadogan. After the usual exchange of greetings, Cadogan said: "Mr. Ambassador, I invited you here in order to give you an extremely important message. Please take a sheet of paper and write what I dictate." Then Cadogan read out information from British intelligence about the redeployment of formations of the German-fascist armies in the direction of the Soviet border. Returning to the embassy, Mayskiy immediately encoded Cadogan's message and sent it to Moscow. On June 13, the Soviet ambassador in London was again invited to the Foreign Office, this time to see the minister of foreign affairs, A. Eden. The minister delivered still another warning to Mayskiy. Eden informed Mayskiy that if Germany attacked the Soviet Union, and the British government considered this a possibility, it was ready to give aid to the USSR, first by the operations of British aviation against Germany, secondly by the dispatch of a military mission to Moscow, the members of which would have had great experience in military operations in the current war, and thirdly by giving whatever economic aid was possible in practice.[16]

Thus the attempts of Hitler's Germany to achieve a "truce" with England before attacking the USSR ended in failure. England made the choice which favored her national interests.

At the beginning of June, the most widespread point of view in international political circles was that Stalin, impressed with German military might, was ready to do practically anything to avoid war in the summer of 1941.[17]

The counselor of the German embassy in Moscow, Hilger, summarizes his impressions of that period as follows: "Everything pointed to the fact that he [Stalin—A.N.] considered that Hitler was preparing to play a game for the purpose of extortion, in which, after threatening troop transfers, there would follow sudden demands for economic or even territorial concessions. He apparently believed that he would be successful in coming to an agreement with Hitler, when these demands were presented." [18]

From L. M. Sandalov's memoirs we learn that a similar point of view was also widespread in the high command of the Red Army. In June the commander of the Fourth Army, A. A. Korobkov, declared at a conference at army headquarters after his return from the military district headquarters: "Germany will not dare to break the Nonaggression Treaty. She is pulling troops toward our borders mainly because she is afraid of us. . . . But on the other hand," the commander continued after a moment's pause, "One can fully allow that the concentration of German troops on our border must strengthen Germany's 'arguments' in deciding various political questions with us." [19] If these impressions truly reflected the state of affairs, they are only a confirmation of Stalin's lack of a realistic idea of the world situation and also testify to his fears in connection with the lack of preparedness to parry the German blow. But no matter what conclusions Stalin drew, nothing can justify his refusal to take elementary precautionary measures in case Germany's attack should come after all. In practice this should have been expressed by the implementation of a rearguard action plan. The reports from the frontier indicated the urgent necessity of taking emergency precautionary measures.

In the last days of May and at the beginning of June, enough signs of approaching war were noticed in the border military districts. The ever increasing flights of German aircraft over the Soviet borders were constant reminders. According to the information of army intelligence, there was a significant increase in the activities of the Germans in areas contiguous to the Soviet border.

Thus, in a report from the intelligence section of the staff of the Western Special Military District, Army General G. D. Pavlov * was informed on June 4, 1941, that Germany's military preparations against the USSR recently, particularly since May 25, 1941, were being carried out intensively. The report drew attention to an increase in German groupings in the area of Ostrlenok, Krasnyshi, Mlava, and Tsekhanov by two to three infantry divisions and by two SS armored divisions; to the increase in artillery units, tank formations and automobiles, and antitank and antiaircraft defense measures in the direction of the border. The arrival of German military aviation in Warsaw and Koenigberg and an increase in the number of training flights were noted. The increase of troops in the frontier zone and the resettlement of inhabitants from the border regions to the rear was mentioned. Army intelligence reported about the covert mobilization of German officials for future positions in the western regions of the USSR. The conclusion of the report emphasized that "The information on the intensive preparations of a

---

* Soon to be executed on Stalin's orders.—V.P.

theater of war and on strengthened troop concentrations in the zone opposite the Western Military District is deserving of trust."

Similar information was available to the commands of other border districts. For instance, it was known that in the zone of the Soviet Fourth Army, the strength of the Germans brought up to the border was three times greater in ground forces, and even more in the air, than that of the Soviet.

The headquarters of the Fourth Army had information about the concentration of significant German forces. This information was received from the border detachment and construction units working on the border. "From time to time" the headquarters also received information from higher echelons. In addition, German spies and saboteurs, who confirmed the alarming reports about the German army's preparations for attack, were caught in the army's zone. In information possessed by the military district headquarters on June 5, 1941, it was stated that about forty German divisions were concentrated on the border of Byelorussia, including twenty-four divisions opposite Brest.[20]

On June 2 the Main Directorate of Border Troops informed higher headquarters that in the course of April and May the Germans had concentrated eighty to eighty-eight infantry divisions, thirteen to fifteen motorized divisions, seven armored divisions, sixty-five artillery regiments, etc., near the Soviet frontier. On June 6 it again reported that there were about four million German troops concentrated near the Soviet borders, and eight German armies were concentrated on Polish territory.

In May and June the Germans carried out extensive reconaissance along the Soviet frontier—photography, topographical survey, and measurement and depth of border rivers.

The whole atmosphere in the border regions testified to the coming of war. This is how the situation in the Brest area was described by L. M. Sandalov, whose memoirs are characterized by their objectivity, accuracy, and a wonderful knowledge of the situation, and sincerity: "The rumors that the Germans would come soon circulated everywhere among the local population. Lines crowded outside of stores. Flour, sugar, kerosine, and soap sold out. The owners of private tailor, shoe, and watch shops gladly took new orders, but were not in a hurry to deliver overcoats, suits, boots, and watches to their customers. The orders placed by military personnel were especially delayed. Among the troops this caused alarm, but from the military district headquarters came the most contradictory instructions.[21]

The command of the Leningrad Military District already had information about a concentration of German troops, transferred from Norway and Germany, opposite Murmansk and Kandalaksha. German ships, putting in at the Leningrad port, were not unloaded, and began to go back home. There were other, more minor, but noteworthy symptoms. For instance, the personnel of the German consulate in Leningrad canceled their orders to Leningrad tailors.[22]

On the Karelian Isthmus the border guards noticed the appearance of many new officers on the other side of the border. A large number of towers were built on the Finnish side. However, the command of the military district apparently ignored these reports. Here, for instance, is what the district's chief of engineer troops, General B. Bychevskiy, wrote: "We were used to this type of information and did not attach much meaning to it because we did not believe that Finland would go for a repetition of its military adventure."[23]

Bychevskiy's statement is confirmed by higher military leaders such as, for instance, Army General I. V. Tyulenev, the commander of the Moscow District. "Yes, we, particularly the higher military circles," he writes, "knew that war was not far beyond the hills and was knocking at our gates. And still, one must honestly admit, that misinformation like the above-mentioned denial of TASS [see below—A.N.], the persistent propaganda that 'if there is war tomorrow, if tomorrow there is a campaign, we will be ready for the campaign today,' * led to a certain complacency. The idea that the powerful concentration of German troops on our borders was only a provocation, to which one should not react in a morbid manner, that supposedly the German government was only 'playing' on our nerves, cast a spell over us to a certain extent, the commanders of military districts and the People's Commissariat of Defense, which possessed the opportunity of putting together an accurate prognosis of the 'military climate' on June 22, 1941." [24]

Tyulenev's testimony is extremely important. However, he apparently was mistaken in attributing this mood to all the military district commanders. From the memoirs of other participants in the events, and from materials of other kind, we know what worry, for instance, was felt by the command of the Kiev Special Military District. The commander, Colonel General Kirponos, and a member of the military council, M. F. Lukin, expected in the middle of June that the war would start any minute. "The district commander said," Major General A. A. Lobachev relates, "that the armies of fascist Germany have been brought up to the Bug River. The border in the defense area of the Kiev Special Military District is being violated every day. German planes are flying over our territory. In the old fortified regions the armaments have been removed as obsolete, and not replaced by new equipment. The leaders of the district were worried by the circumstance that they had practically no real

---

* From a popular soldiers' song of the period, "Yesli Zavtra Voyna."— V.P.

possibility of providing a clear instruction to the command personnel of individual units and formations." [25]

The same point of view was also held by the chief of the operational section of the district staff, Colonel I. Kh. Bagramyan (later Marshal of the Soviet Union). "In Bagramyan's opinion, one could no longer doubt that Hitler would violate the Nonaggression Pact," A. A. Lobachev emphasizes. M. P. Kirponos sent a letter to Stalin. He wrote that the Germans were concentrating on the Bug River and that the German advance would soon begin. He proposed the evacuation of 300,000 persons of the population from the threatened regions, the preparation of positions there, and the construction of antitank defenses. To this Kirponos received an answer that preparations of this sort would be a provocation to the Germans, and no excuses for an attack should be given.[26]

Marshal of the Soviet Union R. Ya. Malinovskiy writes: "Requests by some district troop commanders for authority to bring their troops to combat readiness and move them closer to the frontier were personally turned down by J. V. Stalin [meaning that there were such requests!—A.N.]. The troops continued to be trained in peacetime fashion: the artillery of infantry divisions was in artillery camps and ranges, antiaircraft weapons on antiaircraft ranges, and sapper units in engineer camps, and the "naked" infantry regiments of divisions were located separately in their camps. With the threat of war approaching, these most crude mistakes bordered on the criminal. Could this have been avoided? It could have and should have been." [27]

There still were commanders who were worried by the situation. They tried to get permission from higher commanders to move at least part of their troops to occupy more convenient positions in case of attack. On this score we have, in particular, the convincing testimonies of I. Kh. Bagramyan and R. Ya. Malinovskiy. The latter relates that, being at that time a corps commander, he insisted on the redeployment of his unit. On June 7, 1941, he moved out of the Kirovgrad and Pervomaysk area, with corps headquarters and one infantry division, to the Beltsy area of Moldavia, which he reached on June 14, a week before the beginning of the war. On the eve of war the movement of the army commanded by I. S. Konev from the North Caucasus to the Ukraine was completed, and later the shift of part of the forces of another army from the Trans-Baikal region. With the permission of the People's Commissar for Defense, the command of the Kiev Special Military District began to move five infantry corps to the border. In Marshal I. Kh. Bagramyan's opinion, these facts were evidence that Moscow was undertaking serious measures "for the strengthening of the western borders of our country." And the initiative of local commanders, although it had importance under the circumstances, was really not the whole show. From the beginning of June on, a general movement of troops from the depths of the country to the western regions was begun. But these measures had an extremely inconsistent character. I. Kh. Bagramyan relates, for instance, that when, on June 10, the troops of the Kiev Military District began to occupy the line of the unfinished frontier fortified areas, from Moscow "came a stern reprimand: 'Cancel this order immediately and report who, specifically, issued this unauthorized, arbitrary order.' " [28]

The Last Week

June 14. The attention of readers opening their papers on June 14 was attracted by an announcement from TASS. The announcement categorically denied the assertions of the British and other foreign press that Germany had allegedly presented demands of a territorial and economic nature to the Soviet Union and that "negotiations are in progress between Germany and the USSR regarding the conclusion of a new, closer, agreement between them." The foreign press asserted that these demands had been rejected by the Soviet Union, after which Germany had started concentrating its troops at the Soviet borders for an attack on the USSR, and the Soviet Union, for its part, also was "urgently preparing for war with Germany and concentrating troops at the borders." Calling these rumors "clumsily concocted propaganda by powers hostile to the USSR and Germany, who are interested in a further widening and unleashing of war," TASS, by authority of responsible circles in Moscow, announced that Germany had not presented any demands to the Soviet Union and there had been no proposals about a new "closer agreement"; that "Germany is observing the conditions of the Soviet-German Nonaggression Pact just as rigidly as the Soviet Union, in view of which, in the opinion of Soviet circles, the rumors of Germany's intention to break the pact and undertake an attack on the USSR have no foundation whatever, and the recent transfer of German troops, freed from operations in the Balkans, to the eastern and northeastern regions of Germany is connected, it must be supposed, with other motives having nothing to do with Soviet-German relations." In the communiqué it was confirmed that the Soviet Union was observing as before and intended to observe the terms of the Soviet-German Nonaggression Pact, in view of which the rumors about the USSR's preparations for war with Germany are "false and provocative." In conclusion, the communiqué pointed out that it would be, "to say the least, absurd," to represent as hostile to Germany the summer musters of Red Army reserve contingents then taking place and the coming maneuvers which are held every year.[29]

This TASS communiqué is an extremely curious document. In

the first place, its text shows definitely that the transfer of German troops closer to the Soviet borders was well known to the Soviet government. Therefore the matter at hand concerned only the interpretation of the purpose of this transfer, and the fact itself did not evoke any doubts. In this way Germany was given the opportunity to confirm the opinion, stated in the TASS communiqué, that the concentration was connected, ". . . *it must be supposed* [italics mine—A.N.] with other motives having nothing to do with Soviet-German relations." The choice of motives was up to Germany itself. Such a formulation testified to a readiness to accept any explanation. Furthermore, the communiqué did not exclude the possibility of opening new negotiations between the Soviet Union and Germany. It simply stated that negotiations about the conclusion of "any new, closer, agreement" had not been proposed by Germany, ". . . *in view of which* [italics mine—A.N.] the negotiations on this subject could not have taken place."

TASS's announcement gave Germany the opportunity of suggesting new negotiations, or of associating herself with TASS's denial, or both.

But the German side preferred to maintain silence. The *New York Times* reported on June 14, a few hours before the publication of TASS's communiqué, that a small exposition about the blitzkrieg in the Balkans, including photographs of the bombing of Belgrade and the occupation of Athens, was opened in the German embassy in Moscow.[30]

One cannot help but remember that a few days before the German assault on Norway, the German ambassador in Oslo showed a film about the blitzkrieg in Poland.

In Germany the TASS communiqué was not published. But the day this message appeared in the Soviet press, Hitler convoked the last big military conference before the attack on the

USSR. On that day Halder wrote in his official diary: "A big conference at the Fuehrer's. Reports of the commanders of army groups, armies, and tank groups, on 'Plan Barbarossa'! The Fuehrer gave a big political speech in which he explained the motivation of his decision regarding the attack on Russia and stated that with the crushing of Russia, England would be forced to stop fighting." [31] At the conference, the date of the attack was once again confirmed: On June 22, at the arranged signal "Dortmund," the German-fascist armies were to invade the territory of the Soviet Union.

All Soviet military leaders assert unanimously that the TASS statement had a pernicious, demoralizing effect on the army. For instance, L. M. Sandalov writes: "The anxious mood, which had reached a particular acuteness in the middle of the month, was somehow dampened by the well-known statement of TASS, published in the newspaper *Pravda* on June 15. . . . An article of this type from an authoritative state agency blunted the vigilance of the troops. It created among the commanders a certainty that there existed unknown circumstances which allowed our government to remain calm and confident as to the security of the Soviet borders. Commanders stopped spending the night in barracks. Soldiers began to undress at night. . . ." I. Kh. Bagramyan writes, "The organizational passivity to which Stalin and the chiefs of the Commissariat of Defense had condemned the troops of the border military districts was aggravated by the hour by unintelligent propaganda, which disoriented the soldiers and blunted their vigilance. This was also furthered by the special announcement of TASS published on June 14. . . ." [32] Commenting on the TASS statement, the *Manchester Guardian* stressed the fact that this statement did not deny the concentration of German troops on the borders of the USSR. On June 14 the British and American newspapers reported that the Germans had sent fresh troops to Finland by sea. "Although these reports are unconfirmed," the *Manchester Guardian* wrote, "they are viewed as probably correct." [33]

June 15 and 16. Rumors crept in from Ankara about an imminent attack on the Soviet Union by Germany. These rumors, apparently, were connected with the Turco-German negotiations regarding the conclusion of a neutrality pact. The *Manchester Guardian* reported on June 16 from Ankara: persons arriving there from Hungary and Romania were saying that German propagandists in those countries were predicting an inevitable clash between Germany and the Soviet Union within the next two weeks. The correspondent emphasized that bets were even being made at the odds of five to one on this score.[34]

June 17. A German reconnaissance plane flew over the main base of the Northern Fleet at Polyarnyi at a low altitude. Even the identifying markings were visible. But the antiaircraft batteries were silent. Not a single shot was fired. The commander of the Northern Fleet, Admiral A. G. Golovko, wrote in his diary on that day, "Having visited the batteries, I asked the commanders one and the same question: Why didn't they fire, in spite of the instructions to open fire. I received one and the same answer: They didn't open fire out of fear of causing confusion in some way. That is, instructions are instructions, but the consciousness of most of us mechanically continued to go along with the main direction of the past years: not to fall for a provocation, not to furnish an excuse for an incident which could cause a conflict in any degree and serve as a formal excuse for the unleashing of war.

"But the Hitlerites are already unleashing it, operating in the air only for the time being, and brazenly certain that here in the North we cannot put out aircraft of equal worth against them." [35]

On the western border, in the zone of the Eighth Border

Guard Detachment, a group of enemy agents was arrested; they had the mission of blowing up the railroad beds at the following points: Stolbtsy, Baranovichi, Osipovichi, Lida-Molodechno, and Lupinets. Stalin was informed that fascist Germany's attack would occur on June 21–22. But Stalin, as before, was deaf to warnings.[36]

The Finnish newspaper *Helsinken Sanomat* included an article by the former Finnish minister of foreign affairs, Erkko, in which he wrote that the military situation in the Baltic was ripe for surprises which would probably affect Finland, but he did not specify what he meant. In Finland rumors circulated about the movement of troops along the Soviet-Finnish border.

June 18. In the area occupied by the Fifteenth Infantry Corps, a German defector in the rank of sergeant appeared. He fled because while drunk he had struck an officer, and he was in danger of being shot. The sergeant informed the chief of the border guard detachment, and then repeated to the commander of the Fifteenth Infantry Corps, I. I. Fedyuninskiy, that at four o'clock in the morning of June 22, Hitler's troops would go into an offensive along the whole length of the Soviet-German border. The commander of the Fifth Army, Major General M. I. Potapov, to whom the defector's statements were reported, declared: "You are sounding the alarm for nothing." However, after urgent requests, he agreed to move two regiments closer to the border and recall the artillery regiments from the ranges.[37]

In the zone of the Eighty-seventh Border Guard Detachment a group of saboteurs was caught. Their mission consisted of derailing trains and creating a block at the Lupinets station to facilitate the operations of German aircraft.

Reports from Ankara: Turkey has signed a friendship pact with Germany. The *New York Times* publishes a number of reports about German-Soviet relations. In the report from Ankara it is stated: "It is considered that the war between the Reich and the Soviets is drawing closer." And then a report from Moscow: "Today there are no signs of a general or partial mobilization in Russia, but this does not in any way signify that the Soviet Union is not prepared to meet any surprise which might arise out of the international situation." [38]

June 19. People's Commissar for Defense C. K. Timoshenko orders the commander of the Kiev Special Military District, M. P. Kirponos, to transfer the district headquarters to Tarnopol. The district command is informed of the possibility of a German attack within days without a declaration of war. But at the same time there follows no order to bring the troops to full military preparedness. [39]

Then the military council of the Twelfth Army, on June 18, queries the chief of staff of the Kiev Special Military District about an order: " 'Anti-aircraft guns may open fire only in conformity with the command post system of Antiaircraft Defense (PVO) by special order of the military council of the district.' Unclear. Explain." On June 19 the clarification follows: "You may open fire: 1) if there is a special order from the military council of the district, 2) in the event mobilization is declared; 3) if the covering force plan is put into action, unless there is a special prohibition, 4) it is known to the military council of the Twelfth Army that we do not fire on German planes in peacetime."

A correspondent of an American radio broadcasting company, the Columbia Broadcasting System, files a report that Germany has already attacked the USSR at fifteen points along the border! Obviously somebody has been overcome by impatience.

In the world press there was a profusion of every possible kind of rumor including one about an ultimatum served by

Germany on the Soviet Union, one of the demands of which was the admission of German "technical experts" to the Ukraine and the Caucasus.

The correspondent of the *New York Times* in Lisbon wrote that a diplomat arriving from Berlin had stated that in Berlin a general conviction was paramount that within a few days a Soviet-German conflict would begin and some circles were even predicting its start within forty-eight hours.

The widespread rumors about the coming attack of Germany on the USSR forced the German authorities to take measures to stop the leaks of information. On the evening of June 19, telephone and telegraph communications with Switzerland, and also with Bucharest and Sofia, were cut off. Reporting this, newsmen emphasized with alarm that such measures were extraordinarily rare.

But in the reports from Moscow the correspondents drew attention to the calmness and confidence reigning in the Soviet capital. "The population of Moscow," the *New York Times* wrote, "is busy with its usual, every-day affairs, it is working and shopping in stores well stocked with goods and attending the football games so popular in the Soviet Union. Nothing in the mood of the Russians points to the approach of a Soviet-German conflict, while the official position confirms that the Soviet Union is firmly and completely following its independent foreign policy." [40]

The general tone of the international press was this: If the Germans attacked the Soviet Union, they would encounter a serious defense.

"The summer rest of the workers," was the name of *Pravda*'s lead article on June 19. [41]

Six saboteurs were caught in the zone of the 87th Border Guard Detachment. They had been charged with penetrating to the area of Grudo and Zazhechany (thirty-five kilometers east of Byelostok), creating an illegal base in the forest, and carrying on intelligence work from it in the Byelostok and Volkovysk area. At the start of military operations they had the mission of seizing or destroying bridges.

June 20. Six German planes carrying bombs violated the Soviet border in the West.

The headquarters of the Odessa Military District is uneasy. Officers awakened by an alarm, in field uniforms, suitcases in hand, discuss it: "Probably staff exercises. But it might be war. But with whom?!"

The District Commander, Colonel General Ya. T. Cherevichenko, tells the newly arrived commander of the airborne brigade, Major General A. I. Rodimtsev: "There is information that Romanian and German troops are concentrating at our borders." [42]

In the Leningrad Military District information is received about the concentration of Finnish troops at the border. The chief of staff of the district, Major General D. N. Nikishev, orders the engineer troop commander to prepare some areas for defense. [43]

"Germany and Russia face to face"—this is the headline which opens the international reports in the London *Times* of June 20, 1941. Afterwards came the subheadlines: "Troops concentrated along borders," "A smokescreen of rumors," "Reports that demands made to Kremlin." [44] *New York Times* correspondent Sulzberger reports from Ankara: "Diplomatic sources from two different countries bordering the Soviet Union have been informed that a German military attack on Russia can start within forty-eight hours. . . . The Germans, supported by the Romanians and Finns, may begin a powerful advance along the whole distance from the Black Sea to the Arctic." [45]

On June 20 in Helsinki a call for reservists up to forty-four years of age is announced. Cadets in military schools are suddenly commissioned as officers. Civilian railroad communications are sharply curtailed in order to facilitate military shipments. Addressing the population, the bourgeois Finnish press writes: "Every Finn must obey without hesitation, as it was in 1939."

In these last hours the German command tries to confuse the Soviet Union. An official German representative in Berlin, denying reports of clashes on the Soviet-German border, states: "The mere fact that these rumors are of foreign origin show that they are without foundation."

The Reuter agency reports from Moscow: "Here nothing is known about any German demands to the Soviet Union. Responsible observers in fact have reason to believe that neither Germany nor Romania have made any sort of proposals to Russia. In the Soviet capital there are no signs of a crisis." [46]

The newspaper *Pravda,* in a lead article entitled "Against Chatterboxes and Good-for-Nothings," calls for a struggle for efficiency in work, against gossip and chatter which mask inactivity.[47]

June 21. Sulzberger telegraphs from Ankara: "The countries of Central Europe, from Slovakia to Sweden, are taking measures not to be caught by surprise by the German-Soviet war. Three Romanian warships, cruising in the Black Sea, have received orders to stay where they are. German circles predict that a more important event than the Turco-German pact will occur within two or three days."

In Bucharest almost all the foreign missions are transferring their bank deposits out of the Romanian capital. People coming from Constantsa are saying that the roads are crowded with evacuees.

In Helsinki all reservists up to age forty-four have been called up. The evacuation of children has begun.

In Bratislava (Slovakia) mobilization of all men between the ages of eighteen and twenty-seven has been declared. German divisions located in Slovakia are being transferred in an easterly direction. In Sweden intensive military preparations have begun.

Anne McCormick writes in the *New York Times:* "Apparently it is believed in London and Washington that the crisis in German-Soviet relations is a reality. Yesterday's message of the president was inspired by somewhat more important considerations than the sinking of the 'Robin Moore' [This had to do with F. D. Roosevelt's announcement in connection with the sinking of the American refrigerator ship 'Robin Moore' by the Germans—A.N.]. By the timing of the announcement and by its tone, it was meant to convince Russia that the United States plans to stand against Germany to the end. Similarly voices have been raised in England to convince that country to support the Soviet Union if it is subjected to an attack by Germany; they are also trying to strengthen Russian resistance to Hitler's demands." [48]

Hitler decides, finally, to inform his main partner, Mussolini, about his intention to attack the Soviet Union. In Hitler's opinion, England has already lost the war, and her warlike spirit is being supported only by hopes of America's aid. "We have no chance of eliminating America. But it does lie in our power to exclude Russia. The elimination of Russia means, at the same time, a tremendous relief for Japan in East Asia and thereby the possibility of a much stronger threat to American activities through Japanese intervention." [49]

An official of the secretariat of Minister of Foreign Affairs Ribbentrop, Bruns, writes a memorandum by order of the minister: the minister will not be able to receive the Russian ambassador in the afternoon because he has left Berlin and will not return until evening. After his return, he will inform the ambassador when it will be possible to see the minister.[50]

But Ribbentrop does not receive the Soviet ambassador at all that day. In his stead this is done by State Secretary Weizsaecker. The ambassador hands Weizsaecker a verbal note of protest from the Soviet government against the violation of the Soviet border by German aircraft. Weizsaecker, fully informed that war would start on the next day, brazenly denies the facts and in his turn accuses the USSR of violating the German border.[51]

At about the same time a note of protest is handed to Germany's ambassador to Moscow, Schulenburg. The People's Commissar for Foreign Affairs asks him what it is that dissatisfies Germany and how German-Soviet affairs stand at the moment.[52]

It is an anxious time on the Soviet-German border.

In the zone of the Eighty-seventh Border Guard Detachment a group of enemy saboteurs numbering ten men is apprehended. The group has a mission to seize and hold the bridges across the Narev River at the Lapa station, on the Byelostok-Chizhev railroad line, at the start of military operations, and also two bridges on the Byelostok-Belsk highway.

In the Leningrad Military District most of the command personnel are in the field. The chief of staff confirms his order to the engineer units to prepare barriers on the border.

In the Baltic Military District the population is mobilized to dig trenches and emplacements on the border with East Prussia. The district's sapper units are busy building pillboxes at the same time. There were no ready defensive works.[53]

In the zone of the Vladimir-Volynsk Border Guard Detachment, reinforced details go out to defend the border. At eleven o'clock in the evening, in the zone of the Fourth company, a German soldier of the Two Hundred and Twenty-second Infantry Regiment, Seventy-fourth Infantry Division, Alfred Liskow, has voluntarily crossed to our side. Liskow is interrogated at detachment headquarters at 0030 hours, and states that on June 22 at four o'clock in the morning the German army will go to the offensive. The German artillery has occupied fire positions, and the infantry, assault positions. This is immediately reported to the chief of the border troops of the NKVD of the Ukrainian Military District, the headquarters of the nearest army at Lutsk, and the commander of the division in Novograd-Volynsk.

In the zone of the Lyubomirsk Border Guard Detachment, before dark, on the opposite bank of the Western Bug, a peasant woman appears. She shouts: "Comrades, come, because the Germans have already prepared the bridges—they want to attack you." Seeing a German officer, she shouts loudly, pretending to be shouting at the geese in the river: "Come on, comrades. The Polish overlords have fled, they are afraid of you, and we are waiting for you and have prepared something to eat for you." This incident is long discussed by the border guards at their post. That evening they get ready for a night of entertainment.

The border guards of the Rava-Russkiy Detachment are returning from the club late in the evening. The officers' wives, having assembled for a delegates meeting, are looking at the movie "Vesyolye Rebyata" ("Gay Fellows"). June 22 has been declared a day off, the first one in the whole summer of 1941.

June 21. Minsk. The officers' club. The commander of troops of the Western Special Military District, Army General D. G. Pavlov, with his deputy, General I. V. Boldin, is watching a show. The chief of the intelligence section of the district staff appears in the box. Bending down to the commander's ear, he whispers something to him. Boldin continues the story: "That can't be," was heard in answer.

"The chief of the intelligence section departs.

" 'What nonsense,' Pavlov said to me in a low voice. 'Intelligence reports things are very alarming on the border. The German troops have supposedly been brought to full combat readiness and have even begun to fire on individual points of our border.' " [54]

In Brest, the commander of the 4th Army, A. A. Korobkov, and his chief of staff, L. M. Sandalov, go to headquarters late in the evening. At about 2300 hours, the chief of staff of the military district telephones. No special orders are received. However, it is known that one must be on the alert. [55]

In the evening an alarming message is received at the main base of the Black Sea Fleet in Sebastopol: three German transports, which have made regular trips between Soviet ports and the ports of Romania and Bulgaria, are in the harbor. The fleet command is informed of this. [56] A few hours later operational alert No. 1 is declared in the fleet.

"Climbing the headquarters staircase," reminisces a responsible official of the Chief Political Directorate, I. A. Azarov, "I remembered by chance a recent conversation with N. M. Kulakov [a member of the military council of the Black Sea Fleet—A.N.]. He said then that another defector had been detained by the Danube naval flotilla (I had already known in Moscow about the first defector, who had crossed the border at the beginning of June). Both defectors warned of Germany's exhaustive preparations for an attack on the USSR." [57]

Late in the evening of June 21 the fleet commanders are informed by the People's Commissariat of the Navy of a possible attack by fascist Germany on the USSR. Cables are sent to the fleets to bring all forces up to full military preparedness.

In Moscow, at first glance, everything is calm. But tension is rising. By evening there is still more alarming information about German preparations. Stalin telephones Army General

I. V. Tyulenev, the commander of the Moscow Military District. He asks how things are with the antiaircraft defense of Moscow. He orders the combat preparedness of the troops of the Moscow antiaircraft defenses to be brought up to 75 percent. Tyulenev receives the impression that Stalin has received new information about the German military plans. Tyulenev issues an order to his deputy for antiaircraft defense, Major General M. S. Gromadin, to bring the antiaircraft artillery into full combat readiness.

A little later Tyulenev visits the People's Commissar for Defense, Marshal S. K. Timoshenko, and learns that "the alarming symptoms of approaching war are being confirmed." Employees of all ranks in the German embassy are hurriedly leaving city limits by car.

In the opinion of the General Staff: according to the reports of the military district headquarters, everything seems to be quiet on the western border. The commanders have been warned about the possible invasion by Hitler's Germany. People's Commissar Timoshenko has reported the situation to Stalin.

Stalin's opinion: "We are starting a panic for nothing."

Maybe it is really for nothing. After all, in the General Staff they think that the Germans do not have a general preponderance of forces.[58]

At midnight on June 22, the Berlin-Moscow express passes, as usual, through Brest.

At three o'clock in the morning all the border point commanders reported by telephone to the commander of the Vladimir-Volynsk Border Guard Detachment that a strong roar of motors is audible along the entire opposite bank of the Western Bug, but everything is quiet at the border itself.

In the direction of Kovel, almost all border points of the Lyubomilsk Border Guard Detachment report by the end of the night that there was a loud roar of motors beyond the Bug, and a series of red rockets. All details are assembled at the border points. They prepare for combat.

Meanwhile, the fascists are only waiting for the signal to attack. The muzzles of thousands of artillery pieces are pointed east. Thousands of tanks have come out to assault positions. Only minutes remain before the agreed signal.

The group of German forces intended for the attack on the USSR numbers 190 divisions, of which 153 are German; 29 divisions and 16 brigades belong to the allies of Hitler's Germany. Included in the grouping are 17 armored and 13 motorized divisions.

The fascist forces are colossal in their number. Counting reinforcement units, rear area, naval and air force, it has 4,600,000 men, fully armed with modern weapons, including 50,000 guns and mortars, about 5,000 aircraft (4,000 of them German), 3,712 tanks. The German ground forces with their reinforcement units number 3,300,000 men.

In the far north, Army "Norway" is concentrated (commander, General Dietl); farther south, Army Group "North" (commander, General Field Marshal Leeb); Army Group "Center" (commander, General Field Marshal Bock); and Army Group "South" (commander, General Field Marshal Rundstedt).

Army Group "North" is supported by the First Air Force (1,070 combat aircraft); Army Group "Center" by the Second Air Force (1,670 planes); Army Group "South" by the Fourth Air Force (1,300 planes).

The German forces contain, in addition to the general headquarters reserve numbering twenty-four divisions, special troops of the so-called security service, which have the special "mission" of unmasking and destroying communists and political workers of the Red Army.

In Hitler's headquarters there are no doubts of success.

The victorious outcome of the expedition to the East was doubted by few. The German fascists and their generals were ready to throw themselves into the most adventurist of all the shady ventures ever undertaken by German militarists. However, they were not throwing themselves into this venture rashly. Although all the plans of the German high command of that period bore the stamp of underestimation of the capabilities of the Soviet Union and overestimation of their own capabilities, the preparations of the German-fascist troops for the attack on the USSR had been carried out with exhaustive care. Dozens of new divisions, including motorized ones, were the pride of the German General Staff. The most modern armament. Especially careful preparations were carried on in the armored divisions, destined for the breakthrough. Ideological preparation was carried out among the troops. Although in order to preserve military secrecy the soldiers were not told straight out when and against whom the new offensive would be launched, it was hammered into their heads in every way that the Wehrmacht was invincible. The whole world had been convinced of this after the victories of German arms in the West and in the Balkans. Germany above all. Germans above everyone. The German soldier must be cruel and merciless to the enemy. From him only full and unquestioning obedience is demanded: after all, the Fuehrer has taken upon himself the full responsibility for the operations of the army. And these were not just words. The monstrous violence and crimes of the German-fascist soldiery in Poland and other countries were encouraged by the commanders. Plunder, burn, rape—the Fuehrer answers for everything! After the crushing of Poland, many German officers received as a reward landed estates with the cheapest slave labor in the world. And farther east, there, "in that barbaric Russia," were endless spaces of the most fertile lands. And all this had to be German, all of it must belong to Germany—Poland, Russia, and then the whole world. So said the Fuehrer. On the buckles of the soldiers' belts was the inscription: "God is with us!"

Facing the German force were the troops of five border military districts. On the eve of the war there were 170 divisions in these districts. The troop strength of these districts comprised about 54 percent of the whole Red Army.

All the troops of the border military districts were spread over a large territory. The troops of the first echelon numbered fifty-six divisions and two brigades and were deconcentrated to a depth of up to 50 kilometers. The troops of the second echelon were located 50 to 100 kilometers from the border, and the reserve formations up to a distance of 150 to 400 kilometers.[59]

The first echelon of the German-fascist armies outnumbered the strength of the first Soviet echelon by almost two to one.

The enemy was able to create a significant preponderance of forces in the area of his main blows. In the Kaunas-Daugavpils sector there were thirty-four German divisions against eighteen Soviet ones; in the direction of Brest-Baranovichi the enemy had sixteen divisions against seven Soviet divisions; in the Lutsk-Rovno sector the enemy had nineteen divisions and the Soviet forces nine.[60]

The Day the War Started

At 0030 hours on the night of June 22, the People's Commissar for Defense finally issued a directive placing the armed forces on a state of combat readiness (only 180 minutes remained to the troops after this warning). But some military districts only found out about Directive No. 1 after the beginning of military operations. The directive itself had a strange and contradictory character. In it, like two drops of water, the doubts and vacillations of Stalin found a reflection—his unjustified hope that the war somehow still could be avoided. To count on this on the night of June 21–22 was the same as to hope for a miracle. And no miracle occurred.

Still another report had just been received from Soviet military intelligence in Berlin—the invasion was scheduled for June 22. The directive spoke of a possible surprise attack of German troops against the troops of the Soviet western military districts on June 22–23. This attack could begin from a provocation. The directive demanded that the commanders of military districts not fall for any provocations, "which could call forth serious complications." How was this directive to be understood? There was an explanation in another of its parts. The commanders of border military districts were instructed to occupy secretly, in the course of the night of June 21–22, "the weapon emplacements of the fortified areas of the borders" with troops. To disperse all aircraft among the military airfields, carefully camouflaging them. To bring units to combat readiness, disperse them, and camouflage them. To bring antiaircraft defense to combat readiness "without additional mobilization of territorial reserves. To prepare all measures for the blackout of cities and installations." The last point of the directive stated: "No other measures are to be taken without special orders." [61]

Marshal Malinovskiy reminisces: "To the question of clarification whether one could open fire if the enemy invaded our territory, the answer followed: Don't give in to provocation and don't open fire!" [62]

0315 hours. Artillery fire begins from the German side. German bombers are in the air. In the course of forty-five minutes, from 0345 to 0400 hours of the morning, the fascist aggressor begins his offensive along the whole Soviet border.

The first blows fall on the Soviet border posts. The border guards, suffering enormous losses, fight to the last against the enemy and accept unequal battle bravely. The Hitlerites try to cross quickly to the Soviet side of the border. It turns out that the bridges are not mined! After furious fights the fascist troops secure the crossings. Hitlerite tanks hurry to break through into the depth of the defenses.

It is already ten hours since Senior Lieutenant Maksimov's border point at Vydranok station, on the bank of the Western Bug, has been fighting the enemy. The fascists have carried on artillery fire for several hours. Then they go into an advance. But the border guards do not surrender. The last man alive, Master Sergeant Parkhomenko, already wounded, throws a grenade at a passing German staff car. There is an explosion. Bodies of German soldiers and officers lie around the smashed vehicle, among them a colonel and a lieutenant colonel.

A fierce fight takes place at the border town of Sokal. Soviet soldier Korneychuk, throwing a burning cloak soaked with gasoline around him, dives under an enemy tank. The other German tanks retreat, frightened.

Battles flare. Soviet soldiers fight bravely. But here and there is confusion.

German Army Group "Center" intercepts an alarming question from a Soviet military transmitter: "They are shooting at us. What shall we do?" The reply comes from headquarters: "You must be sick. And why wasn't your message encyphered?" [63]

Moscow. On the morning of June 22 the commander of antiaircraft defense troops (PVO), N. N. Voronov, visited Peo-

219

ple's Commissar Timoshenko. The Deputy People's Commissar, L. Z. Mekhlis, was present. "I was struck," Voronov wrote later, "that in such a serious situation the People's Commissar gave no orders and did not give any mission to the PVO. It seemed to me then that he did not believe that the war had started." [64]

Sebastopol. A conversation between the commander of the Black Sea Fleet, Admiral F. S. Oktyabrskiy, and Moscow: "Oktyabrskiy said in an unusually harsh voice:

" 'Yes, yes, they are bombing us. . . .'

"There was a strong explosion; the glass in the windows rattled.

" 'Just now a bomb landed somewhere not far from headquarters,' Otkyabrskiy continued in an excited voice.

"We exchanged glances.

" 'In Moscow they don't believe that Sebastopol is being bombed,' said Kulakov in a choked voice." [65]

Moscow. After issuing Directive No. 1, the People's Commissar for Defense begins to telephone the military districts to clarify the situation. In the space of a short time, Timoshenko calls the headquarters of the Western Special Military District for the fourth time. The deputy commander, General Boldin, reports the latest information. Hearing him out, the People's Commissar says, "Comrade Boldin, bear in mind that you must not take any actions against the Germans without our knowledge. I am informing you, and ask you to tell Pavlov, that Comrade Stalin does not permit the opening of artillery fire on the Germans." Boldin shouts into the receiver: "How can that be? Our troops are being forced to retreat. Cities are burning, people are perishing!" Boldin insists on the immediate use of mechanized infantry and artillery units, particularly antiaircraft. The answer of the People's Commissar is: "Do not take any measures other than reconnaissance in enemy territory to a depth of sixty kilometers." [66]

On the morning of June 22 everything seems to be as usual in Moscow. Everyday matters are discussed in the newspapers. *Pravda*, for instance, publishes a lead article entitled "The People's Care about Schools," and an article by Irakliy Andronnikov about the centenary of the death of M. Yu. Lermontov. And here is a line from the poet's famous poem "Borodino": "Not in vain does all Russia remember the day of Borodino!"

And on the last page there is a small notice: near Leningrad, in Lesnoy, on the territory of the Physics and Technical Institute of the USSR Academy of Sciences, the first Soviet cyclotron has been built, designed for experiments to smash the nucleus of the atom.[67]

Beyond the ocean the newspapers are printing enormous headlines: "Germany attacks the Soviet Union." But not for a few more hours does the grave voice of the announcer sound: "All the radio stations of the Soviet Union are speaking. . . ."

Three hours had already passed since the beginning of the war. At 0715 hours on June 22, the People's Commissar for Defense issued a directive: "Open active offensive operations against the enemy. All forces are ordered to attack the enemy and destroy him wherever he has crossed the Soviet border." But in Moscow, as before, the German army's invasion was regarded as a mere provocative action, and not as the start of war! This is clear from the fact that this same directive did not authorize the crossing of the border without special orders.

"Only on the evening of June 22," writes Marshal of the Soviet Union M. V. Zakharov, "when a threatening situation was created on the flanks of the Western Front because of the deep wedges made by German tank groups, the front commanders received an order to deliver deep counterblows to smash the main forces of the enemy and transfer the action to his territory." [68]

The directive ordered the air forces to deliver blows only to a depth of 100 to 150 kilometers, and to bomb Koenigsberg and Memel. But this directive, too, was issued too late and did not take into account the peculiarities of the situation which had arisen. The initiative had been seized by the Hitlerites, whose advance was still only developing, under the cover of German aviation. The German air force had already begun to bomb Soviet airfields at dawn on June 22. Sixty-six airfields belonging to the border military districts were subjected to bombing. By noon on June 22, the Soviet air force had lost twelve hundred planes, of which eight hundred were destroyed on the ground. The losses of the air forces belonging to the Western Special Military District were especially heavy.

At the end of the first day of war, the enemy was able to break through to the Dubisa River in the northwest (thirty-five kilometers, northwest of Kaunas) and to ford the Neman River sixty kilometers south of Kaunas. On the left flank of the Western Front, Soviet Fourth Army troops had to retreat and abandon Brest. But the fortress of Brest defended itself heroically for a long time. The details of this brave struggle with the fascist invaders became known only many years after the end of the war. The defense of the fortress has entered the history of the Great Patriotic War as a legendary feat of arms, testifying to the limitless patriotism of Soviet soldiers. The Hitlerites were not able to take the fortress by assault; they blockaded it and bypassed it; the defenders of the fortress held out heroically for many days.

In the Brest sector, German tanks moved forward from fifty to sixty kilometers on the first day of war and occupied Kobrin. In the Southwestern Front area the enemy succeeded in advancing fifteen to twenty kilometers. In the direction of Lvov the Hitlerites advanced ten to fifteen kilometers. Stubborn fighting developed on the other parts of the front.[69]

The situation which existed at the end of the first day of war excluded the possibility of carrying on offensive activities against the invader who had invaded our motherland. It was essential to organize a defense immediately. However, the troop command structure had broken down. The leadership of the People's Commissariat of Defense and General Staff was receiving incomplete information and apparently incapable of forming a correct opinion of the situation at the front. As a result, at 2115 hours, June 22, the People's Commissar for Defense issued a directive to the military councils of the Northwestern, Western, and Southwestern Fronts to attack. But this order was absolutely unrealistic and impossible to carry out.[70]

The first hours of the war had already shown that Hitler's political efforts to isolate the Soviet Union in a war against Germany had completely collapsed. Only the Turkish minister of foreign affairs, Saracoglu, learning of the attack on the USSR, exclaimed joyfully: "This is not a war but a crusade!"

The reaction of the governments of England and the United States of America was completely different. By that time the situation in England had become much more complicated. Only a year had passed since the British army had returned to England, after abandoning the dunes of Dunkirk and leaving there all its arms and equipment. Much had been done in that year. The main thing was that England had been able to stand up against the German air attack. But on the flanks of the British Empire, England suffered one defeat after another. An extremely grave situation was shaping up in the Near East. In

April the broadly conceived operation of General Wavell failed. England suffered a defeat in Greece and was forced to abandon Crete with large losses. This signified the complete banishment of England from the European continent. Wavell's attempt in the Near and Middle East to recapture the initiative ended in failure. The campaign which was supposed to become a "turning point" for the British collapsed. "Our defeat," writes the English historian D. Butler, "was a cruel disappointment." A tense situation was created in Iraq in connection with the pro-German revolt of Rashid Ali El Gailani.* The threat of an attack on Gibraltar by Germany in collusion with Spain seemed real. The battle of sea communications grew sharper, particularly in the Atlantic. As a result, the supplying of England with raw materials and food had become greatly complicated. The economic blockade interfered with the development of military production. Lend-lease deliveries from the United States of America were barely beginning to come through. England was living through one of the most dangerous moments of the war. For this reason the very first reports of Germany's proposed attack on the Soviet Union were received by Churchill's cabinet with relief. It was obvious that the Soviet Union's participation in the war would substantively improve England's position and afford her a certain breathing spell. Actually the experts in London anticipated that the breathing spell would be a short one. The most pessimistic appraisal of the length of the war against the USSR was six weeks; the most optimistic, three months. And only very few people, literally a few individuals, considered that if Hitler decided to attack the USSR this would be the most insane of all the decisions he had ever taken and would end with a catastrophe for Germany.

---

* Rashid Ali's regime was recognized by the Soviet government shortly before the German invasion.—V.P.

A few hours after receiving the report of Germany's attack, British Prime Minister Winston Churchill spoke on the radio. He declared that nobody had been a more convinced foe of communism for the last twenty-five years than he, Churchill. But now all this had to be put aside, because England "has but one aim and one single, irrevocable purpose. We are resolved to destroy Hitler and every vestige of the Nazi regime. . . . Any man or state who fights on against Nazidom will have our aid. Any man or state who marches with Hitler is our foe. . . . Hitler's invasion of Russia is no more than a prelude to an attempted invasion of the British Isles. . . . The Russian danger is therefore our danger and the danger for the United States, just as the cause of any Russian fighting for his hearth and home is the cause of free men and free peoples in every quarter of the globe. . . ." Churchill declared that England would give the Soviet Union "whatever help we can." [71]

The British prime minister, in making this declaration, was certain that the president of the United States of America, in spite of strong anti-Soviet tendencies in the American government, Congress and Senate, would also take a similar position.

In the few hours which had passed since the moment of Hitlerite Germany's treacherous attack on the Soviet Union, the whole life of the country had received a new direction. War had come, a cruel and merciless war. And everyone understood this. At the call of the Communist Party and in response to the imperatives of duty and heart millions of Soviet citizens arose to defend their motherland on the very first day of the war. Displaying miracles of heroism and self-sacrifice, Soviet people fought to the death against the insidious enemy.

All the thoughts of the people were imbued with one aspiration. It was formulated in short form in the headline of the lead article in *Pravda* on June 23, 1941: "Fascism will be destroyed."

The Great Exploit of the People

On June 22, 1941, Hitler's Germany treacherously attacked the Soviet Union.

On May 8, 1945, the German armed forces unconditionally surrendered to the powers of the antifascist coalition—the Soviet Union, Great Britain, and the United States of America. The fascist Reich ceased to exist. The peoples of the world triumphantly celebrated the victory.

Between these two events there had passed four years of grave war which caused the Soviet people to strain all of its powers and make enormous sacrifices.

Fascist Germany began the war against the USSR with a massive blow, which, because of its tactical surprise, caused enormous damage to the ground and air forces, crushed the antiaircraft defense, and disorganized movement on railroads and highways to a great degree. The fascist armies did not encounter a serious defense at the frontier, although Soviet soldiers fought heroically, to the last round, to the last breath. There, on the border, in the very first hours of battle, there was born the heroism which enabled the Red Army to survive the terrible blows and vicissitudes of war and finish its liberating march in prostrate Berlin.

The swift advance of the fascist troops, their seizure of the strategic initiative, and their mastery in the air made the concentration and deployment of Soviet troops enormously difficult.

The reasons for the Soviet army's failures in the initial period of the war also were rooted in the fact that fascist Germany hurled against the USSR a huge, completely mobilized army,

226

which had had great experience in waging modern warfare. Germany also had prepared for the war economically. She had harnessed the economies of the European countries she had conquered to the needs of her military machine. At that time the Soviet Union had not placed its economy on a military footing to the necessary extent and had not completed the rearmament of its troops on a broad scale. The Soviet armed forces were not brought to a condition of top military preparedness in the face of the obvious threat.

The Central Committee of the Communist Party of the Soviet Union in its resolution of June 30, 1956, "On Overcoming the Cult of Personality and Its Consequences," pointed out that a serious mistake was made by Stalin "in the organization of the country's preparation for the repulse of the fascist invaders." [1]

For all of these reasons, the initial successes of the German-fascist troops in the war against the USSR became possible. It is quite obvious that the war would have started and developed very differently if Hitler's army had been stopped on the territory of the border military districts.

The German fascists were convinced that under the blows of the Wehrmacht the Soviet Union would fall apart like a "house of cards," and that all would be over within two or three months. Their opinion was also shared by military and political circles considered competent in the United States of America, England, and some other countries.

In these calculations and "prognoses" a deep political ignorance was demonstrated, a lack of understanding of the very essence of the Soviet social system. The German militarists miscalculated crudely not only in their evaluation of the combat capacity of the Red Army but also of the capabilities of the Soviet economy and the productive powers of the Soviet nation. Ignorance of the psychology of the Soviet people and lack of understanding of the sources of its patriotism constituted the crudest mistake of the Nazis. The Soviet people carried on a defensive war against an aggressor who had broken into the territory of the Soviet motherland without a declaration of war. Aspirations for conquest and aggressive designs are alien and hateful to the Russian people and to all Soviet people. The Soviet people carried on a just war for the independence of their state, for their freedom, for life itself. And this was the source from which ever greater strength was derived.

The moral purity of the cause which the Soviet people were defending in the years of the Great Patriotic War was an extremely important factor in their inexhaustible bravery, unprecedented heroism, and supreme readiness for self-sacrifice.

From their convictions of their rightness came patriotism, pride of the people in their country, and loyalty to their socialist state.

The high morale of the people was strengthened by the military and economic might of the state. It is a fact that, in spite of certain weaknesses and shortcomings in our economy before the German attack, in the war years our industry coped fully with the most difficult and exacting problems of supplying the Red Army with armament, equipment, and military materials without interruption. And all this was done in spite of the fact that in the initial period of the war extremely important economic regions were lost, having fallen into the hands of the enemy. The creation of new arsenals on the Volga, in the Urals, and in Siberia was a very great achievement of the Communist Party, the working class of our country, and the whole Soviet people. Those who labored in the rear under incredibly severe conditions fought for victory every day and every hour. When the war was over, a medal called "For Valiant Labor in the Great Patriotic

War" was instituted, as if symbolizing that labor in the rear was equal in its significance to exploits on the field of battle.

The just nature of the war against the German-fascist invaders created the mass heroism of the Soviet soldiers. Their courage did not abandon them either in the grave days of 1941 and 1942, or during the cruel battles on the Volga, at Kursk, and Berlin. History has not known such massive heroism as Soviet soldiers demonstrated in the years of the Great Patriotic War. Millions of them gave their lives in the struggle with the mortal foe of the Soviet nation and all freedom-loving humanity.

History also has not known a precedent for such a mass partisan movement in the enemy's rear as that which developed on Soviet territory occupied by the foe. Hundreds of thousands of people who found themselves on the territory occupied by the invaders took part in this movement.

Leaning on the support of the population, the partisans, closely connected with underground organizations and led by the Communist Party, carried on a merciless struggle against the occupiers and their hangers-on, the Ukrainian and other nationalists, traitors, and turncoats. This unprecedented scale of partisan warfare made it impossible for the invaders to create a secure rear area in the occupied Soviet regions and forced them to pull considerable forces away from the front, a fact which substantially eased the Red Army's problems in smashing the fascist hordes and chasing them out of our country.

Victory in the Great Patriotic War was achieved by the selfless activities of the armed forces of the Soviet Union and the military leadership skills of their commanders, by the heroic labor of the working class, the peasantry, the intelligentsia, by the struggle of the partisans and the operations of the underground in the Soviet territory occupied by the enemy.

The Communist Party of the Soviet Union unified and directed all the efforts of the people. Communists were the steadiest, bravest fighters wherever they were in the years of the Patriotic War. In battles and in labor alike they always marched in front, not sparing their own lives, carrying the people along after them by their personal example.

On the fields of battle the might of the most dangerous foe of socialism and all progressive mankind—German fascism—was broken.

The Soviet people freed not only their own country but all other states and peoples from the threat of enslavement by the fascist barbarians. The road to independence and socialism opened for many of them.

In the victory over the Hitlerite invaders the Soviet people played the principal, decisive role.

This great exploit of our people will not fade throughout the ages.

Aleksandr Moiseyevich Nekrich
June 22, 1941

Confirmed for printing by the editorial collegium for scholarly-popular literature of the Academy of Sciences of the USSR

EDITOR: Yu. A. Redko

COVER: by artist L. G. Larskiy

ART EDITOR: A. P. Guseva

Delivered for typesetting 1 April 1965

Approved for printing 27 August 1965

CIRCULATION: 50,000 copies

Summary production plan for social-political literature for 1965, No. 965

PRICE: 30 kopeks

PUBLISHING HOUSE: "Nauka," Moscow K-62, Podsosenskiy Per. 21

Typeset in the 2nd typography of the "Nauka" Publishing House, Moscow G-99, Shubinskiy Per. 10.

Printed in Moscow Typography No. 8 of Glavpolitgrafprom of the State Committee for the Press of the Council of Ministers of the USSR, Khokhlovskiy Per. 7.

Abbreviations

DGFP   Documents on German Foreign Policy, 1918–1945. From the archives of the German Foreign Ministry, Series D (1937–1945)

FR   Foreign Relations of the United States. Diplomatic Papers

IMT   Trial of the Major War Criminals before the International Military Tribunal, Nuremberg

OKW   Das Oberkommando der Wehrmacht (High Command of the German Armed Forces)

OKH   Das Oberkommando des Heeres (High Command of German Ground Forces)

SD   Sicherheitsdienst (Security Service)

Notes*

From the Author

1. *Twentieth Congress of the Communist Party of the Soviet Union,* stenographic report, Vol. II, Moscow, 1956, p. 498. *Twenty-second Congress of the Communist Party of the Soviet Union,* stenographic report, Vol. III, Moscow, 1962, p. 220.

Part One

1. *The Testament of Adolph Hitler,* London, 1961, p. 64.
2. Hermann Rauschning, *Hitler's Aim in War and Peace,* London, 1940, p. 27.
3. Hermann Rauschning, *Gespraeche mit Hitler,* Zurich, 1940, pp. 37, 46.
4. *Vierteljahrhefte fur Zeitgeschiche,* Stuttgart, 1959, No. 4, pp. 434 ff.
5. Colonel General Franz Halder, *The Diary of the Chief of General Staff of the German Ground Forces* (hereinafter cited as *Halder's Diary*), entry for October 18, 1939.
6. *Ibid.,* June 2, 1940.
7. *Ibid.,* July 22, 1940.
8. W. Ansel, *Hitler Confronts England,* London, 1961, pp. 152–153.
9. *Halder's Diary,* July 3, 1940.
10. *Ibid.,* July 13, 1940.

---

* Russian titles are given in English translation.—V.P.

11. *Ibid.*, July 18, 1940.

12. *Ibid.*, July 22, 1940.

13. Walter Warlimont, *Im Hauptquartier der deutschen Wehrmacht, 1939–1945*, Frankfurt am Main, 1962, p. 126.

14. *Ibid.*, p. 127.

15. *Halder's Diary*, July 26, 1940.

16. *Ibid.*, July 31, 1940.

17. D. M. Proektor, *War in Europe, 1939–1941*, Moscow, 1963, p. 403.

18. Maurice Hindus, *Hitler Cannot Conquer Russia*, New York, 1942, p. 23.

19. *Halder's Diary*, September 3, 1940.

20. *Ibid.*, May 5, 1941.

21. D. M. Proektor, *op. cit.*, pp. 406–407.

22. IMT, Vol. XXVII, No. 1229-PS, p. 72.

23. DGFP, Vol. XI, No. 532, pp. 899–902.

24. F. N. Telegin, "Hitlerite Germany's Military-Economic Preparations for War Against the USSR," *Novaya i noveyshaya istoriya*, 1961, No. 3, p. 37.

25. DGFP, Vol. XI, Nos. 192, 193.

26. Walter Bartel, *Deutschland in der Zeit der faschistischen Diktatur, 1935–1945*, Berlin, 1956, p. 200.

27. *German Imperialism and the Second World War*, Moscow, 1961, pp. 193–194.

28. B. Mueller-Hillebrandt, *Germany's Land Army, 1939–1945*, Moscow, 1957, Vol. II, pp. 62–63.

29. F. M. Telegin, *op. cit.*, p. 40.

30. *Ibid.*, p. 41.

31. I. M. Faingar, *Survey of the Development of German Monopoly*, Moscow, 1958.

32. *German Imperialism and the Second World War*, p. 131.

33. *Ibid.*, p. 225, *Voyenno-istoricheskiy zhurnal*, 1964, No. 7, p. 120.

34. *Juni 1941*, Berlin, 1961, p. 37.

35. *The Nuremberg Trial of the Principal German War Crimi-*

nals. Collection of materials in seven volumes, Moscow, 1958. Vol. III, p. 401.

36. *Ibid.,* p. 407.

37. *Ibid.,* p. 405.

38. *Ibid.,* p. 408.

39. *Ibid.,* Vol. V, p. 30.

40. *Juni 1941,* p. 38.

41. IMT, Vol. XXVI, No. 1058–OS, p. 610.

42. *Nuremberg Trial,* Vol. V, p. 25.

43. *Ibid.,* p. 439.

44. *Ibid.,* Vol. III, p. 438.

45. *Ibid.,* p. 439.

46. Walter Warlimont, *op. cit.,* pp. 169–172.

47. *Nuremberg Trial,* Vol. III, p. 23.

48. *Ibid.,* Vol. I, pp. 428–429.

49. *Ibid.,* Vol. V, pp. 36–37.

50. *Ibid.,* Vol. III, p. 95.

51. *Ibid.,* Vol. V, p. 115.

52. Paul Leverkuehn, *Intelligence and Counter-Intelligence Service: Results of the Second World War,* Moscow, 1957, p. 273.

53. Walter Schellenberg, *Memoirs,* London, 1956, p. 318.

54. Paul Leverkuehn, *De geheime Nachrichtendienst der deutschen Wehrmacht.* Frankfurt am Main, 1957, p. 129.

55. *History of the Great Patriotic War of the Soviet Union, 1941–1945,* Moscow, 1965, Vol. 6, p. 134.

56. L. B. Valev, *The Bulgarian People in the Struggle Against Fascism,* Moscow, 1963, p. 315.

57. Walter Schellenberg, *op. cit.,* p. 158.

58. *Ibid.,* p. 205.

59. *Ibid.,* pp. 205–206.

60. *Ibid.,* p. 206.

61. *Ibid.,* p. 215.

62. *Ibid.*

63. *Ibid.,* p. 216.

64. DGFP, Vol. XII, No. 126, pp. 221–227. A record of the

conversation between Reichsmarshal Goering and General Antonescu (in the Belvedere Palace, Vienna, March 5, 1941). Berlin, March 8, 1941.

65. *Ibid.*, No. 249, p. 433. The operation section of the high command to the chief of the German military mission in Bucharest. Berlin, April 1941.

66. *Ibid.*, No. 416, pp. 656–658. The minister in Romania to the ministry of foreign affairs, Bucharest, April 28, 1941.

67. *Ibid.*, No. 431, p. 685.

68. *Ibid.*, No. 572, pp. 926–927. Memorandum of the director of the political department. Berlin, May 30, 1941.

69. *Ibid.*, No. 614, pp. 996–1006. Schmidt's memorandum on the conversation between Hitler and Antonescu in Munich, June 11, 1941, in the presence of Keitel and Jodl.

70. *Ibid.*, No. 644, pp. 1047–1049. Adolf Hitler to General Ion Antonescu, June 18, 1941.

71. A. I. Pushkash, *Hungary in the Second World War*, Moscow, 1963, p. 113.

72. DGFP, Vol. XII, No. 215, p. 369. Hewel's memorandum of the conversation between Hitler and Sztójay, March 27, 1941. Berlin, March 28, 1941.

73. *Ibid.*, No. 227, pp. 400–401. Horthy to Hitler, Budapest, March 28, 1941.

74. A. I. Pushkash, *op. cit.*, p. 140.

75. DGFP, Vol. XIII, No. 631, p. 1030. Ribbentrop to the mission in Hungary, Venice-Berlin, June 15, 1941.

76. *Ibid.*, pp. 122–126. Letter of the German military attaché in Finland, Ressing, to Colonel G. Matzke of the intelligence directorate of the general staff of ground forces, Helsinki, February 21, 1941.

77. *Ibid.*, No. 250, pp. 433–435. The Minister in Finland, von Bluecher, to the ministry of foreign affairs, Helsinki, April 2, 1941.

78. *Ibid.*, No. 501, p. 787. Ritter's memorandum, Berlin, May 12, 1941.

79. *Ibid.*, No. 554, pp. 879–885. OKW memorandum, Salzburg, May 25, 1941.

80. *Ibid.*, No. 592, p. 963.

81. *Ibid.*, p. 569.

82. *Ibid.*, No. 592, p. 963. Chief of staff of the German army in Norway to the high command of ground forces, Helsinki, June 4, 1941.

83. *Ibid.*, No. 624, p. 1023. Minister in Finland to the ministry of foreign affairs, Helsinki, June 13, 1941.

84. No. 636, pp. 1038–1039. Ritter's memorandum, Berlin, June 16, 1941.

85. DGFP, Vol. XII, No. 675, pp. 1083–1084. Minister in Finland to the ministry of foreign affairs, Helsinki, June 23, 1941.

86. *Ibid.*, No. 514, p. 815. Von Papen to ministry of foreign affairs, Ankara, May 13, 1941. For more details on the position of Turkey, see A. M. Nekrich, *The Foreign Policy of England, 1939–1941*, Moscow, 1963, pp. 174–185, 416–432.

87. *Manchester Guardian*, June 20, 1941.

88. *Times*, June 21, 1941.

89. Walter Warlimont, *op. cit.*, pp. 148–149.

90. DGFP, Vol. XII, No. 617, p. 1012.

Part Two

1. V. I. Lenin, *Complete Works*, Vol. 42, p. 159.

2. G. S. Kravchenko, *The Military Economy of the USSR, 1941–1945*, Moscow, 1963, pp. 20–21; *The People's Economy of the USSR in 1962*. Statistical year book, Moscow, 1963, p. 52.

3. G. S. Kravchenko, *op. cit.*, pp. 21–22.

4. *The People's Economy of the USSR in 1962*, p. 71.

5. *Ibid.*, pp. 66–67.

6. G. S. Kravchenko, *op. cit.*, p. 36.

7. *Ibid.*, p. 39.

8. *The People's Economy of the USSR in 1962*, p. 76.

9. *Agriculture in the USSR*. Statistical collection, Moscow, 1960, p. 196.

10. *The People's Economy of the USSR in 1962*, p. 202.

11. *The Great Patriotic War of the Soviet Union, 1941–1945.* Short history, Moscow, 1965, p. 588.

12. *Pravda*, November 7, 1940.

13. *The CPSU in Resolutions and Decisions of Congresses, Conferences, and Plenums of the Central Committee*, Moscow, 1954, Part III, p. 426.

14. G. S. Kravchenko, *op. cit.*, pp. 63–64.

15. *History of the Great Patriotic War of the Soviet Union, 1941–1945*, Moscow, 1960, Vol. I, p. 414.

16. *Ibid.*

17. *Voyenno-istoricheskiy zhurnal*, 1962, No. 2, p. 80.

18. *Ibid.*, p. 81.

19. *Ibid.*, p. 84.

20. *Ibid.*

21. *History of the Great Patriotic War . . .* , Vol. I, p. 416.

22. N. Vozensenskiy, *The War Economy of the USSR in the Period of the Patriotic War*, Moscow, 1948, pp. 78–79.

23. *History of the Great Patriotic War . . .* , Vol. I, p. 464.

24. *Ibid.*, p. 439.

25. A. I. Todorskiy, *Marshal Tukhachevskiy*, Moscow, 1963, p. 90.

26. A. Nikitin, "The Reconstruction of the Work of the USSR's War Industry in the First Period of the Great Patriotic War," *Voyenno-istoricheskiy zhurnal*, 1963, No. 2, pp. 11–12.

27. *Ibid.*, p. 12.

28. I. I. Fedyuninskiy, *Aroused by the Alarm*, Moscow, 1961, p. 6.

29. B. Bychevskiy, "At the Beginning of the War near Leningrad," *Voyenno-istoricheskiy zhurnal*, 1963, No. 1, p. 61.

30. K. Terekhin and A. Taralov, "On the Beginning of the Great Patriotic War," *Voyenno-istoricheskiy zhurnal*, 1963, No. 8, p. 86.

31. Walter Schellenberg, *Memoirs*, London, 1956, pp. 46–47.

32. *Pravda*, June 11, 12, 13, 1937.

33. *History of the Great Patriotic War of the Soviet Union, 1941–1945*, Vol. 6, Moscow, 1965, p. 124.

34. I. Bagramyan, "A Difficult Summer," *Literaturnaya gazeta,* April 17, 1965.

35. John Erickson, *The Soviet High Command: A Military-Political History, 1918–1941,* London, 1962, p. 433.

36. *History of the Great Patriotic War . . . ,* Vol. 6, p. 125.

37. *The Foreign Policy of the USSR,* Vol. IV, No. 361, pp. 451–453; No. 358, p. 449; No. 361 G, p. 453.

38. *Ibid.,* No. 403, p. 491; No. 484, p. 537; see also *Pravda,* February 18, 1940.

39. M. Andreyeva and N. Dmitriyeva, "The Soviet Union and Swedish Neutrality in the Years of the Second World War," *Mezhdunarodnaya Zhizn,* 1959, No. 9, p. 92; A. S. Kan, *The Latest History of Sweden,* Moscow, 1964, p. 169.

40. *Parliamentary Debates, House of Commons,* Vol. 347, col. 1840.

41. *The Foreign Policy of the USSR,* Vol. IV, No. 426, p. 506; No. 427, pp. 506–507.

42. *Ibid.,* No. 402, pp. 490–491.

43. *Ibid.,* No. 409, p. 498.

44. *History of the War in the Pacific,* Moscow, 1958, Vol. III, p. 35.

45. W. S. Churchill, *The Second World War,* London, 1950, Vol. II, pp. 119–120.

46. *Parliamentary Debates, House of Commons,* Vol. 365, col. 1300.

47. *Pravda,* September 30, 1940.

48. *Ibid.,* October 5, 1940.

49. *Ciano Diaries,* London, 1947, p. 300.

50. *The Foreign Policy of the USSR,* Vol. IV, No. 452, p. 522.

51. L. V. Pozdeyeva, *Anglo-American Relations in the Years of the Second World War,* Moscow, 1964, pp. 263–264.

52. *Ibid.,* p. 267.

53. L. B. Valev, *The Bulgarian People in the Struggle Against Fascism,* Moscow, 1963, p. 175.

54. *Ibid.*

55. *Ibid.,* p. 179.

56. *The Foreign Policy of the USSR*, Vol. IV, No. 487, pp. 538–539.

57. *Ibid.*, No. 497, pp. 544–545.

58. DGFP, Vol. XII, No. 121, pp. 213–215. Schulenburg to the ministry of foreign affairs, Moscow, March 3, 1941.

59. *The Foreign Policy of the USSR*, Vol. IV, No. 501, p. 547.

60. DGFP, Vol. XII, No. 70, p. 127. Ritter to the embassy of the USSR, Berlin, February 22, 1941.

61. *The Foreign Policy of the USSR*, Vol. IV, No. 483, pp. 536–537.

62. DGFP, Vol. XII, No. 176, p. 306. Memorandum of Minister Saucken, who headed the German delegation at the negotiations over the demarcation of the Soviet-German border; No. 181, p. 317. Memorandum of Wermack, the director of the political department of the German ministry of foreign affairs, Berlin, March 18, 1941.

63. *Pravda*, April 6, 1941.

64. *The Foreign Policy of the USSR*, Vol. IV, No. 505, p. 549.

65. L. N. Kutakov, *The History of Soviet-Japanese Diplomatic Relations*, Moscow, 1962, p. 263.

66. *Ibid.*

67. *Ibid.*, p. 265.

68. *Ibid.*, p. 273.

69. DGFP, Vol. X, No. 672, p. 1131. Memorandum of Hitler's conversation with Mussolini in Berghof, January 19, 1941.

70. *Ibid.*, Vol. XII, No. 8, p. 10. Schmidt's memorandum about Hitler's farewell reception for Japanese Ambassador Kurusu.

71. *Ibid.*, No. 125, pp. 219–220.

72. *Ibid.*, No. 222, pp. 388–389. Hitler's talk with Matsuoka, March 27, 1941.

73. *Ibid.*, No. 218, pp. 379–380. Ribbentrop's talk with Matsuoka, March 27, 1941.

74. *Ibid.*, No. 233, p. 413. Ribbentrop's talk with Matsuoka, March 29, 1941.

75. *Ibid.*, pp. 266, 455. Hitler's conversation with Matsuoka, April 4, 1941, No. 278, p. 473. Ribbentrop's conversation with Matsuoka, April 5, 1941.

76. *History of the War in the Pacific,* Moscow, 1958, Vol. III, pp. 211–213.

77. *The Foreign Policy of the USSR,* Vol. IV, No. 506, pp. 549–551.

78. *History of the War in the Pacific,* Vol. III, p. 218.

Part Three

1. *History of the Great Patriotic War of the Soviet Union, 1941–1945,* Moscow, 1960, Vol. I, p. 478.

2. *Ibid.,* pp. 478–479.

3. N. N. Voronov, "In Difficult Times," *Voyenno-istoricheskiy zhurnal,* 1961, No. 9, p. 64.

4. *History of the Great Patriotic War . . . ,* Vol. I, p. 479.

5. DGFP, Vol. XII, No. 381, pp. 602–603. The chargé d'affaires of the German embassy in Moscow, Tippelskirch, to the ministry of foreign affairs, Moscow, April 22, 1941.

6. Record of conversation between A. M. Nekrich and Major General I. A. Susloparov, February 11, 1965.

7. *Ibid.*

8. *Pravda,* September 4, 1964.

9. Cordell Hull, *Memoirs,* New York, 1948, Vol. II, pp. 967–968.

10. Ladislas Farago, *op. cit.,* p. 122.

11. FR, 1941, Vol. I, p. 714. Secretary of State Hull to the ambassador in Moscow, Steinhardt, Washington, March 4, 1941.

12. *Ibid.,* p. 723. Welles, memorandum, Washington, March 20, 1941.

13. W. S. Churchill, *The Second World War,* Vol. III, London, 1950, p. 151.

14. A. M. Nekrich, *The Foreign Policy of England, 1939–1941,* Moscow, 1963, pp. 488–489.

15. Ladislas Farago, *op. cit.,* p. 124.

16. *History of the Great Patriotic War of the Soviet Union, 1941–1945,* Moscow, 1965, Vol. 6, p. 135.

17. Record of the conversation between Marshal of the Soviet Union F. I. Golikov and A. M. Nekrich, September 25, 1964.

18. I. Bagramyan, "A Difficult Summer," *Literaturnaya gazeta,* April 17, 1965.

Part Four

1. DGFP, Vol. XII, No. 260, p. 446. Memorandum of the representative of the ministry of foreign affairs to the supreme commander of ground forces, April 3, 1941.

2. *Ibid.,* No. 333, p. 537. Schulenburg to the ministry of foreign affairs, April 13, 1941.

3. *Ibid.,* No. 420, pp. 662–663. Killinger to the ministry of foreign affairs, Bucharest, April 28, 1941.

4. *Ibid.,* No. 423, pp. 666–669. Schulenberg's memorandum of his conversation with Hitler, April 28, 1941.

5. Gustav Hilger and Alfred G. Meyer, *The Incompatible Allies: A Memoir-History of German-Soviet Relations, 1918–1941,* New York, 1953, p. 328.

6. *Halder's Diary,* May 5, 1941.

7. DGFP, Vol. XII, No. 399, p. 632. The German naval attaché in Moscow to the high command of the navy, Moscow, April 24, 1941.

8. *Times,* May 1, 1941.

9. DGFP, Vol. XII, No. 433, p. 687. Schulenburg to the ministry of foreign affairs, Moscow, May 2, 1941.

10. *Ibid.,* No. 446, pp. 668–669. The chief of political section IM of the ministry of foreign affairs, Cramarge, to the embassy in Moscow. Berlin, May 2, 1941.

11. John Erickson, *The Soviet High Command: A Military-Political History, 1918–1941,* London, p. 579.

12. A. M. Nekrich, *op. cit.,* p. 479.

13. *Sunday Express,* July 23, 1961.

14. *Times,* May 16, 1941.

15. Gustav Hilger and Alfred G. Meyer, *op. cit.,* pp. 331–332.

16. FR, 1941, Vol. I, p. 171. Johnson, chargé d'affaires of the U.S. embassy in London to Hull. London, June 13, 1941.

17. *Manchester Guardian,* June 7, 1941.

18. Gustav Hilger and Alfred G. Meyer, *op. cit.,* p. 330.

19. L. M. Sandalov, *What We Lived Through.* Moscow, 1961, pp. 74–75.

20. *Ibid.,* pp. 71–73.

21. L. M. Sandalov, *op. cit.,* p. 74.

22. B. Bychevskiy, "At the Beginning of the War Near Leningrad," *Voyenno-istoricheskiy zhurnal,* 1963, No. 1, p. 60.

23. *Ibid.*

24. I. V. Tyulenev, *Through Three Wars,* Moscow, 1960, p. 140.

25. A. A. Lobachev, *By Difficult Roads,* Moscow, 1960, p. 127.

26. *Ibid.*

27. R. Malinovskiy, "The Twentieth Anniversary of the Start of the Great Patriotic War," *Voyenno-istoricheskiy zhurnal,* 1961, No. 6, pp. 6–7.

28. I. Bagramyan, "A Difficult Summer," *Literaturnaya gazeta,* April 14, 1965.

29. *Izvestiya,* June 14, 1941.

30. *New York Times,* June 14, 1941.

31. *Halder's Diary,* June 14, 1941.

32. L. M. Sandalov, *op. cit.,* p. 78; I. Bagramyan, *op. cit.*

33. *Manchester Guardian,* June 14, 1941.

34. *Ibid.,* June 16, 1941.

35. A. G. Golovko, *With the Fleet,* Moscow, 1960, p. 17.

36. I. Bagramyan, *op. cit.*

37. I. I. Fedyuninskiy, *Aroused by the Alarm,* Moscow, 1960, pp. 11–12.

38. *New York Times,* June 19, 1941.

39. *History of the Great Patriotic War of the Soviet Union, 1941–1945,* Vol. 6, p. 135.

40. *New York Times,* June 19, 1941.

41. *Pravda,* June 19, 1941.

42. A. Rodimtsev, "The Fifth Airborne Brigade in the Defense of Kiev," *Voyenno-istoricheskiy zhurnal*, 1961, No. 8, p. 64.

43. B. Bychevskiy, *op. cit.*, p. 60.

44. *Times*, June 20, 1941.

45. *New York Times*, June 10, 1941.

46. *Times*, June 20, 1941.

47. *Pravda*, June 20, 1941.

48. *New York Times*, June 21, 1941.

49. DGFP, Vol. XII, No. 660, pp. 1066–1069. Hitler to Mussolini, June 21, 1941.

50. *Ibid.*, No. 654, p. 1059. Memorandum of an official of the secretariat of the ministry of foreign affairs, Berlin, June 21, 1941.

51. *Ibid.*, No. 658, pp. 1061–1062. Weizaecker's memorandum, Berlin, June 21, 1941.

52. *Ibid.*, No. 662, pp. 1071–1072. Schulenburg to the ministry of foreign affairs. Moscow, June 22, 1941.

53. B. Bychevskiy, *op. cit.*, p. 61.

54. I. V. Boldin, *A Page of Life*, Moscow, 1961, p. 81.

55. L. M. Sandalov, *op. cit.*, p. 90.

56. N. Rybalko, "The First Day of the War on the Black Sea," *Voyenno-istoricheskiy zhurnal*, 1963, No. 6, p. 63.

57. I. I. Azarov, "The Beginning of the War in Sebastopol," *Voyenno-istoricheskiy zhurnal*, 1962, No. 6, p. 80.

58. I. V. Tyulenev, *op. cit.*, pp. 140–141.

59. *History of the Great Patriotic War of the Soviet Union, 1941–1945*, Vol. I, pp. 384–385; Vol. 6, p. 25.

60. *The Great Patriotic War of the Soviet Union, 1941–1945.* Short history. Moscow, 1965, p. 53.

61. *History of the Great Patriotic War of the Soviet Union, 1941–1945*, Vol. 2, p. 11.

62. R. Malinovskiy, *op. cit.*, p. 7.

63. *Fatal Decisions*, Moscow, 1958, p. 83.

64. N. N. Voronov, *op. cit.*, p. 65.

65. I. Azarov, *op. cit.*, p. 82.

66. I. V. Boldin, *op. cit.*, p. 86.

67. *Pravda,* June 22, 1941.

68. M. Zakharov, "The Initial Period of the Great Patriotic War and Its Lessons," *Voyenno-istoricheskiy zhurnal,* 1961.

69. *History of the Great Patriotic War of the Soviet Union, 1941–1945,* Vol. 2, p. 16.

70. *Ibid.,* p. 30.

71. W. S. Churchill, *The Unrelenting Struggle,* London, 1943, pp. 179–180.

The Great Exploit of the People

1. *The CPSU in Resolutions and Decisions of Congresses, Conferences, and Plenums of the Central Committee,* Moscow, 1960, Part IV, p. 322.

THE DISCUSSION

The sensational document which follows, is an unusual one. It purports to be a protocol or, rather, notes of a stormy discussion of Nekrich's book at the Institute of Marxism-Leninism (IML) taken by one (or several?) of those present and later on smuggled out to the West like so many other colorful and revealing documents of similar nature which have been pouring out of the Soviet Union recently. The channels by which such documents come out, by their very nature, are secret; those who publish them do not reveal how the material was received; nor do they print facsimiles of these notes, appeals, protocols, etc., since this would enable the KGB to track down and punish the culprits. In at least one instance, involving the notes taken down in Moscow during the trial of the two Soviet writers Sinyavsky and Daniel in February 1966, which were also smuggled abroad and widely publicized, the culprits were apprehended, put on trial, and sentenced to prison terms in January 1968. At no time did Soviet authorities question the accuracy of the notes themselves.

Because of this unusual situation, the authenticity of the document offered here must be taken on faith. It probably came in two versions, sometime during 1966. One of them appeared in several translations: in *La Sinistra* in Italian, in *Le Nouvel Observateur* in French, in *Der Spiegel* in German, and in *Survey* (No. 63) in English. Another version, presumably in the original Russian, published (in January 1967) by the Russian émigré weekly *Possev* (Stuttgart), differs somewhat from the version published in the translations mentioned above. It is shorter, but at the same time it contains passages which are absent in the *Survey* text. I use here the latter, with the additions from the *Possev* text given in the footnotes.

The issue of the authenticity of the "protocol" is, of course, important. One reason why I am inclined to believe that it is essentially authentic is that Western correspondents in Moscow have established that its copies did circulate in manuscript form in the Soviet capital, at least in student circles, throughout 1967. But in addition there is also a substantial, albeit indirect, evidence which permits us to take the document seriously. Let us consider it, item by item:

(a) The names of many participants are known to Western Sovietologists.

(b) Two of the speakers, Professor Deborin and Major General Telpukhovskiy, wrote later a programmatic article containing a devastating attack on Nekrich in the September 1967 issue of *Voprosy istorii KPSS*—many months *after* the "protocol" became available in the West.

(c) There has been no attempt, direct or indirect, in the Soviet Union to denounce the "protocol" as a forgery although if there had been any, this would not have necessarily been conclusive one way or the other.

(d) The nature of the discussion not only helps to understand the conflicting trends among Soviet military historians and appreciate the significance of the debate concerning Stalin's role in the war, but it also allows us to explain the *subsequent* unhappy fate of A. M. Nekrich.

(e) If this "protocol" is a forgery, it is very difficult to imagine who (either in the West or in the Soviet Union), and for what reason, would undertake to concoct such a story.

(f) If we dismiss this "protocol," we would have to dismiss a great number of other similar documents recently published abroad, reflecting the turmoil among the Soviet intelligentsia, and we know that the authenticity of at least some of them has been recognized by the Soviets themselves.

If the reader of this volume happens to be an unreconstructed skeptic, inclined to think that the "protocol" of the IML meeting printed here is a forgery, he would still have to recognize the significance of the fact that many Soviet citizens believe it to be authentic. In the long run this might be the only thing that truly matters.

One is tempted to wonder about the rather violent character of some of the remarks recorded in the "protocol." Soviet scholars as a rule are known to be more restrained in their expressions, and the reported "cries from the hall" like "Cowards and swine!" or "Old windbag!" may sound strange. On the other hand, this was what is known in the Soviet Union as a "closed" meeting, with no outsiders present, and the subject of the discussion was such as to provoke passionate responses. Not only were some of the participants defending their own records (both as historians and as individuals), but their very careers were at stake. Finally, several of the speakers had valid personal reasons for being excited. A. V. Snegov, for example, had spent long years in Stalin's concentration camps, and so probably had Pyotr Yakir, son of one of the top Red Army commanders executed in June 1937 together with Marshal Tukhachevskiy and post-humously rehabilitated after the Twentieth Party Congress. Professor Deborin's father, academician A. M. Deborin, was also a victim of Stalin's purges.

Insofar as it could be established, the speakers were historians, mainly from the Institute of Marxism-Leninism, the Soviet General Staff, and from the Institute of History of the Academy of Sciences. Some held the rank of general or colonel, and several are known to have published historical books and articles on the war, Soviet diplomacy, and international affairs. The document states that there were 130 persons in the audience but does not explain who they were. We may assume that they were General Staff officers, historians, researchers, and employees of either IML or the Academy of Sciences, or some other Moscow institutions, in one way or another

involved in the study of history and in evolving its "correct" ideological interpretation.

An interesting thing about the discussion of Nekrich's book is
that not a single speaker ventured to defend Stalin unequivocally.
Some of them found certain extenuating circumstances, and several
pointed out that other prominent military and political leaders of
the period ought to share the blame for the tragedy of 1941. On the
other hand, there were those who felt that Nekrich had not gone far
enough in his criticism of Stalin and if the "voices from the hall"
reflect the consensus of the audience, we are compelled to recognize
that it was strongly and overwhelmingly for the condemnation of
Stalin and his associates.

Significant as this might be, the "protocol" per se does not
warrant broad generalization going beyond what it actually contains. We may conclude from it that a resistance to anything suggesting Stalin's rehabilitation is strong among Soviet historians.
From what we know from other sources, we may also assume that
similar sentiments exist among a large number of intellectuals in
major metropolitan areas of the Soviet Union. But what it all adds
up to and what it bodes for the future direction of the Soviet society
are questions which cannot be answered satisfactorily on the basis
of this evidence.

A Meeting of the Division of History of the Great Patriotic War of the Institute of Marxism-Leninism of the CC CPSU, February 16, 1966

AGENDA: Discussion of A. M. Nekrich's book *June 22, 1941*. Audience of 130. On the platform: Major-General E. A. Boltin, Major General B. S. Telpukhovskiy, Professor G. A. Deborin, and Professor of History A. M. Nekrich. Chairman of the session: Boltin.

DEBORIN: [1] The principal purpose of today's meeting is to seek the causes of our army's reverses at the beginning of the war. In the first part of his book, with the heading "What They Hid from Us," [2] Nekrich adopts an erroneous position; he explains everything by the obstinate stupidity of Stalin himself. That is a superficial analysis, from which it would follow that the problem is no longer of any interest, since Stalin is dead. This is incorrect: Stalin is not the only person involved.

He relies in one passage of his book on an assertion by General Golikov who was, at the time, head of the information services of the Red Army staff. But Golikov did not so much inform the government as lie to it. His reports were in many cases completely untrue. They were always in two parts: in the first part he reported

---

1. In the *Possev* version, Deborin's remark begins as follows: "The division of history of the Great Patriotic War of the Institute of Marxism-Leninism regards the Nekrich book as an accomplishment on balance. In this, the opinion of the IML differs from that of the Committee for the Affairs of the Press [the central political censorship administration in the Soviet Union.— V.P.] which takes a negative attitude. Of course, Nekrich's conclusions are correct but there are a number of contradictions in the book."

2. An obvious error which does not exist in the *Possev* version. Deborin refers to Part Three, not One, of the book, entitled "Warnings That Were Disregarded."

information which he classified as "from reliable sources"; here, for example, he included everything that supported the forecast of Germany's invading Great Britain. In the second part of his communications he reported information "from doubtful sources": for example, information from the spy Richard Sorge about the date on which Germany would attack the USSR. One must expand the criticism of the personality cult and say that certain people composed their reports in such a way as to please Stalin, at the expense of truth.

The TASS Agency communiqué of June 14, 1941, is a normal diplomatic maneuver. It was a question, at that time, of testing the reactions of the German government. In view of the internal situation people accepted that communiqué as true.

In estimating Stalin's action it is unnecessary to refer to Khrushchev's declarations, which are not objective. For example, it is difficult to accept the statement that Stalin was afraid of war. Insofar as he received false information, Stalin reached false conclusions. He placed too much hope in the German-Soviet pact, while the Germans, protected by the pact, were getting ready to attack. But Stalin's estimate of German intentions was endorsed by all those around him. So Stalin cannot be considered solely responsible for his mistakes.

Moreover, Nekrich commits serious errors of fact; for example, in the matter of the forty-five millimeter guns. I must point out that these guns were useless against the German tanks, and the government halted their production for that reason.

VOICE FROM THE HALL: It's not true. The forty-five lasted all through the war. It worked marvelously. It was criminal to stop producing it. We fought the German tanks with our bare hands. At the beginning of the war there was a complete lack of antitank weapons.

DEBORIN: Besides, it was known by Bluecher and others that the Tukhachevskiy-Yakir group were innocent; and yet they condemned them.

VOICE FROM THE HALL: They knew it perfectly well.

DEBORIN: All the same, comrades, I think no one can deny that Voroshilov and Budennyi, who took part in the trial, were men of conscience and honor.[3]

VOICE FROM THE HALL: Voroshilov was not at the trial. And how much honor and conscience did that lot have? Cowards and swine!

(*Excitement in the hall. Deborin leaves the rostrum.*)

ANFILOV (*of the General Staff*): As for Voroshilov and Budennyi, I must assert that they were men without honor. There are a number of documents in our archives which cannot at present be made public, but which lead us to an entirely negative judgment of these two men's activity. I will mention only one little incident. At a meeting, about the middle of 1937, Stalin said: "Myself and Voroshilov, we came to Tsaritsyn in 1918, and within a week we had unmasked all the enemies of the people." By that phrase Stalin was referring to a number of former staff and front-line officers who were honestly serving the Soviet regime.

VOICE FROM THE HALL: And they were all drowned in the river, without trial!

ANFILOV: "While you," Stalin went on, "are not even capable of unmasking your neighbors." Voroshilov then intervened to express entire agreement with Stalin and to invite us to denounce our own friends and colleagues. It makes me feel sick, at parades, when I see Voroshilov at the tribune.

And now let us come to the beginning of the war. If all our forces had been completely ready for action, which was entirely Stalin's responsibility, we should not have begun the war with such disasters! And in general the war would not have been so long, so bloody, and so exhausting.

One must certainly also take into account the responsibility of

---

3. The last two Deborin remarks, according to *Possev*, went as follows: (a) "Besides, from Nekrich's book follows that Stalin, Voroshilov, Bluecher and others knew about the innocence of Tukhachevskiy, Yakir, etc., but nevertheless condemned them." (b) "There is no need to doubt that Voroshilov and Budennyi, who were present at the trial, had both honor and conscience."

important military chiefs. Golikov and Kuznetsov [4] appear as heroes in their own speeches and memoirs. The truth is that Golikov gave Stalin a report dealing at length with "Plan Barbarossa," but with the comment that it was a fake by *agents provocateurs* who wanted to push the USSR into war with Germany. And Kuznetsov has written that when he received from Vorontsov, the Soviet naval attaché in Berlin, a report giving plans and dates of the German attack, he immediately gave the information to Stalin. True enough, but in what light did he present it? If you could read it, you would see that he claims Vorontsov's communication to be a trick of the German counterespionage.

Nevertheless, Stalin remains the chief culprit. Not long ago I had a conversation with Zhukov. He told me that Golikov was directly responsible to Stalin and made no reports to anyone else, not even to the chief of staff (Zhukov) or the Commissar for Defense, Marshal Timoshenko. These two knew nothing about the plans and dates of the German attack. I have not been able to talk to Timoshenko: he talks to nobody.

ZASTAVENKO (*of the Institute of Marxism-Leninism*): The people around Stalin did not help him to get a true idea of the situation. On June 5, 1941, Kalinin [5] could still say in a speech at the political-military academy that "The Germans are preparing to attack us, but we are ready. The sooner they come, the better: we will wring their necks."

VOICE FROM THE HALL: Eyewash!

ZASTAVENKO: Anyway, that is what the Politburo thought; they underestimated the German power. So Stalin is not the only one to blame for what happened.

(*Murmurs in the hall*)

DASHICHEV (*of the General Staff*): Deborin was not correct about the forty-five millimeter gun. At the beginning of the war its projectiles could pierce right through the armor of every type of German armored vehicle. To stop its production was to disarm our units,

---

4. Admiral Kuznetsov, People's Commissar of the Navy.
5. Mikhail Kalinin, Chairman of the Presidium of the Supreme Soviet.

because no other type of antitank gun was produced to replace the forty-five. So the army found itself without artillery or antitank munitions.

What is most serious is that Soviet sources for everything relating to that period are not always accessible. For example, in order to discuss the report of the Soviet attaché in Berlin that war would break out on June 22 one has to consult the books of the English historian Erickson. When shall we finally be given access to all the sources? It should be possible to find in the archives of the ministry of foreign affairs some information about the meeting between the German ambassador Schulenburg and Molotov, accompanied by Pavlov—a meeting in the course of which Schulenburg betrayed his own country by announcing that Germany would attack the USSR on June 22.[6] Schulenburg was weeping; he begged that the Red Army should be alerted so as to prevent Hitler from carrying out his plan. But Schulenburg was not believed.

Now a word about the trial of our military leaders (the Tukhachevskiy-Yakir group). The forgery on which they were condemned was prepared by the Gestapo, but the idea was Stalin's; he had suggested it to the fascist leaders through General Skoblin.[7] Unfortunately the documents relating to this are still inaccessible. Golikov was a criminal not only because he wrote his reports so as to please Stalin, but also because he got our best counterespionage agents abroad arrested.

A VOICE FROM THE HALL: Including Sorge!

DASHICHEV: Has Nekrich's book completely cleared up the causes of the tragedy of June 1941? He should have gone deeper. It was Stalin who was chiefly responsible for this tragedy. It was he who

---

6. This is an obvious error which does not exist in the *Possev* version. Nekrich accurately reported (from Gustav Hilger's memoirs) that Schulenburg gave warning to Dekanozov, the Soviet ambassador to Berlin, and not to Molotov. The name of Pavlov, Stalin's personal interpreter, was not mentioned.

7. A Soviet secret agent in Paris, White émigré Skoblin collaborated with the Gestapo on Moscow orders in framing the Tukhachevskiy group. He disappeared after the kidnapping by the Soviet of General Eugene Miller, head of the Federation of Tsarist Army Veterans, on September 23, 1937.

made the situation in which the country then found itself. Stalin's greatest crime was to have eliminated the best cadres of our army and our party. All our leaders understood the international situation, but not one of them was courageous enough to fight to get the necessary measures taken for the defense of the country. That is their terrible guilt before the party and the people. There are people who still say that one ought not to speak badly of Stalin, that he was not the only one. That is not true. The driver of the bus is responsible for every accident that happens through his fault. Stalin assumed the responsibility of sole driver. His guilt is immense.

It is also necessary to define more precisely the reasons that determined the attitudes of Churchill, Schulenburg, Halder, and Raeder (the two latter, key men on Hitler's staff, were opposed to a war with the USSR). It was not any love for our country that motivated these men. Hitler strongly influenced the decision of the German military when he declared at a summit meeting: "The Red Army has been decapitated; 80 percent of its leaders have been liquidated; the Red Army is weaker than it has ever been." That was the fundamental factor influencing his decision; he had to make war before the new cadres were formed. Every historian should have the courage to tell the truth.

ROSHCHIN (*of the Institute of Marxism-Leninism*): I am not in agreement with what Deborin said about the TASS Agency communiqué; it was not a diplomatic maneuver but a crime. This communiqué morally disarmed the population. Stalin and those around him did everything to prevent the Soviet people from preparing for war. When Kuznetsov told Malenkov [8] that the fleet had made certain preparations to be "on a war footing," on June 17, 1941, Malenkov laughed at him and said: "You're behaving as though war was going to break out tomorrow." Zhdanov,[9] who was present at this meeting, had a more serious attitude, but he too did nothing. Malenkov canceled all the measures taken by Kuznetsov. But it is impossible to acquit our military leaders from equal responsibility.

---

8. Georgiy Malenkov, member of the Politburo of the CC CPSU
9. Andrei Zhdanov, member of the Politburo of the CC CPSU

MELNIKOV (*of the Institute of History of the Academy of Sciences*): [10] If we are to believe Deborin, Nekrich's book exaggerates Stalin's faults. On the contrary, he underestimates them.

Let us consider a problem which is so heavily taboo that it is still impossible to mention it. I mean the negotiations between Molotov and Hitler at Berlin in November 1940. To recall the situation: preparations for "Barbarossa" were entering their final phase, and German troops were being moved towards the Soviet frontier. In the Balkans and Finland the Hitlerian diplomats were redoubling their activity. To hide these preparations from the Soviet government, Hitler then proposed a meeting at the highest level. The chairman of the Council of People's Commissars, Molotov, went to Berlin. Hitler expounded to him a very broad general plan for dividing up the world. Molotov claimed the Straits, Bulgaria, Romania, and Finland, but Hitler was unwilling to go into so much detail, for fear of "leaks" to his future allies. His reply to Molotov's demands was an invitation to the Soviet Union to join the Rome-Berlin-Tokyo axis.

VASILENKO (*of the Institute of Marxism-Leninism*): Objectively, we possessed everything necessary for resisting the German attack. But Stalin ruined everything. And afterwards, to explain away his disgraceful defeat, he advanced the ridiculous theory that the aggressor is always the better prepared for war.[11]

KULISH (*editor of Voyenno-istoricheskiy zhurnal*): To ask whether Stalin's guilt was total or limited is still a typical attitude of the personality cult. One is still concentrating on Stalin. We should look into the problem more deeply. We should ask how such a situation was able to come about. How did the government, under Stalin's

---

10. In the *Possev* version, Melnikov begins by arguing against Deborin's contention (not recorded in either version) that Hess's flight to England justified Stalin's mistrust of Churchill. Melnikov insists that in the light of new documentation there is no reason to believe that the Hess episode had any significance.

11. According to *Possev*, Vasilenko added: "On May 5, 1941, Stalin addressed the Frunze military academy and stated that we were not ready for war yet. Not only was he weak himself, he discouraged others as well, including military commanders."

direction, govern the country? How did it defend our people against the danger? Was it equal to its responsibilities? The answer is: NO. We must analyze the process which allowed Stalin, who was not equal to his task, to become head of the party and the state, with unlimited powers.[12]

GNEDICH: Nekrich's book is good. I had not intended to speak, but the discussion has taken a turn which obliges me to intervene. It was I who for two years delivered to Stalin and Molotov the reports of the information services. All of them passed through my hands. It is quite true that Golikov was a "misinformer." But that is not the point. All the "reliable" parts of Golikov's regular reports appeared in one form or another in our official press. Stalin, however, on principle was only interested in the information classed by Golikov as "doubtful." Stalin knew everything and his policy was to take no measures. Golikov is responsible for the repression which fell upon the GRU (Chief Directorate of Intelligence) cadres; but he is not responsible for the fact that no defense measures were taken. In our histories we read that Stalin became head of the government on May 5, 1941 in order "to prepare for the country's defense." But there is nothing to justify such a statement. The fact is that Stalin did nothing to strengthen the country's defensive capacity. There is every reason to believe that Stalin took over the government not to prepare for the country's defense, but to reach an agreement with Hitler.

SLEZKIN (of the Institute of History of the Academy of Sciences): I was at the front and took part, at the age of nineteen, in the June 1941 fighting. There can be no hesitation in saying that Stalin's behavior was criminal. There was a vicious circle of personality cult, provocation, and repression. Everyone tried to please his superior by supplying only the information that might gratify him, or

---

12. According to *Possev*, Kulish added: "There is one more error. In all of our literature, the inclusion of the Western Ukraine and Byelorussia [in the USSR.—V.P.] is viewed as a factor which improved the defensive capacity of our country. This is not so. For a number of well-known reasons, the acquisition of the *Predpolye* made the frontier more difficult to defend. Therefore, in evaluating the annexation of the western regions it would be better to talk about the liberating, internationalist role of the Red Army."

playing down anything that might annoy him. No one attempted to give a personal opinion. All this was the cause of immeasurable damage to the country, and everyone is guilty in his own way, if only for not daring to say what he thought. And the responsibility is heavier in proportion to one's place in the hierarchy, because the greater one's privileges the greater the crime of suppressing the truth to safeguard them. Stalin is the chief culprit. The 1939 pact was perhaps inevitable, but it was a crime to base any hopes on this pact and, above all, to stop the fight against fascism. And that is what Stalin ordered.

YAKIR (*of the Institute of History of the Academy of Sciences*): [13] Some of the speakers who have preceded me have referred to "Comrade Stalin." It is an improper expression. Stalin was nobody's comrade and, above all, not ours. Stalin impeded the development of our armaments by eliminating many eminent technicians, and among them the creators of our artillery: Ikhomirov, Lannemann (the inventor of the "Katyusha"), Kurchevskiy, Bekhauri. We should also look at the question of the concentration camps and study it from an economic standpoint. We were at war, and in the concentration camps there were millions of able-bodied men, specialists in every department of the country's economic and military life. And the task of guarding them absorbed considerable forces.

TELEGIN: Nekrich shows no evidence of critical spirit as regards foreign sources, and in particular as regards memoirs which contain very little truth.

---

13. According to the *Possev* version, Yakir begins by saying: ". . . the Nekrich book is very good. Some speakers here touched upon the case of Tukhachevskiy, Yakir, and other comrades. I consider all these talks about fascist provocation, and about the 'red folder' with its incriminating documents, useless and even harmful. Such talks lead us away from the facts. There was no 'red folder' at the trial, and it is not to be found in the records of this hasty affair. All the defendants were judged guilty on the basis of Stalin's unsubstantiated declarations at the meetings of the Military Council on June 1–4, 1937. Then, some of the speakers who have preceded me have referred to 'comrade Stalin.'" The reference to the "red folder" apparently has to do with the forged documents which were supplied to the Soviets by the Gestapo, to incriminate the Tukhachevskiy group. The speaker, Pyotr Yakir, is the son of one of the executed generals.

A VOICE FROM THE HALL: And what about our own memories?

TELEGIN: In our own memories too there is a great deal of nonsense (*laughter*), and one should recollect that in those memoirs there are obvious traces of the exaggerations of the Khrushchev period (*murmurs*).[14]

PETROVSKIY: (*of the Institute of Historical Archives*): We must remember that fascism first appeared during Lenin's lifetime: Mussolini in Italy, the Kapp putsch, etc. Lenin designated fascism as the chief enemy. Stalin paid no attention to Lenin's view and said that the chief enemy was social democracy. His theory was broadcast far and wide, and it set millions of workers against one another all over the world. That is what enabled fascism to win power. Stalin is a criminal.

BOLTIN: Comrade Petrovskiy, in this hall and on this platform one must watch one's language. Are you a communist?

PETROVSKIY: Yes.

BOLTIN: I am not aware of any text, or directive, or party resolution, which obliges us to consider Stalin as a criminal.

PETROVSKIY: The Twentieth Party Congress decided to remove Stalin from the mausoleum because of his offenses, his crimes against the party. Therefore he is a criminal.

SNEGOV: Nekrich's book is honest and useful. If a unit is disorganized on the eve of combat, with the rifles in one place and their bolts in another, and the scouts and sentries asleep, then that unit suffers a defeat. The head of such a unit is generally shot by order of the high command, and there's no more to say. Stalin was both the

---

14. In the *Possev* version, after Telegin there was one more speaker (before Petrovskiy), Major General Telpukhovskiy of the IML: "The events must be presented objectively. Almost all the statesmen had underestimated Hitler. However, after the fall of France the old criteria were revised; they had to be revised. Stalin had calculated that if Hitler would not break his neck in the West altogether, he would at least get tied down there. When France fell, other statesmen reconsidered their views. Not Stalin. When the war had already begun, Stalin continued his futile efforts to avert the conflict. There is no other way of explaining the three conflicting directives of the high command on the first day of the war. Stalin is the chief culprit, but the others aren't free of blame either. Render unto Caesar only what is Caesar's. . . ."

supreme commander and the head of the unit; and that unit, in a state of disorganization, was our whole country. Stalin ought to have been shot. Instead of which, people are now trying to whitewash him.

Why is Nekrich's book, which accuses Stalin, so hurriedly criticized and even condemned, while the book by the notorious falsifier of history, I. Petrov, which credits Stalin with merits he never possessed, has still, after years, not come up for criticism? Why has Deborin tried to justify Stalin? When Hitler was preparing to attack Poland, Stalin helped him. He had all the Polish communists in the USSR shot, and outlawed the Polish Communist Party. Why was the fourth partition of Poland described as a Liberation? How can one be a communist and speak smoothly about Stalin—who betrayed and sold communists, who eliminated nearly all the delegates of the Eighteenth Congress and nearly all the central committee members elected by it, and who betrayed the Spanish Republic, Poland, and all communists in all countries?

DEBORIN (*summing up*): It has not been my task to defend or justify Stalin. What is needed is to examine the personality cult more deeply in all its aspects. As for Snegov's contribution, we have heard more than once what he told us about Poland; but we heard it from the opposite camp. It is the thesis of the West German professor Jacobson, among others. It is strange that Snegov should hold the same point of view. Comrade Snegov, you ought to tell us which camp you belong to!

SNEGOV: The Kolyma camp.[15]

DEBORIN: Such things need to be gone into.

A VOICE FROM THE HALL: D'you want the telephone number too? Like in the good old days?

(*Uproar. Deborin is shouted down.*)

NEKRICH: I am grateful for your observations. Deborin certainly does not hold the views that have been attributed to him; but in the heat of discussion there is a tendency to exaggerate. It is Stalin who bears the chief responsibility for the heavy defeat and all the trag-

---

15. A famous gold-mining concentration camp in northeastern Siberia.

edy of the first part of the war. All the same, nobody ought to provide his own superiors with inexact information because it will give them pleasure. Stalinism began because of us, the small people. Stalin wanted to trick Hitler; but instead of that he got himself into a maze which led to disaster. He knew better than anyone about the elimination of the leading cadres and the weaknesses of the army.

SNEGOV: I thought this was to be a scientific discussion; but instead of scientific demonstration Deborin has produced 1937-type arguments. But it's not easy to frighten us with concentration camps. We won't let ourselves be intimidated. Times have changed, and the past won't come back. (*Applause.*)

BOLTIN (*summing up*): The meeting has elicited much that is new and interesting on the general problem. The interventions by Comrades Snegov and Petrovskiy were very passionate. One may agree with much that Comrade Snegov said, but not with all of it. One cannot attribute to our country the intention of depriving Poland of its independence and dismembering it. That is the view of bourgeois historians and White émigrés. The fact is that we defended the independence of Poland. Certain comrades have described as exaggerations the criticisms of the personality cult that were made during the Khrushchev period. That is a radically mistaken view. The Twentieth and Twenty-second Congress resolutions on the personality cult are not exaggerations due to the Khrushchev period; they are of vital importance for every communist.

THE PRAISE

The review of Nekrich's book by G. Fedorov, a translation of
which is offered here, was the only major favorable reaction to
June 22, 1941 published in the Soviet Union. If we take into
account that the book's appearance did not pass unnoticed, and that
it evoked lively discussion in military and scholarly circles, the conclusion is inescapable that the editors of newspapers, magazines,
and professional journals, were instructed to ignore it. "Silent
treatment" of politically controversial works is an old technique in
the Soviet Union.

That G. Fedorov's review appeared in *Novyi mir* (No. 1, 1966) is
characteristic. This journal, for reasons unknown to us, has been
permitted to stay in the forefront of publishing nonconformist articles, short stories, memoirs, etc., ever since Stalin's death. Its circulation has been reduced by about 50 percent in the last few years, to
its present seventy thousand copies, which is quite small by Soviet
standards. As before, its every issue sells within a few days, if not
hours, after hitting the newsstands.

There is no question that if the party leadership wanted to replace
the "liberal" editorial board of *Novyi mir* with the more orthodox
communists, it could have done it a long time ago. It is possible to
speculate that this step has not been taken in order to avoid the
inevitable outcry, both in the Soviet Union and abroad, that the last
remnants of The Thaw are being eliminated. This hypothesis, how-

ever, does not appear very convincing: the leadership of the CPSU has rarely been deterred by such considerations in the past. And although nothing drastic has happened so far, there have been signs that the editorial board of *Novyi mir* has been under political pressure in the last two years: we know that several works by controversial writers (or on controversial topics), presumably accepted for publication, have failed to appear.

G. Fedorov's review of Nekrich's book speaks for itself and does not require special analysis. It is interesting because of its unequivocal endorsement of the book and the unusually warm praise for its author. But it is more interesting for the peculiar roundabout style which Fedorov employs in order to attract attention to the main unstated thesis of *June 22, 1941*, i.e., that Stalin is not alone to be blamed for the blunders of Soviet policy on the eve of the war. Fedorov does it by devoting much space to German developments and by reiterating the point that since Nazi military and political leaders had concurred with Hitler's criminal decisions, they should be held "fully responsible" for the consequences of these decisions.

The author does not say in so many words that Stalin's decisions were also criminal. But he poses his "difficult question": whether the colossal sacrifices of the nation were avoidable, or should they be regarded as inevitable, predetermined by a fatal combination of "objective factors." Fedorov answers this question with an unqualified and resounding "No" and with a reference to the CC CPSU resolution of June 30, 1956, "On Overcoming the Cult of Personality and Its Consequences." A normally intelligent Soviet reader has no difficulty in catching the implication that (a) Stalin and his associates must bear direct responsibility for the tragedies of the war, and (b) that the Communist Party had recognized that much at the Twentieth Party Congress.

A Measure of Responsibility

A. M. Nekrich, June 22, 1941. *"Nauka," Moscow, 1965. 174 p.*
By G. Fedorov, Doctor of Historical Science

In his preface to his book *June 22, 1941,* A. Nekrich writes:

It is easier and simpler to speak of victories. To describe the flash of a solemn salute in honor of battles won is, of course, more pleasant than the bitter sorrow of defeats. . . . A historian who has taken the task of researching the war is obliged to remember not only the way it ended but how it started. . . . The reasons which led to the defeats of the initial period of the war must not be passed over quickly because such an approach not only damages historical truth, not only reduces the heroism shown by Soviet soldiers in the initial period of the war and the grandeur of our victory which began under such extraordinarily unfavorable circumstances, but also objectively harms the interests of our state, leading to incorrect conclusions from the lessons served up to us by history.

These courageous and truthful thoughts stated by the author are far from empty words, as his book shows. It is they, these words, which lie at the very basis of the study, give it authority and objectivity, and make A. Nekrich's book useful and necessary for the widest circle of readers.

The author begins with a memorable episode. It is May 1940. A large part of Europe is under the heel of fascism. In the small town of Bastogne in the Ardennes, at the headquarters of von Rundstedt, commander of German Army Group "A," which is advancing on the western front, a Hitler drunk with successes once more returned to the idea of attacking the Soviet Union.

This idea was not a matter of chance. The most consistent ideological foe of fascism, the Soviet Union, had been and remained an invincible obstacle to the triumph of fascism in the world and the evil which it was bringing to mankind.

A few years ago, American historians found among captured

German materials and later published (under the title of *Hitler's Second Book*), a manuscript by the fascist Fuehrer about the foreign policy of Germany. *Hitler's Second Book* appeared only recently, but the "ideas" contained in it had been repeated thousands of times by fascist propagandists. They contained a venom with which the Hitlerites were able gradually to poison the consciousness of millions of Germans and lead them along the path of bloody crimes.

Immediately after crushing of fascist Germany and up to our own time, the generals of Hitler's former Wehrmacht and their biographers have tried to relieve themselves of the responsibility for these crimes, for the planned preparation of the war against the USSR, and for the monstrous crimes in cold blood, against prisoners-of-war and the peaceful civilian population of the occupied territories of the USSR. We know that among the officers of the Wehrmacht, and particularly among the participants of the anti-Hitler conspiracy of 1944, there was a group of progressive, patriotic, courageous and bold people who, even in the paws of Hitler's executioners, preserved human dignity in the face of an agonizing death, decisively and angrily condemning National Socialism, its bestial essence, and the misery which it brought to people, including the German people itself. We know the names of Stauffenberg, Moltke, Yorck von Wartenberg, Stieff, and the others, and we give them their due, as was done, for instance, in the monograph of the Soviet historian, D. Melnikov, *The Conspiracy of July 20, 1944, in Germany*. Unfortunately, it was not these officers who determined the position and actions of Hitler's staff of generals.

The late President of the USA, John F. Kennedy, used to say that victory has a hundred relatives, and defeat is always an orphan.

After the defeat of Hitler's Germany, the generals of the Wehrmacht and their defenders began to insist that they were not to blame for the preparations for the bandit-like attack on the USSR, for the preparation and implementation of the war plans, for the inhuman plunder and destruction of defenseless Soviet people, war prisoners and peaceful civilians alike; that only Hitler and his closest Nazi comrades-in-arms were guilty. Such claims are contained in official statements as well as in numerous memoirs of the defeated generals of Hitler's Wehrmacht. Thus, for instance, the chief of the operational section of the General Staff of the German army's ground forces, General Guenther Bluehmentritt, writes in his article "The Moscow Battle": "The first fatal decisions were made by the German command in Russia. From a political point of view, the most important fatal decision was the decision to attack that country."

Well, as one might say, golden words, the holy truth! However it follows from Bluehmentritt's later thoughts that Hitler alone was to blame for the preparation of the war against the USSR and for the unleashing of this criminal war, and the generals had nothing to do with it; moreover, according to him, Rundstedt, Brauchitsch, and Halder tried to dissuade Hitler from making war on Russia. In general, it turns out that if one does not count the fascist Fuehrer who ended his life by suicide, Hitlerite Germany's defeat in the war against the Soviet Union is a complete orphan.

Was it this way in actual fact? A. Nekrich's book answers this clearly and accurately, and one of the virtues of this book consists in his analysis of the issue of responsibility for the war. After all, it was exactly in Rundstedt's headquarters, on May 17, 1940, that Hitler returned to the idea of attacking the USSR and he did not meet any objections there. Furthermore, from the end of May until the end of July 1940, there was a lively exchange of opinion in the highest German military circles, with the participation of the supreme commanders, and the commanders of ground forces, the navy, and the air force, about when and by what means to start the war against the USSR. This plan of war against the USSR did not call forth any objection in principle among any of the generals. On July 22, 1940, at a conference of the high command of the German army with the participation of Hitler, the commander of the ground forces Brauchitsch was already reporting the practical guidelines developed by the General Staff officers regarding war with the USSR. By December 1940, Hitler's generals had completed a plan for "lightning-like war" against the USSR, signed by Hitler on December 18, 1940, and given the code name of "Plan Barbarossa." All these, and other eloquent facts in the book, proving the responsibility of Hitler's Wehrmacht in the preparations for the attack on the USSR, are based on actual entries in the official diary of General Halder, the chief of general staff of Germany's ground forces, and on other incontrovertible documents.

Hitler's generals carry full responsibility for the crimes against the Soviet people during the war. Thus, after the war had already started, on July 16, 1941, Keitel issued an order to all German army units to carry out unfailingly the directives which condemned millions of our countrymen to hunger and death. And as early as May 12, 1941, the high command of the German ground forces issued a directive according to which Soviet army political workers and commissars captured in the coming war were to be destroyed. In a cynical addition to this directive, Jodl not only agreed with it, but issued instructions on the perfidious way this criminal "measure" was to be carried out. As we see, in anticipation of the coming victories, the plans of attack on the USSR had more than enough "relatives" among Hitler's generals.

A careful analysis of our country's situation as of June 22, 1941, allows the author to show that the Hitlerites, in preparing their attack on the motherland of socialism, made at least two fatal mistakes: in the first place, they underestimated the military and economic power of the Soviet state, and, secondly, in their contempt for the people, they could not imagine that the popular masses, united and inspired by high ideals, "in the name of these ideals were ready for the most incredible sacrifices, suffering, and deeds."

Many of the facts cited have been widely known and many are published by A. Nekrich for the first time. But his presentation of the question [of responsibility] itself is totally new in principle.

It is known that we lost about twenty million lives in this war, and the most significant of these losses occurred in the first period of the war, when our troops retreated almost to Moscow itself, and whole huge territories and millions of peaceful citizens and war prisoners fell into the hands of the enemy. And here a difficult question arises:

could such colossal losses have been averted, or were they unavoidably dictated by a fatal combination of circumstances and by inexorable objective reasons?

An absolutely honest, straight answer to this was given in the decisions of our party, in particular in the resolution of the Central Committee of the CPSU of June 30, 1956, entitled "On Overcoming the Cult of Personality and Its Consequences," where the serious mistake of Stalin "in the organization of the preparations of the country to repel the fascist aggressors" is discussed in plain terms.

Yes, the number of victims could have been significantly less if the heroic efforts of the people, on all its levels, in preparing for the coming struggle with fascism had not been slowed down by the circumstances resulting from Stalin's cult of personality. For the first time the reader may find a number of facts confirming this view in Nekrich's book. The record of the author's conversations with Marshal of the Soviet Union F. I. Golikov, Major General I. A. Susloparov; information gleaned from talks with other participants of the events; materials from the archives of the German ministry of foreign affairs, most of which are being published in Russian for the first time; all this data throw new light on these events. Enormously interesting are the warnings made by the German ambassador to Moscow, Schulenburg, concerning the impending attack, to the Soviet ambassador in Berlin, Dekanozov; Schulenburg's reports to Ribbentrop; and the record of the ambassador's conversation with Hitler. It is also impossible to overlook the author's opinion regarding l'Affaire Tukhachevskiy. "Those who gave the order about their arrest and trial must have known that the accusations were groundless and the documents forged." The facts presented about the warnings regarding Hitlerite Germany's coming attack on the Soviet Union from other sources are unknown or only slightly known to the Soviet reader.

All the previously known and newly published facts, accurately qualified and described, whether in the field of foreign relations, intelligence, the preparations of the border defensive fortifications, the distribution of strategic stockpiles, or the fate of military leaders

—all these facts combined create an earth-shaking impression. Above all, they engender a feeling of pride for our people which, under the experienced leadership of its party, with the communists in the front ranks of the fighters, was able to stop and then smash the very powerful enemy in spite of extremely unfavorable circumstances.

The closer the fateful day of June 22 approaches, the more tense is the book's style. In such chapters as "Warnings That Were Disregarded," and "On the Eve," months and weeks literally become hours and minutes. The world press publishes reports about the concentration of German troops near the Soviet frontier under huge headlines. Fascist aircraft increase their overflights in the frontier zone. Our border guards keep catching spies and saboteurs. Some Soviet division commanders request higher headquarters to permit them to make essential redeployments. But there comes a categorical "No": Germany could take this as a provocation.

This "No" is also heard in the first directive issued by the People's Commissar of Defense at 0030 hours on June 22, 1941, on bringing the armed forces into combat readiness. Ordering essential measures, the directive at the same time is silent about opening fire.

At dawn on June 22 the Germans began an offensive along the entire front. The perfidious enemy, tearing up the Soviet-German agreement, invaded our country. The book tells about the first day of the war with feeling. That tragic and heroic epic is resurrected.

The book was written by a knowledgeable historian and specialist. However, through the clear, level rhythm of carefully measured and balanced statements the reader always perceives the excited voice of a contemporary to the events—of a patriot of his country, its historian and its defender, an officer who has returned to his peaceful scholarly profession after the victorious war, who had not forgotten or lost part of the thoughts and feelings which had consumed him while the war was still on. And this communicates a special dramatic suspense to the book, fills it with that atmosphere of authenticity and trustworthiness which cannot be faked, and gives it an enormous force of emotional influence.

A. Nekrich is known as the author of solidly researched monographs such as *The Foreign Policy of England in the Years of the Second World War,* and also popular publications such as *The War That Was Called "Strange"* and others. The book *June 22, 1941* has been published in the popular series of the publishing house "Nauka." However, it is difficult to relate it only to popular publications, since it combines a clear, understandable, and interesting account of the described events and occurrences, with a method of strict scholarship and a number of new and interesting conclusions.

THE ATTACK

The Deborin and Telpukhovskiy article in the September 1967 issue of *Voprosy istorii KPSS,* the translation of which follows, appeared in the section of the journal entitled "Reviews and Surveys." Normally, this section contains book reviews and review articles on subjects related to problems of communist ideology and party history. In this instance, however, such a modest place in no way diminished the significance of the article as an official party statement on a highly controversial subject. Its very length, the names of its authors, the fact that *Voprosy istorii KPSS* is concerned exclusively with matters of importance to the CPSU leadership, and the personal nature of the attack on Nekrich, reminiscent of the Stalin era, all indicate the party's exceptional preoccupation with the *political* heresies imbedded in *June 22, 1941.*

The names of the two authors are known to us from their part in the discussion at the Institute of Marxism-Leninism of the CC CPSU of February 16, 1966. Professor G. A. Deborin, Doctor of Economic Sciences and senior associate of the Institute, took a somewhat equivocal position towards Nekrich on that occasion. He endorsed *June 22, 1941* on the whole but defended Stalin against some of Nekrich's charges, saying that Stalin's judgment was impaired because of the misleading information he was receiving from Marshal Golikov, his military intelligence chief. Major General B. S. Telpukhovskiy, also an associate of the IML, took a similar line, finding extenuating circumstances to explain Stalin's behavior. He insisted that Stalin was guided by a desire to avoid war, adding that whatever his failures were, others around him were also responsible.

The article in *Voprosy istorii KPSS* covers enormous ground and has all the markings of a "guideline" for all the writers venturing into the history of the Great Patriotic War. By disregarding all the protestations of Nekrich's loyalty to the socialist motherland contained in his book as obviously inadequate, the article in effect demands that this loyalty must be overriding in all the examinations of the subject. The stress must be on the "ideological and political unity of the Soviet people and the role of the Communist Party." Nekrich, who failed to concentrate on this aspect, according to *Voprosy istorii KPSS* "has cut himself off from a fully scientific examination of historical laws." This is a very grave charge indeed.

In discussing specifics, Deborin and Telpukhovskiy see Nekrich's major sin as his juxtaposition of the tragic beginnings of the war and its victorious end, and as his unwarranted concentration on the former. This is an unmistakable call for a return to the orthodox treatment of the war's history as it existed during the last years of Stalin's life. As if in recognition of the changing times the authors feel compelled to go into explanations of some of the actions of the Soviet government which Nekrich criticized in his book. But in doing so, they do not hesitate to distort established facts or to interpret them in a way which few independent-minded historians would find acceptable.

Item. "The Soviet government agreed to a nonaggression treaty with Germany only when the unwillingness of the British and French leaders to resist German aggression had become obvious." In actual fact, Stalin's agents in Berlin began searching for a rapprochement with the Third Reich in April 1939, *after* the Western powers had committed themselves to resisting Germany by extending unilateral guarantees to Poland and Romania.

Item. "This [nonaggression] treaty broke apart the Munich front of Germany and Italy with England and France, supported by the USA." In fact, "the Munich front" (with which the US had nothing to do) broke apart with the German annexation of Bohemia and Moravia in March 1939, five months *before* Ribbentrop's trip to Moscow.

Item. "The fault for there having been no improvement in [Soviet-British and Soviet-American] relations is completely that of the reactionary governments of the USA and England, and the monopolies whose will was carried out by these governments, which stuck to the same old anti-Soviet course even after the defeat of France." There is no mention here that during this period in the eyes of the democracies the Soviet Union was a friend and ally of the Nazi Germany, hardly an appealing object for courtship.

Most revealing for our understanding of Stalin's thoughts and attitudes during 1940–41 are the pages of the article which deal with Churchill and his efforts to warn Stalin about the coming German invasion. The authors insist that Stalin had solid reasons for questioning Churchill's motives. They point out that even Nekrich was "forced to admit" that Churchill was anxious to see Germany embroiled with the Soviet Union. Since such was the case, they say, it was natural for the Soviet government to conclude that Churchill wished "to push" Germany into an invasion of Russia. Viewing this conclusion as wholly justifiable, the authors make the next "logical" supposition, namely that since Churchill did harbor such a criminal wish, he could not possibly have had a "nobility of purpose" in warning Stalin. To support this thesis, the authors cite several "progressive" Western writers testifying to Churchill's infinite perfidy. And they again bring up the case of Rudolf Hess—so much belabored by Soviet historians—insisting, in disregard if all that we know, that Hitler sent Hess to England to negotiate a common front against the Soviet Union and that the British government "undertook negotiations" with him. This episode, according to *Voprosy istorii KPSS*, was "an important component part of the general evaluation of the international situation before Germany's attack on the Soviet Union," thus indicating that it was uppermost in Stalin's mind when he dismissed Churchill's warnings.

While impeaching the British motives (and, to a somewhat lesser extent, those of the US government), the authors make no attempt whatsoever to discredit Nekrich's endless list of the warnings which came from bona fide communist and Soviet intelligence sources. Nor do they make any reference to the famous TASS communiqué of June 14, 1941, which, according to Nekrich (and numerous Soviet war memoirists) totally disoriented the military commanders and lulled them into complacency one week before the attack.

Among other major subjects of *June 22, 1941* which *Voprosy istorii KPSS* does not discuss at all is the effect that the Red Army purge had on the Soviet preparedness for war, and the sordid episode of the Gestapo collaboration with the NKVD in fabricating evidence against the Tukhachevskiy group. Also left without rebuttal are Nekrich's revelations about Stalin's ill-fated decisions to dismantle the fortifications along the old Soviet-Polish border, to build army supply depots too close to the frontier, and to discontinue production of certain antitank weapons.

The article attacks Nekrich personally on several grounds. It sternly takes him to task for his criticism of the Soviet strategic doctrine, as it existed in 1941, for its optimistic expectation that the toiling masses in capitalist countries would rush to the defense of the Soviet Union if the latter were attacked by imperialists. Nekrich, intone the authors, "in his blindness . . . does not take notice that this political line originated with V. I. Lenin himself," and that "the peoples of many countries," while fighting for their national interests, did indeed help the Soviet Union when it was confronted with the "mad onslaught of Hitler's hordes." Nekrich is also scolded for assuming (along with Western historians) that Stalin's appointment as chairman of the Council of People's Commissars in May 1941 was a manifestation of Soviet weakness in confronting Hitler. The authors assert that on the contrary, this appointment "had the aim of unifying the country and people to an even greater degree before a possible German attack." Not noticing their own contradiction, the authors, in the same breath, declare that even if Stalin did in fact want to placate Hitler, there was nothing wrong with it since it proved only his love for peace.

Voprosy istorii KPSS charges Nekrich with throwing "a monstrous accusation at Soviet fighting men" by suggesting that "the fascist armies did not encounter a serious resistance at the frontier"; according to the magazine, this "is still another example of slander such as few falsifiers of history permit themselves." The article concludes by stating that Nekrich had betrayed "the scientific principles of Marxist historiography, and therefore historical truth as well." And it reprimands the publishing house of the Academy of Sciences of the USSR for "displaying irresponsibility in undertaking the publication of this politically harmful book."

Probably the main charge leveled against Nekrich—and one which is clearly a warning to all other communist historians—is that instead of relying on "objective" Soviet sources, he utilized Western documentation which, by definition, is unreliable and tainted with hostility towards the Soviet Union. Time and again, references are made in the article to the party-approved *History of the Great Patriotic War* as a repository of both the proven facts and correct interpretation, and to the theses of the CC CPSU published on the occasion of the fiftieth anniversary of the October Revolution for everybody's political guidance in historical matters.

There is one interesting twist in the article, however, which permits us to think that the official reaction to *June 22, 1941* perhaps would not have been so violent if the above did not attract so much attention among the anti-Stalinist opposition at home and the Russia-watchers abroad. Not only the title, "In the Ideological Captivity of the Falsifiers of History," suggests this; the authors explicitly accuse Nekrich of the "crime" of having his "little book" used "by foreign reactionary propaganda for anti-Soviet purposes." Similar charges, we may recall, were made against such Soviet writers as Boris Pasternak and Sinyavsky and Daniel after their books had been published abroad "illegally"; the latter two writers were actually sent to prison for seven and five years, respectively, on exactly the same charge. A. M. Nekrich, of course, made no attempt to have his book published abroad: *June 22, 1941* appeared in the Soviet Union, with the approval of the appropriate authorities. This being the case, his accusation of aiding and abetting the enemies of the Soviet Union in the face of his legal innocence was bound to have serious repercussions for his future as a historian, of which his expulsion from the Communist Party was perhaps the most significant.

Although Nekrich's professional career had been fatally impaired, it is perhaps too early to say that his misfortune, which has been closely followed by all other Soviet historians, had been decisive in laying the ground for the second revision of Stalin's role in history. Those historians who are primarily concerned with advancing their own careers in the changing political climate, have undoubtedly drawn the necessary lessons. But there are others who are seemingly resolved to stand by their professional integrity, and who may persist in treating Stalin as a fundamentally negative figure, at least until the party openly repudiates the decisions of the Twentieth Party Congress regarding the "cult of personality." The ability of the writers belonging to the latter group to have their works published will be a conclusive test of the direction of the communist policies in the cultural field in months and years to come. And if de-villainization of Stalin becomes an accomplished fact, we would be able to conclude that the era of relative liberalization in the Soviet Union had come to an untimely end.

In the Ideological Captivity of the Falsifiers of History

By G. A. Deborin and B. S. Telpukhovskiy

A correct interpretation of the history of the Great Patriotic War is of great scholarly and political significance. An analysis of the events preceding the war, of its course and its military and political results, and their influence on the later developments of the world, makes it possible for the peoples and statesmen to derive instructive lessons. It is not by chance that the history of the last war has become the subject of a sharp ideological struggle between socialism and capitalism.

This struggle is carried on in questions connected not only with the lessons of the Great Patriotic War, but with the evaluation of the power relationships in the international arena in the prewar period and in the initial period of the war.

The Great Patriotic War of the Soviet Union was a heroic episode in the fifty-year history of the socialist state created by the October Revolution. In an incredibly difficult, bloody war, the Soviet Union came out victorious over German fascism, a very strong foe, whose armies had been able to conquer a significant part of the European continent by 1941. The legendary exploit of the Soviet people, which saved world civilization from destruction and all mankind from the horrible fate prepared for it by the German-fascist barbarians, has entered the annals of world history forever.

A profound analysis of the results of the war was given in the theses of the Central Committee of the CPSU, entitled *Fifty Years of the Great October Socialist Revolution*. The theses state: "The results of the Great Patriotic War of the Soviet Union have shown in the most convincing way that there are no powers in the world able to crush socialism, or to put on its knees a people faithful to the ideas of Marxism-Leninism, devoted to the socialist motherland,

united around the Leninist party. These results are a stern warning
to the imperialistic aggressors, a severe and unforgettable lesson of
history." [1]

The subjects of the Great Patriotic War are attracting the attention of scholars and will continue to do so. Soviet historiography
objectively reflects the great exploit of the Soviet people in pointing
out the inevitability of the Soviet victory in this war. Among bourgeois scholars there are some honest people in whose works various
concrete problems of the war are to a certain extent correctly
illuminated. But many bourgeois authors, in the interests of the
imperialist powers, try to minimize the role of the Soviet Union in
the smashing of Germany and portray its victory in the war as not
inevitable. Soviet historiography successfully carries on a struggle
with the bourgeois falsification of the history of World War II,
making its contribution to the general cause of the defense of
peace.

The publication by the publishing house "Nauka" of a little book
written in the spirit of bourgeois historiography is therefore all the
more surprising. We refer to A. M. Nekrich's work, *June 22,
1941.* [2] Its author, employing an erroneous methodology, has departed from the Communist Party spirit in research and has shown a
lack of scruple in his selection and evaluation of factual material. It
is no coincidence that Nekrich's book has met with approval on the
pages of the most reactionary press in the capitalistic countries,
which has even published a portrait of the author. For what qualities does Reaction praise A. M. Nekrich's book? It does it for the
fact that he denies the inevitability of the Soviet victory in the Great
Patriotic War, for his deliberate distortion of the foreign and
domestic policy of the CPSU and the Soviet government on the eve
of the war and at its start. This book is being used by foreign
reactionary propaganda for anti-Soviet purposes.

The most important requirement of Marxist-Leninist methodology consists of not limiting oneself to a simple account of events,
but of finding and uncovering objective laws of development which
condition social-economic processes. Bourgeois authors often cite
an enormous number of facts in their studies, but they do not draw

the underlying conclusions from them because the discovery of objective laws does not conform with their class position. The Marxist historian, on the other hand, cannot and must not limit himself to a simple statement; he is obliged to analyze the whole totality of facts, and to draw conclusions conforming to a principled, Marxist-Leninist position.

The Great Patriotic War was the gravest and most cruel of all the wars ever experienced by our motherland. The Hitlerites made use of a number of temporary advantages; their army, crazed with the poison of chauvinism and racism, penetrated our territory deeply. Of course, the discovery of those circumstances which led to the serious failures of our troops at the start of the war has important significance. But one must not stop there. One must show that the failures had a temporary character, that there were factors of decisive significance which made the victory of the USSR inevitable.

But in A. M. Nekrich's book the victory of the Soviet Union and the defeat of Germany are presented as accidental, and not the result of historical laws. This is exactly what the West German revanchists are striving for when they try to prove in every way that the war against the USSR can be repeated, and that success can be achieved under a new combination of chance circumstances.

The victory of the USSR was assured by objective factors, which had been functioning before the war started.

Of course, historical laws by themselves do not mean predetermination. The Soviet people's victory over Hitler's Germany did not arrive by itself; it was forged in violent battles with a powerful, dangerous, and perfidious enemy. The Soviet people needed enormous effort and mobilization of all their strength to win the victory. The decisive role in the realization of the objective opportunities for victory belonged to the policy and organizational activity of the Communist Party.

The main source of the Soviet Union's inner strength in the face of fascist Germany's attack was the presence of a socialist social and governmental regime, the triumph of which was the result of enormous transformational activity by the party and the masses led by it. The victory of socialism in the USSR meant basic changes in the economics and politics of the country and in the ideology and morale of its people. The superiority of the socialist system over the system of capitalism was the most important objective factor in the Soviet victory in the war against Germany.

But this factor is not only ignored in A. M. Nekrich's little book, it is, in fact, denied. The author does mention in passing that the Soviet people were *building* socialism. However, he does not mention so much as a single word about the fact that socialism *had been built*, about its superiority, about the very deep changes which occurred in the internal and international position of the Soviet Union with the victory of socialism. But it was precisely the victory of socialism in the USSR that was the decisive factor which made the country invincible.

For instance, in comparing the economic capabilities of the USSR and Germany, A. M. Nekrich does not mention the difference in their social systems. But this difference substantively influenced their power relationship. The economic potentialities for waging war were determined not only by the material resources present in Germany and the USSR, but by their productive reserves and by the ability of the state to mobilize all the existing economic capabilities and to use them in the most effective way. These capabilities depend directly on the nature of the social and governmental order and the attitude of the popular masses toward it. The more progressive the social and political order, the more completely it satisfies the basic interests of the people, the more the state is able to create a coordinated economy, capable of surviving all the trials of war.

In all this the Soviet Union, even before the war, significantly excelled Germany as well as all the other capitalist states, a fact about which A. M. Nekrich is silent. In the prewar years the Soviet Union had moved to the first place in the world in the ratio of high quality steel production to the total of steel production. It is known that during the war years Soviet engineers, technicians, and workers solved a problem which the metallurgy of no other country was able to solve: they learned how to make high quality armor steel in ordinary open-hearth furnaces.[3] These facts alone incontrovertibly testify that it is the superiority of the socialist system, and first of all the heroism of the working class, which makes it possible to achieve greater production with a smaller industrial base. And when the Soviet Union was subjected to enemy invasion, each machine, each tool, each kilogram of steel and other materials was used much more effectively than in Germany. Thus another Soviet "miracle" became possible: with a smaller industrial base, the Soviet Union, beginning with the end of 1942, began to produce more equipment, arms, and ammunition than were produced by Hitler's Germany and by the countries she occupied.

It was also very significant that before the war in the Soviet Union there was a constant process of broadened socialist production, and that a basic re-equipment of industry on the basis of modern technology for that period was carried out. The economy of the USSR developed rapidly and did not know crises and depressions. If A. M. Nekrich mentions this, he carefully avoids the question of the influence of the victory of socialism on industrial production and on the condition of the country's economy.

It must be pointed out that, from the very beginning of the war, the socialist system of people's economy facilitated the solution of the complicated problems of the creation and development of war economy. The national economy of the USSR was quickly switched to wartime tracks. About a year was required for the creation of a coordinated war economy. And this took place while there was war on the territory of the USSR, while the Donbas—the leading coal-metallurgical base of the country—was under enemy occupation, when large heavy industry installations and military industries had to be moved from the western parts of the country to the far rear areas, and to be rebuilt and put into operation in new places. No other country had ever had to solve such a gigantic problem. By contrast, the problem of creating a military economy had been solved by Germany in good time, before the war, a process which required about seven years, while the USA and England needed about four to five years during the war.*

The decisive role in the achievement of victory over Hitler's

---

* It is characteristic of the times that neither Nekrich nor his critics say a single word about the sizable economic-military assistance rendered to the Soviet Union by Great Britain and, especially, by the United States from 1942 through 1945.—V.P.

Germany was played by the heroic working class of the country, led by the Communist Party, the most conscientious and organized detachment of the workers of the USSR. The great exploits performed by the workers were not accidental. They resulted from that new, socialist attitude toward labor, which was formed in the prewar years and found its personification in socialist competition, which later played a large role during the war period. But in this book no place has been found even for an evaluation of the meaning of socialist competition in the years of the first five-year plans. It says nothing about the stability of the collective farm system, which later became apparent in the course of the war even in the regions occupied by the fascists. The author's subjective approach to the exposition of his material is once more obvious here.

A. M. Nekrich does not attach significance to the ideological and political unity of Soviet society which arose on the basis of the victory of socialism. But this unity is a qualitatively new phenomenon in the interrelation of the masses of people, and also between the masses and the state. This ideological and political unity signified an unprecedented solidarity of the Soviet people, a transformation of society into one mighty whole, a unification of the desires, will, and actions of the masses of many millions.

War is a continuation of a certain policy. Politics, in V. I. Lenin's words, "is the relationship between classes." [4] In a society built on the antagonism of class interests, war serves to develop the indignation of the masses against the policies of the government. In Soviet society, founded on the unity of the workers' and peasants' class interests, war united the masses around the policies of the Communist Party and the Soviet government.

The party incessantly educated the masses to love their native land, to be devoted to the socialist order, to believe in the righteousness and invincibility of their cause, to a deep and universal ideological conviction. It educated Soviet people in the spirit of solidarity with the workers of all countries, in the spirit of the ideas of Soviet patriotism and proletarian internationalism.

The solidarity of the Soviet people with the Communist Party was formed over a period of many years. But in the days of grave trials the role of this mighty factor grew day by day, because the strength of the party is in its connection with the masses, and the strength of the people is in its solidarity with the party. And it is no accident that the greatest flow of Soviet people into the party at the front and in the rear took place at the hardest moments.

By ignoring the ideological and political unity of the Soviet people and the role of the Communist Party, A. M. Nekrich has cut himself off from a fully scientific examination of historical laws which were demonstrated with special force in the war days. He has not shown the factors of extraordinary stability and inner power of Soviet society and the outstanding mass heroism of our people, although he does mention the organizational and educational work of the party.

The departure from Marxist methodology also appears in the way the author explains the heroism of the soldiers of the Soviet nation. He does not recognize that the Great Patriotic War was a military clash between socialism and capitalism.

A. M. Nekrich did not want to understand that the basis of the steadfastness of Soviet soldiers above all rested in their loyalty to the ideals of socialism, to the cause of the Communist Party. As a result of the victory of socialism, the interests and aspirations of Soviet people had become identical with the concept of a socialist motherland. This deep devotion to the socialist cause was transformed into an important dynamic force in the actions of Soviet man. The mass heroism of Soviet soldiers, workers in the rear, partisans, and underground fighters was clear evidence of this. The nature of our people was even more clearly demonstrated in the Great Patriotic War—their beauty of soul, their belief in victory, their hatred of fascism and imperialism, their love for the socialist motherland, the Communist Party, and the whole of Soviet society, their devotion to the ideals of proletarian internationalism. Soviet man arrested and destroyed the military machine of fascism.

Marxist methodology assumes the study of historical phenomena in their development. The first months of the Great Patriotic War were not merely a time of serious failures. It already became clear during those months that Hitler's military venture was doomed to failure. June 22, 1941, and May 9, 1945, these two historic dates, are inseparably connected.

A. M. Nekrich's little book is, actually, constructed on a contrast between the beginning of the war and its victorious finish. In his preface, pleased beyond all limits with his own "boldness," the author says that he has undertaken a hard task; to tell of the "bitter sorrow" of defeats although "it is easier and simpler to speak of victories," "to describe the flash of a solemn salute" to victory. This sham boldness sent the reviewer of the magazine *Novyi mir* into ecstasy; he saw in the tendency of the book some kind of special "objectivity." [5] Not having understood the contents of the book, he used it as an excuse to come out in the press with his own thoughts, which are far removed from the basic historical truth. There can be no objectivity when the military misfortunes of the first months of the war are considered separately from the course of events that followed, as is the case with A. M. Nekrich's book. The attempt to stress the shortcomings, mistakes, and oversights in a one-sided and exaggerated manner, and to belittle and suppress the achievements, self-sacrifice, and heroism of the Soviet people—this is not a new approach by their open enemies and so-called friends.

Having refused to examine objective factors, A. M. Nekrich moves a subjective factor to the fore and even then narrows it down to shortcomings, mistakes, and oversights, interpreting these in an extremely tendentious manner and explaining all the difficulties and failures of the Soviet troops in the early period of the Great Patriotic War only in this way. A. M. Nekrich has concentrated and presented in a deliberately exaggerated way all the shortcomings, all the difficulties of the growth of the Soviet nation.

The departure of the book's author from Marxism is also seen in the lack of a class approach in his description of events. Like a regular bourgeois historian, the author concentrates his attention on personalities, leaving aside the social classes which stand behind these personalities. Such a method of research is particularly subjective and alien to Marxist-Leninist historical scholarships.

Having read his fill of memoir-type exercises of the raving Fuehrer's accomplices and his speeches, the author assures us that Hitler was the creator of fascist Germany's successes. And these successes, A. M. Nekrich declares for all to hear to be "absolutely fantastic." If one is to believe the author, Hitler was an oracle with the capability of calculating and foreseeing things more correctly than anyone else. Characterizing the policy and actions of Germany A. M. Nekrich writes: "This development of events was unexpected by the highest political leaders: for Churchill in England, for Roosevelt in the United States. And it was not foreseen by J. V. Stalin either." And later the author discusses the "staggering successes of the fascist Wehrmacht." Not once does A. M. Nekrich recall the German monopolies which created Hitler and directed his activities. He does not reveal the class nature of the fascist regime and its terrorist methods in ruling Germany.

Having cited the fascist chieftain's speech at the Berghof conference on July 31, 1940, A. M. Nekrich writes: "Hitler was constantly dominated by fear of the possible creation of an anti-German coalition between England, the Soviet Union, and the United States of America. In order to prevent this, it was necessary first of all to knock out the most important of the potential participants, the Soviet Union. These were the main reasons why Germany had to attack the USSR." But if the *main reason* for Germany's attack on the USSR consisted only of this, if one is to hold to such a conception, all the plans of the German monopolies to destroy socialism, to seize the territory and riches of the USSR, to enslave its population, disappear. In a quasi-objective manner A. M. Nekrich puts forth not only Hitler's speech, but even the thesis that Germany had to attack the USSR to protect itself against the anti-German coalition that might arise. Such a presentation puts a trump card into the hands of the ideologists of aggression who have tried to prove that the attack on the USSR was a preventive, defensive war. It is known that this false version is still adhered to by the present official West German historiography which portrays the attack on the USSR as a preventive action against the alleged military threat of Bolshevism. But this threat did not exist; that much was admitted by even the fascist defendants and witnesses at the Nuremberg trial.

The author also presents the conclusion of the Soviet-German

Nonaggression Treaty in a distorted light. He writes: "In August 1939, trying to rid himself of the danger of a two-front war, Hitler proposed a nonaggression pact to the Soviet Union. But Hitler viewed the pact only as a deft diplomatic maneuver." Thus, according to A. M. Nekrich, there was for Germany in 1939 a real danger of a two-front war, that England and France were preparing to fight her in all seriousness. Even the bourgeois falsifiers of history do not go that far.

It is known that the governments of England and France did not want to fight Germany. They wanted to place the Soviet Union under the blows of the German-fascist war machine so as either to stay out of the war, or even to help Germany. It is precisely because of this that the British and French governments turned down all the Soviet proposals to conclude an effective mutual assistance treaty.

The Soviet government agreed to a nonaggression treaty with Germany only when the unwillingness of the British and French leaders to resist German aggression had become obvious. The Soviet-German treaty gave the USSR the opportunity to avoid a two-front war in an unfavorable international situation, to win time, and to prepare conditions for the defeat of the fascist aggressor. This treaty broke apart the Munich front of Germany and Italy with England and France, supported by the United States.

Casting a one-sided light on the Soviet-German treaty, A. M. Nekrich is carried away with admiration for Hitler's skill, portraying matters as if the treaty was useful only for Germany. The author is silent about those extremely important considerations which prompted the Soviet Union to conclude the Nonaggression Pact with Germany, and about the role which the pact played in the subsequent development of events. It is possible that Hitler evaluated the conclusion of the treaty as a success for himself, but in the final analysis the treaty meant the defeat of Germany in the area of foreign policy and diplomacy; it meant a victory not for Germany but for the Soviet Union and all freedom-loving peoples.

A. M. Nekrich also interprets the policy of England and the USA and the conduct of Roosevelt and Churchill from a non-class position, completely ignoring in this case, too, the class forces which they represented. As a result, the reasons for our country's relations with the USA and England having remained tense before Germany's attack on the USSR disappear from our field of vision. A. M. Nekrich, in fact, whitewashes the actions of the American and British governments. He writes that "unfortunately, affairs did not reach a state of genuine rapprochement with England and the USA, or even a serious improvement in relations with them." But to put it in this way is not to state the main issue: *who was to blame for this?* The fault for there having been no improvement in relations is completely that of the reactionary governments of the USA and England, and the monopolies whose will was carried out by these governments, which stuck to the same old anti-Soviet course even after the defeat of France. It is these governments which did not move toward any rapprochement with the USSR, not even in the cultural field.

A. M. Nekrich states: "In the summer and autumn of 1940 and the first months of 1941, American-Soviet relations began to improve a little." There was a "movement on the part of the United States of America to grow closer to the USSR." But this statement of the author is directly contrary to the facts.

There was no such movement. The American government's policy toward the USSR was made perfectly clear in the State Department's cable of June 14, 1941, addressed to the American embassies in London and Moscow. This malice-filled document stated: "We do not intend to suggest any negotiations to the Soviet government. . . . If Soviet Russia offers concessions in order to improve Soviet-American relations, we must turn them down." [6] * In this

---

* In a fashion rather typical of this sort of writing, the authors considerably distort the story. For one thing, this "document" is to be found not in Hull's memoirs but in the *Foreign Relations of the United States* series, Vol. 1, 1941, p. 758. For another, the cable was addressed to the London embassy only. It was a reaction to Ambassador Steinhardt's cable from Moscow of June 12, 1941, who—correctly—reported that in spite of the likelihood of the German invasion, Stalin was "undoubtedly prepared to satisfy any reasonable German demands." The United States policy with regard to the Soviet Union, as stated by Hull, was: "1. To make no approaches to the Soviet Government; 2. To treat any approaches which the

official document of the American government it is unequivocably stated that the USA would turn down any move by the USSR aimed at rapprochement, and would make no move itself. That is how the USA made its "conciliatory gestures" toward the USSR. Maybe Nekrich evaluates this telegram of the State Department, too, as a "conciliatory gesture."

It is known that the US government, even after its announcement of support for the Soviet Union when it was subjected to Germany's attack, continued to hinder the export of goods to the USSR until August 1941, while it winked at the shipment of strategic materials from the USA to Spain and Vichy France for subsequent transshipment to Germany. Right up to December 1941, the US government strongly tried to provoke an attack on the Soviet Union by Japan, and for this purpose held secret conversations with the latter.* It is curious that A. M. Nekrich does not mention a single word about these Japanese-American negotiations. In connection with similar "silences" of Nekrich, the question involuntarily arises: what is this —an ignorance of the facts, or a premeditated falsification of history? But the text of the book forces one to draw the conclusion that the numerous "silences" are the expression of a definite system of views.

A. M. Nekrich expends great effort to present the policy of the British government in the best possible light. Churchill's policy, in

Soviet Government may make towards us with reserve until such time as the Soviet Government may satisfy us that it is not engaging in manoeuvers for the purpose of obtaining unilaterally concessions and advantages for itself; 3. To reject any Soviet suggestions that we make concessions for the sake of 'improving the atmosphere of American-Soviet relations' and to exact a strict *quid pro quo* for anything which we are willing to give the Soviet Union; 4. To make no sacrifices in principle in order to improve relations; 5. In general, to give the Soviet Government to understand that we consider an improvement in relations to be just as important to the Soviet Union as to the United States, if not more important to the Soviet Union; 6. To base our day-to-day relations so far as practicable on the principle of reciprocity." This policy, obviously, was quite different from what the Soviet authors try to present it for, judging from their "quotation." It should be added that President Roosevelt reversed it completely within ten days after the dispatch of this cable.—V.P.

* This is factually untrue.—V.P.

his opinion, even before fascist Germany's attack on our country, was determined by a desire to help the Soviet Union. For instance, what is the worth of the following words of an author who so characterizes the actions of the government of Great Britain and its motives? "The international position of the Soviet Union had deteriorated greatly. . . . The Nonaggression Pact between the Soviet Union and Germany could not in itself serve as a sufficiently reliable guarantee against attack under the conditions of the headlong growth of Germany's economic might and the incredible self-satisfaction of the German fascists. Taking these circumstances into account and striving to ease England's serious position, the new British War Cabinet, formed in mid-May by Winston Churchill, decided to try to mend relations with the USSR."

Thus A. M. Nekrich considers that England changed her policy toward the USSR because the Soviet Union had no dependable guarantee against attack by Germany. Churchill almost turns into a defender of the USSR against aggression.

The author offers no proof in substantiation of this. But twenty to thirty pages later he relates in dramatic tones how in April 1941 the British ambassador to Moscow was unable to see the head of the Soviet government for two weeks to hand him Churchill's letter. "Two priceless weeks were lost. Churchill in his message warned of the attack being prepared against the USSR," exclaims A. M. Nekrich.

The text of this message of Churchill's is not cited in A. M. Nekrich's book, but he repeats the version of the objectives and sense of the message which many British reactionary historians adhere to. Churchill, Nekrich insists, decided to send a warning to J. V. Stalin so that "the German attack would not catch the Russians by surprise, and the struggle in the East should continue as long as possible." With this aim in mind the British prime minister used the information received by him about Yugoslav Prince Regent Paul's conversation with Hitler during which the latter stated that "the attack on the Soviet Union was scheduled for June 30."

It is possible that Churchill possessed this information along with other. But he did not share it in his message to the head of the

Soviet government, and in general this message can in no way be regarded as a warning. The message merely stated the following: "I have received reliable information from a trustworthy agent that the Germans, after they had decided that Yugoslavia was already in their net, that is after March 20, began to transfer three of their five armored divisions in Romania to the southern part of Poland. As soon as they learned of the Serbian revolution, this transfer was canceled. Your Excellency will easily evaluate the meaning of these facts." [7] What did Churchill wish to convey in his message? In any case, this was not an attempt to warn the Soviet Union about the danger hovering over it.

Representing this extremely suspicious message of Churchill's as an expression of his supposedly benevolent attitude toward the Soviet Union, Nekrich accuses the Soviet leadership of a boundless lack of trust in the actions of the British government. In A. M. Nekrich's opinion, J. V. Stalin "considered the main enemy of the Soviet state in the prewar years to be England." Yes, there were years—1919 and 1927, for instance—when the British government took upon itself the unseemly role of main instigator of anti-Soviet activities. All the more reason for suspecting Churchill's nobility of purpose on the eve of Germany's attack on the USSR. One asks what Churchill preferred: to remove the danger of Germany's attack on the USSR or, on the contrary, to push her into such an attack, in order to repair the affairs of Great Britain at the expense of the Soviet Union. The answer to this question is obvious. Actually the author himself is not able to avoid an indirect admission of this conclusion when he speaks of Churchill's attempts to develop a struggle of as long duration as possible in the East. Why then is it necessary to weep for "lost" weeks?

The provocative game of the British government is also attested to by the fact that, in "warning" the USSR about German actions directed against it, the government of England simultaneously gave the German fascists false information that the Soviet Union was preparing an attack on Germany. Montgomery Hyde, who during World War II was a responsible official of British intelligence in the USA, states that the chief of this intelligence service, William

Stephenson, in close contact with the American Federal Bureau of Investigation, saw to it that the German embassy in the US received, in April 1941, a document which stated: "From completely reliable and trustworthy sources it has become known that the USSR intends to undertake immediate aggressive military measures as soon as Germany is involved in any kind of large-scale military operations."[8] Is it permissible for a Soviet historian to evade and maintain silence in regard to this and similar facts?

For its own provocative purposes the British government undertook negotiations with Rudolf Hess, when he landed in the British Isles in May 1941. There was a time when A. M. Nekrich recognized the seriousness of Hess's mission.[9] But this former point of view was not suitable to the line which he follows in *June 22, 1941*, and it had to be changed. Now A. M. Nekrich states that the significance of his mission "is exaggerated," and that "Hess undertook his flight to England on his own responsibility and risk, on his own initiative."

The question of Hess's mission is an important component part of the general evaluation of the international situation before Germany's attack on the Soviet Union. This situation was a greatly complicated one. It was hard to know what the British and American governments would do. The German leaders considered that they would be able to prevent the participation of these powers in European affairs. These considerations were set forth in detail by none other than Hitler himself in a narrow circle of his retainers. "The conclusion of peace," he reasoned, "would allow us to prevent the intervention of the Americans in European affairs . . . , and Germany, having secured its rear, could devote itself body and soul to the goal of my whole life, to the essence of National Socialism— the destruction of Bolshevism. This would result in the conquest of a large territory in the East."[10] British historians justly remark that on the eve of the attack on the USSR, "Hitler toyed with the idea of normalizing relations with England, in order to free his hands for waging a one-front war in the East."[11]

In connection with the failure of Hess's mission the German government put out the story that this most intimate henchman of Hitler had carried out his flight to England in a fit of temporary insanity. This version is supported up to the present time by all those who are interested in whitewashing the prewar policy of England. And A. M. Nekrich has turned up in this colorful group of deliberately unobjective authors.

All the bourgeois scholars who are at least partially objective, and progressive authors all the more so, note the complete seriousness of Hess's mission. The Englishman Paul has called Hess's mission "the last attempt" of Hitler to attract England to his side." [12] Another British scholar, Ingram, called it an attempt "to influence the official position, or at least to effect a split which would weaken the government which had decided to carry on the war." [13]

The study of the Englishman Leasor, who has discovered rich factual material, is of great interest. Leasor declares that "Hess accomplished what the Fuehrer wanted and with Hitler's knowledge," [14] and therefore on his orders.*

The position of Churchill's government was ambiguous. As a result of Hess's mission, the German fascists acquired a solid certainty that even if England would not help Germany in a war against the USSR, she would not, in any case, enter an alliance with a socialist government. By its position in regard to Hess's mission, Churchill's government was pushing Germany to attack the USSR.

Nekrich tries to prove that England and the USA were striving to improve relations with the Soviet Union and were taking the necessary measures toward this end. We have already pointed out that there is no basis for such a conclusion. The nonsensical quality of this myth has been exposed not only in Soviet historiography, but even in the works of some bourgeois historians.

The accusation, which A. M. Nekrich throws in rather casually, that the Soviet government did not perceive the transformation of Germany into the main enemy of the Soviet Union, is laughable. From the moment the Hitlerites seized power in Germany, right up to the end of the world war, the party, the government, and the whole Soviet people knew that the main enemy of the USSR and of all progressive humanity was Hitler's Germany. In proof of this one

---

* Which, of course, is totally false.—V.P.

can consult the reports of the Central Committee of the party at the Seventeenth and Eighteenth Party Congresses, the speeches of delegates at these congresses, and of the deputies of the Supreme Soviet of the USSR, as well as many other party and governmental documents.*

The departure from class positions, and subjectivism in the evaluation of social phenomena are characteristic of all of A. M. Nekrich's discussions of the Soviet Union. It is no accident that he also evades the question of the class meaning of the Great Patriotic War.

In evaluating the nature of the Great Patriotic War, Nekrich limits himself to calling it a defensive and just war for the independence of the Soviet state. It appears that this war was qualitatively no different from other wars of national liberation. Of course, the Great Patriotic War was also a war of national liberation. But this is not all there was to its nature. It was a gigantic military clash of socialism with the most monstrous spawn of imperialism, fascism. This was a war not only for the liberation of the Soviet Union from fascist invasion, but for the liberation of all peoples who were subjected to aggression. This was a war for the freedom of the motherland, for the defense of socialism.

This is precisely the evaluation of the nature of the war present in all party decisions, and particularly in the theses of the Central Committee of the CPSU, *Fifty years of the Great October Socialist Revolution:* "The war which started on June 22, 1941, forced upon the Soviet Union by German fascism was the greatest military clash between socialism and the shock forces of imperialism. It became the Great Patriotic War of the Soviet people for the freedom and independence of the socialist motherland, for socialism." [15]

In the days of the Great Patriotic War, as in the years of peaceful construction, the Soviet people fulfilled their national, and thereby their international, duty with dignity and honor. In their turn, the workers of many countries also fulfilled their national and international duty, struggling with the fascist occupiers for the freedom and independence of their countries, striving to give what help they

---

* And the secret texts of Nazi-Soviet agreements?—V.P.

could to the Soviet Union and its armed forces. But A. M. Nekrich denies the international unity of the workers of foreign countries with the Soviet people, with the first socialist state in the world. In fishing out defects in Soviet military doctrine, A. M. Nekrich declares that its flaws "were aggravated by the incorrect political assumption of an indubitable armed support for the Red Army by the workers of the capitalist countries."

In his blindness, the author does not notice that this political line originated with V. I. Lenin, that it was confirmed by the experience of the Civil War, by the entire experience of the Soviet state. He also does not want to take into consideration the events of World War II, in the course of which the peoples of many countries, including progressive people in Germany itself, fighting for their national interests, helped the Soviet Union, which was countering the mad onslaught of Hitler's hordes.

The treacherous attack of fascist Germany on the USSR called forth an explosion of indignation against the aggressors and an active struggle on the part of the masses to give all possible help to the Soviet Union. The resistance movement, which had originated before the attack, rose to a new, higher level. The peoples knew and believed that the Soviet Union would smash fascism and liberate them; they sincerely tried to make any contribution in their power to the cause of winning victory. Who can deny that the resistance movement played a substantial role in the course and outcome of the Second World War? Even the most reactionary historians admit this obvious fact.

A. M. Nekrich essentially denies the principal feature of the Second World War; he denies that it was transformed into a great popular war against fascism. And it was this fact that confirmed the very Leninist "political line," which A. M. Nekrich opposes.

The departure from the Marxist-Leninist class position is the characteristic feature of *June 22, 1941* and the principal reason for its scholarly bankruptcy.

There is another important reason for the depravity of this little book's basic assumptions. We have in mind the sources which the author tries to use, his treatment of facts, and also his lack of competence in the questions of diplomacy, economics, politics, and military affairs.

A large number of sources were at A. M. Nekrich's disposal. It was up to him to choose whatever corresponded to reality and to eliminate everything that was unreliable and falsified. He was aided by the fact that he could take advantage of Soviet documentary publications and archival sources, whose objectivity is undeniable. But he followed a different path. He tendentiously picks out facts to support his concept. Soviet publications of documents are used by him to an insignificant degree, often with obvious unscrupulousness. Thus A. M. Nekrich snatches separate sentences out of the memoirs of a number of Soviet authors, leaving out the context wherever it does not fit into his scheme of writing, thereby distorting the true picture of the events described. At the same time he treats all sorts of fabrications and memoirs of reactionary authors as if they were reliable sources, and utilizes them in the widest possible way.

A. M. Nekrich's use of the reminiscences of a Hitlerite diplomat, the adventurer Hilger, can serve as a characteristic example of his unscientific approach. Trying to exaggerate his own importance, Hilger invented a whole fantastic story about how the German ambassador to the USSR, Schulenburg, and he, Hilger, in the beginning of June 1941, secretly met in Schulenburg's residence with the Soviet ambassador to Berlin and informed him in detail about Germany's coming attack on the USSR.

Nekrich relates this story in the following way. First he speaks of it as existing in Western historical literature, which is unreliable by definition. Then he states that the "secret meeting took place," and ends by addressing a lecture to the Soviet government: "No matter how we evaluate Schulenburg's step, it was essential to strengthen military measures to counter an invasion. But "Schulenburg's step" simply did not exist, and now Hilger's concoction has appeared in the pages of Soviet literature. The Hitlerite diplomat and petty swindler probably never counted on such success!

Let us cite still another very revealing fact. In the first volume of *The History of the Great Patriotic War* it is stated that "the valiant

Soviet border guards defended the Soviet land bravely and staunchly," and facts on the numbers of enemy agents destroyed are given. A. M. Nekrich includes these figures and cites the source. But then he tries to convince the reader that "Enemy agents mingled with the construction workers [employed in building defensive border fortifications] and penetrated undetected into Soviet territory." A. M. Nekrich apparently believes that the defensive fortifications were being built directly on the line of the state border, that the Soviet border was open to the enemy, and that enemy agents penetrated into the USSR's territory and flooded the Soviet rear with impunity. One scarcely needs to mention that all this was thought up by A. M. Nekrich from beginning to end. It was not this way in actuality. The Hitlerites miscalculated and suffered a defeat in their attempts to create a widespread secret agent net on Soviet soil.*

The technique of juggling facts and the distortions which A. M. Nekrich generously uses in his book also testify to his unscrupulousness as a researcher. With this work as an example one can see how, through an appropriate selection of material, great achievements can be distorted into shortcomings and neglect of duty.

It is known that enormous efforts were made by the party and the people in the period of the prewar five-year plans to overcome the ineffectual geographic distribution of the country's industrial production, which had occurred as a result of historical development, and to create a second coal-metallurgical and industrial base in the east. Thanks to this, a basic change in the geographical distribution of industry was taking place, expressing itself in its shift eastward. The relative role of the eastern regions in the economy of the country had grown by 1940, in comparison with 1913, by a factor of two in the development of electric power, by almost three in coal production; it was almost four and a half times greater in oil production and one and a half times greater in steel manufacture.[16] This made it possible during the war to increase military production in rear areas far from the front, to relocate evacuated enterprises, and to bring them quickly into production. For the German generals

---

* Nekrich does state that.—V.P.

all this was a complete surprise. In November 1943, at a conference in Munich, General Jodl said: "A decisive factor for us was that we discovered, in the course of our advance into the unexplored spaces of Russian territory, that the enemy controlled not only great human resources, but possessed such a high technical level of war industry that we were forced to wage total war and to multiply our efforts in war industry." [17]

The facts do not suit A. M. Nekrich; he counterposes his own assumptions. Declaring that "by the beginning of the Second World War" the Soviet Union's resources "were actually only beginning to be realized," the author does not show that the Soviet Union possessed the material base needed to repel the enemy. In fact, he reproaches the Soviet government for the fact that the enterprises in the southwest continued to play an important part in the country's economy, and finally states: "From a strategic point of view the concentration of the basic sources of oil in the south of the country near the border, was unsatisfactory." It would appear that this "concentration of the basic sources of oil" did not come about historically, but was the result of somebody's subjective actions.

The efforts of the Soviet government to avoid war with Germany are treated by A. M. Nekrich as a manifestation of "fear of war and uncertainty." He resorts to the same method that our enemies have been using for a long time: they portray the Soviet Union's love of peace as a sign of weakness. Speaking of J. V. Stalin's appointment as chairman of the Council of People's Commissars in May 1941, which had the aim of unifying the country and people to an even greater degree before a possible German attack, A. M. Nekrich restricts himself to mentioning the fact that in foreign circles this appointment was received as a "gesture of invitation to Germany to open negotiations, which he [Stalin] would be ready to carry on personally." Even if such negotiations with Germany had taken place, how could one more attempt by the Soviet Union to preserve the peace be criticized?

Accepting people like Hilger as his sources (we have in mind Nekrich's extraordinary trust in the memoirs of this adventurer), the author sympathetically cites the latter's statement that the Soviet government would have accepted any German demands, even territorial ones, to avoid war. Nekrich himself strengthens Hilger's slander by stating that, allegedly, "a similar point of view was also widespread in the circles of the high command of the Red Army." * But this is nothing but a baseless defamation of the Soviet leadership.

Thus step by step A. M. Nekrich tries to prove that behind the efforts of the USSR to preserve peace there was an unwillingness to defend itself against the enemy. He does not take into account the fact that the events of the Great Patriotic War topple such invidious fabrications by our sworn ideological enemies whose arguments the author broadly employs.

All the distortions and juggling of facts in the little book have a completely definite utilitarian role: they are meant to support the author's absurd thesis that the party and the government allegedly underestimated "the danger of war with Germany." A. M. Nekrich ignores the great labors of preparation to repel an enemy invasion which were carried on in the prewar years and thanks to which the victory over the enemy became possible. It cannot be said that this was unknown to the author since many works published in our country were available to him.

For these purposes of his, Nekrich tries to prove that the party and the Soviet government did not take the necessary measures to speed up the development of industry in the eastern part of the country and to organize a mass production of new military equipment and arms. He paints the situation in industry on the eve of the war in one color: black. In confirmation, A. M. Nekrich gives figures testifying to a certain curtailment of production in some branches of industry, for instance, in the manufacture of tractors. But this curtailment of production was caused by the implementation of preparatory measures in case of war: the tractor industry was getting ready to shift to the production of tanks. For objective reasons, the Soviet nation which had only recently climbed out of the backwardness of centuries, was not yet able to produce both

---

* This distortion of Nekrich's statement is self-evident.—V.P.

peacetime manufactures and military equipment on the scale that was necessary for such a war as was the war with Germany. The author does not take into account the objective difficulties standing in the way of an increase in military production. If he had looked into the decisions of the Eighteenth Party Conference or other party documents, he would have seen a different picture of the development of industry in the USSR in the prewar period. The theses of the CC CPSU, *Fifty Years of the Great October Socialist Revolution,* state: "The Communist Party and the Soviet government saw the danger posed by the policies of the fascist states, took into account the situation which had arisen, and sought measures to strengthen the defensive capabilities of the country. The party implemented important measures directed at the restructuring of work in industry and transport, with the ever growing danger of war in mind. The defense industry created in the prewar years provided the armed forces of the country with modern military equipment." [18]

Presenting the policy of our country in a false light, A. M. Nekrich at the same time does not subject to exposure the policy and strategy of fascist Germany. It is known that Hitler's adventurist policy and the goals of world domination presented by gangster German imperialism determined the depravity of the fascist military command's strategy and tactics. Preparing for aggressive war, the Hitlerites strove to supply the Wehrmacht with military equipment which, in their opinion, would be able to determine the outcome of the war against any enemy, in all theaters of war, with the first powerful blow. Hitler and his strategists planned to win the war against the Soviet Union by one lightning-like campaign. This one-sided theory resulted, in particular, in the underestimation of the significance of such a powerful weapon as the artillery, and in the exaggeration of the role of tank forces. In the first months of the Great Patriotic War the myth of the "invincibility" of the Wehrmacht, and all the calculations of Hitler's politicians and strategists regarding a "lightning-like victory," were buried. The wartime events which A. M. Nekrich undertook to illuminate obligated him to tell about this rather than be carried away with Hitler's "perspicacity."

In characterizing the situation of the Soviet armed forces, the military cadres, and Soviet military doctrine, A. M. Nekrich is silent about the fact that long before the Second World War the basic problems of military science and military art under modern conditions, as well as the principles of the organization of the armed forces of the Soviet state and their preparation for successfully carrying on military operations, had been worked out in our country. The Great Patriotic War showed that the theoretical positions of Soviet military science were completely well founded. It is known that the USSR followed a policy of peace and was not striving for war and that its army did not have the experience of fascist Germany's army. Can the Soviet military cadres be blamed, or Soviet military science blackened, for this?

The Soviet military leadership, generals and officers, quickly and creatively mastered military experience and perfected new forms and methods of armed struggle against a powerful opponent; they perfected the art of war and improved the fighting skills of the army and navy.

Thanks to the superiority of its socialist social and state order, the socialist planned economy, and the ideological-political unity of the people, the Soviet Union was able to obtain a decisive edge over the enemy in the course of the war. This determined the victory over the enemy in spite of the suddenness of fascist Germany's attack and the temporary successes it achieved in the initial period. The war showed that the military organization of a socialist power surpassed the military organization of capitalist countries in every way. Can a genuine scholar who claims to be objective be silent about these facts? The point is that A. M. Nekrich's "forgetfulness" and his conception completely follow from his idealistic, subjective view of the military-political events and the actions of the sides on the eve of the war and in its initial period.

On the eve of Germany's attack, the Soviet military command, understanding the increasing tenseness of the general situation, carried out great work in strengthening the security of the USSR. From 1937 to 1941 the numerical strength of the Soviet armed forces grew from 1,433,000 to 4,207,000 men. In May and June 1941 significant redeployment of Red Army troops was carried out, including the transfer of troops to the frontier military districts from the interior.

All this does not exclude the fact that there were significant omissions in the preparations to repel the first blows of the enemy. To a large degree they resulted from the miscalculations as to the possible timing of Hitlerite Germany's attack on the USSR. This has already been related in historical literature based on party documents. But A. M. Nekrich tries to prove that at the start of the war all of the actions of the Soviet military leadership were in error. He does not spare words and epithets to demean this leadership. One could suppose that it was not the Soviet military leadership that led the armed forces of the USSR to victory over the enemy.

To the Soviet military leadership the author ascribes doubts and vacillations, miscalculations, confusion, and uncertainty. At first he accuses it of not granting permission "to cross the border without special orders" in the first minutes of the war when the situation was still unclear; and then of striving to organize offensive operations at a time when "it was essential to organize a defense immediately." One might think that the Soviet military leadership did not understand the necessity of defense.

A. M. Nekrich does not know and does not understand the interrelationship between defense and offense. He does not know that in order for strategic defense to succeed it must be combined with partial offensive operations, or counterblows. Continuing to lecture the Soviet military leadership, he declares that the situation resulting from Germany's attack "excluded the possibility of carrying out offensive activities against the invader who had attacked our motherland."

To the beginning of the war, which supposedly is the subject of *June 22, 1941*, the author has devoted only four pages! And what pitiful pages they are! A few examples of the heroism of Soviet soldiers can be found in them, examples so selected as to create the impression that the defense against the enemy was disorganized and spontaneous. Moreover, in the concluding pages of his little book, A. M. Nekrich throws a monstrous accusation at Soviet fighting men, declaring that "the fascist armies did not encounter a serious defense at the frontier."

Such an accusation is still another example of slander such as few flasifiers of history permit themselves. At that time, in June 1941, the world was astounded by the bravery of Soviet fighting men who stood to the death. The German fascist conquerors were astounded too. In this regard the testimony of the Chief of General Staff of Germany's ground forces, Halder, is characteristic. On June 24, 1941, he made the following entry in his official diary: "The enemy is resisting almost everywhere in the frontier zone . . . so far there are no signs of an operational withdrawal by the enemy." [19] The next day Halder wrote: "An estimate of the situation in the morning generally confirms the conclusion that the Russians have decided to carry on decisive battles in the frontier zone." [20] The commander of the German Third Armored Group, Hoth, admits: "The troops of the enemy at the border were thrown back but they quickly recovered from the unexpected blow and stopped the advance of the German troops by counterattacks of their reserves and armored units located in the rear." [21] Let us cite, finally, one more testimony by the enemy. The West German reactionary historian Rieker notes that two or three days after the beginning of military operations in the border zone "fierce fighting went on along the whole enormous expanse of the theater of war." [22]

In spite of the suddenness of the attack, in spite of the fact that for the first time in the history of wars such a great mass of men and equipment was put into action simultaneously by an aggressor, Soviet fighting men did not lose their heads, did not lose faith in victory over the enemy and immediately began to put up a decisive defense against him.

Thus, A. M. Nekrich, having found himself in the ideological captivity of the bourgeois flasifiers of history has betrayed the scientific principles of Marxist historiography, and therefore historical truth as well. And it is natural that this little book has become a find for the ideologists of imperialism and has been taken by them as a weapon of hostile propaganda against the Soviet Union and of slander against it. The publishing house "Nauka" has displayed irresponsibility in undertaking the publication of this politically harmful book.

Notes

1. *Fifty Years of the Great October Socialist Revolution,* theses of the CC CPSU, Moscow, 1967. 23 pp.

2. A. M. Nekrich, *June 22, 1941,* "Nauka," Moscow, 1965.

3. See P. A. Belov, *Problems of Economy in Contemporary War,* Moscow, 1951. 73 pp.

4. V. I. Lenin, *Complete Works,* Vol. 43, p. 72.

5. See G. Fedorov, "A Measure of Responsibility," *Novyi mir,* 1966, No. 1., p. 260.

6. C. Hull, *The Memoirs,* Vol. II, New York, 1947, pp. 972–973.

7. *Correspondence of the Chairman of the Council of Ministers of the USSR with the President of the USA and the Prime Minister of Great Britain during the Great Patriotic War, 1941–1945,* Moscow, 1951, Vol. I, p. 391.

8. H. Montgomery Hyde, *Room 3603,* New York, 1963, p. 58.

9. See *World History,* Moscow, 1965, Vol. 10, pp. 89–90.

10. *The Testament of Adolf Hitler,* London, 1959, pp. 33–34.

11. *The Initial Triumph of the Axis,* edited by A. and V. Toynbee. London, 1958, p. 403.

12. L. Paul, *The Annihilation of Men,* London, 1945, p. 34.

13. K. Ingram, *Years of Crisis,* London, 1946, pp. 297–298.

14. J. Leasor, *Rudolf Hess,* London, 1962, p. 122.

15. *Fifty Years of the Great October Socialist Revolution,* theses of the CC CPSU, pp. 18–19.

16. See E. Yu. Lokshin, *USSR Industry, 1940–1963*, Moscow, 1964, p. 32.

17. *Voyenno-istoricheskiy zhurnal*, 1960, No. 10, p. 81.

18. *Fifty Years of the Great October Socialist Revolution*, theses of the CC CPSU, p. 18.

19. See *Voyenno-istoricheskiy zhurnal*, 1959, No. 7, p. 88.

20. *Ibid.*, pp. 89–90.

21. H. Hoth, *Panzer-Operationen*, Heidelberg, 1956, p. 68.

22. K. Rieker, *Ein Mann verliert einen Weltkrieg*. Frankfurt am Main, 1955, p. 31.

APPENDIX

A Story of the Nazi-Soviet Partnership

Based on an article by Vladimir Petrov in the Winter 1968 issue of ORBIS (Foreign Policy Research Institute, University of Pennsylvania)

Western historians seem to have lost interest in the Nazi-Soviet collaboration during the 1939–41 period. After the publication in 1948 of the captured German documents related to this episode, and the appearance of a flurry of memoirs by former German diplomats and soldiers, a few studies attempting to analyze this episode were produced. The subject has also been treated as part of the history of the Third Reich by a generation of scholars specializing in Germany. But there has been no satisfactory study which would have tried to place it into the context of *Soviet* history.

This is understandable. On the one hand, no documentary evidence dealing with the Soviet side of the story, which could have thrown more light onto what we know from the German sources, has emerged from Moscow. On the other hand, because of the politically embarrassing quality of this episode, what seemed to be an appropriate subject for scholarly investigation at the height of the Cold War has come to be regarded as bad taste, if not outright warmongering, once the spirit of peaceful coexistence set in following the death of Stalin. As a result, later studies of Soviet policies and politics of that period, if references to the Nazi-Soviet partnership could not be avoided altogether, treated it, at least implicitly,

305

as a kind of aberration in the otherwise sound foreign policy of the Soviet government.

Such a tendency to skirt one of the most cataclysmic events in modern history is regretful. The subject itself is such as to enable us to gain insight into the relations between the two most powerful countries in Europe as well as into the ways of thinking of the Soviet leaders which, we can guess, have not changed appreciably in the intervening three decades. Furthermore, a dispassionate analysis would probably reveal that, if placed in a proper context, Stalin's decision to enter the compact with Hitler was far from being an aberration but was instead a very logical development, much less sensational than it appeared to the vast majority of contemporary observers. A great many recent Soviet writings dealing with the origins of the "Great Patriotic War," in spite of the paucity of new information they contain, seem to lend weight to precisely this conclusion.

A thorough examination of the Nazi-Soviet Pact should probably begin with Bismarck's policy of alliance with Russia which he inaugurated around 1870 and which resulted in the formation of the "Eastern School" in the German Foreign Office and the General Staff. An integral part of the German political life ever since, this school has been in conflict with another, "Greater Germany" school, whose adherents believed that Germany was strong enough to pursue its goals independently of any foreign power. And although Bismarck's disciples often lost, their struggle against the more jingoistic elements within the subsequent German governments has resulted in many otherwise inexplicable inconsistencies and puzzling reverses in German foreign policy.

It is equally useful, for the understanding of the Nazi-Soviet Pact, to probe into a deep, almost emotional, attachment of Russian Marxists to Germany and German political thought; into Lenin's "defeatism" during the First World War; his ready acceptance of Ludendorff's aid for the promotion of the Bolshevik's fortunes in Russia; and his position regarding the Brest-Litovsk Treaty. Considering Lenin's influence in the party, one should not be surprised at the extent of the pro-German sympathies among the generations of Bolsheviks.

Perhaps more pertinent for our subject would be the story of Rapallo, this *marriage de convenance* of the two states, both painfully humbled and impoverished in the war, both declared and treated as international outcasts, both victims of Anglo-French military interventions, both objects of the systems of alliances and *cordon sanitaires* reinsuring the victors simultaneously against German revisionism and the communist plague. This sense of affinity manifested itself in violent denunciations, in almost identical terms, of Versailles and its principal architects, by the communists and German nationalists alike. And in spite of the resentment against the Comintern's role in fomenting revolution in Germany, governments of the Weimar Republic, prodded by the General Staff which was then a citadel of the "Eastern School," readily embarked upon a far-reaching program of collaboration with Russia in military and economic fields. This collaboration was welcome in Moscow, continually in fear of the hostile "capitalist" encirclement. Nationalist agitation in Germany was a clear asset in Soviet foreign policy, since it was directed against the common enemy, i.e., France and its East European allies.

One should naturally guard against excessive simplifications in discussing the past, and in the case of Germany there were undoubtedly many developments contradicting the picture here outlined. The Locarno Pacts and Germany's entry into the League of Nations marked the end of its formal isolation and probably caused the first serious apprehensions in Moscow as to the reliability of the Rapallo partner. Nevertheless, because anti-German feelings in Western Europe persisted; and because Germany still had many territorial, political, and military grievances, General Hans von Seekt's cooperation with the Red Army leadership and the lively Soviet-German trade continued in spite of the "new" status of Germany. Adherents of the "Eastern School" still dominated the Reichswehr; they were numerous in the Foreign Office; and it is well to remember that most of these men remained in positions of influence even after Hitler's ascent to power.

The proclamation of the Third Reich seemingly introduced a radically new element in the Soviet-German relations. The Nazi propaganda, shrilly denouncing the Versailles system and demanding its drastic revision, also contained sharp attacks against the communists; it was a rare speech in which Hitler failed to elaborate upon the evils of communism. Yet, although the communist propaganda reciprocated wholeheartedly, it can be seriously questioned whether Stalin and his colleagues regarded the declared hostility of the Third Reich with grave concern. Men of communist mentality rarely change their convictions or admit errors of judgment, and there is some evidence to suggest that Soviet leaders had never abandoned their desire for a rapprochement with Germany, even Hitler's Germany.[1] Their cynicism about their own propaganda predisposed them to be equally cynical about Nazi propaganda, to dismiss much of Hitler's oratory as mere lip service to his ideology, and to look, instead, for "hidden messages" expressing his actual aims and desires. There is no doubt, therefore, that Stalin took seriously Hitler's speech of March 23, 1933, in which the Fuehrer voiced his wish "to cultivate friendly relations" with the Soviet Union, indirectly assuring the latter that "the fight against communism in Germany is our internal affair" and that "international political relations with other countries to whom important common interests tie us are not affected by it." It is in this context that one must judge Stalin's speech at the Seventeenth Congress of the CPSU in 1934, with its astounding assertion that while "we are far from enthusiastic about the fascist regime in Germany . . . fascism is beside the point, if only because fascism in Italy, for example, has not kept the USSR from establishing the best of relations with that country."[2] While Stalin was undoubtedly briefed on the contents of

1. See W. G. Krivitsky, *In Stalin's Secret Service* (New York: Harper, 1939), pp. 1–8.

2. For Hitler's speech see Gustav Hilger and Alfred G. Meyer, *The Incompatible Allies* (New York: Macmillan, 1953), p. 262. Stalin's speech at the Seventeenth Congress is quoted by Robert C. Tucker in his introduction to *The Great Purge Trial*, a reprint of the stenographic report of the March 1938 trial of Bukharin *et al.*, edited by Robert C. Tucker and Stephen F. Cohen (New York: Grosset & Dunlap, 1965), p. xxxv.

Mein Kampf, he could continue to discount Hitler's plans for *Lebensraum* in the East, at least so long as Hitler's chief avowed enemy remained the "pluto-democracies" of the West, and Germany remained encircled by France, Czechoslovakia, and Poland. Aware of the German General Staff's opposition to any policy which could have embroiled the Third Reich in a two-front war, the Soviet government could map its politics with considerable freedom.

In evaluating Soviet and German foreign policy statements in the thirties, we should also remember that during those years both dictators were immersed in the internal affairs of their respective countries, struggling with immense economic problems and consolidating their political power. A great deal of the nationalist propaganda served, especially in Germany, to rally the masses around the party. Neither country had yet possessed the industrial and military potential needed to carry out a dynamic foreign policy.

It has been customary to explain the emergence of the Soviet Union from its isolation, beginning with its entry into the League of Nations in the fall of 1934, in terms of its fear of the German—and Japanese—militarism. To a certain extent this probably was the case. However, Litvinov's clamor for collective security at Geneva and Soviet denunciation of the "aggressive powers" made sense from more than one point of view. It is doubtful that Stalin really expected Western democracies to accept the Soviet Union as a full-fledged partner, or hoped that the League would become an effective peace-keeping body. On the other hand, he knew that the Soviet image abroad had been badly marred by the excesses of collectivization of farming in Russia, by the "show trials" and bloody purges, and he heavily counted on the improvement of this image as a result of the declared communist opposition to the Nazis. This posture for a while assured success for the Popular Front tactics, and in many quarters made the communists socially respectable for the first time. The Anti-Comintern Pact might have enhanced Hitler's image as a defender of civilization against communism, but at the same time it put the Soviet Union into the camp of the status quo (or "peace-loving") nations. After Moscow had taken an unequivocal stand in the Spanish Civil War and had begun aiding, albeit modestly, the Loyalists, most liberal Westerners became inclined to forgive Stalin his deeds in Russia while some acclaimed the Soviet regime without reservations.

The most important thing to remember, however, is that the polarization in the national and international politics of that period in no way meant that the Nazis and the Soviet communists were involved in a direct conflict. Both benefited from the erosion of the hated and despised democratic middle ground, gaining adherents and followers not at the expense of each other but through the destruction of the traditional, non-ideological body-politic of Europe. It is true that a few communists left the ranks and became ardent nationalists. But those were beyond Moscow's reach anyway, and their defection only justified in Stalin's eyes the further intensification of the purge of the Comintern, and further assertion of his personal authority.

The absence of a direct confrontation with Germany accounts for the fact that throughout this period Stalin persisted in his secret courtship of Hitler. It can be surmised that in these efforts he had the help of a number of influential people in Berlin, including—at least until the purge of General von Fritsch and others in February 1938—the leadership of the Wehrmacht. The evidence is inevitably scant. But on August 8, 1936, the American chargé d'affaires in Berlin, Ferdinand L. Mayer, wrote in a "strictly confidential" letter to a friend, that from an excellent source he had learned that "there was something stirring toward an improvement in German-Russian relations" and that "negotiations . . . are going on both in Moscow and here." Mayer added that although it was not known whether this was "with the approbation of Hitler," his informant felt that the Fuehrer must have been aware of it, "as the people here could hardly have gone so far . . . without Hitler's knowledge." [3] On August 14, 1936, Prentiss B. Gilbert, American consul in Geneva, reported to the State Department that he was told by "a German source associated with high governmental circles in Berlin" that efforts were being made to diminish the tension between Germany

3. Mayer to Lane, from The Arthur Bliss Lane Collection (New Haven: Yale University).

and Russia and that "the beginning of official communications is imminent." Gilbert noted, that in order to facilitate the rapprochement, all Soviet intelligence operations against the Baltic states had been transferred from Berlin to Stockholm.[4] In September, the minister of foreign affairs of Estonia, Akel, who had recently left his post as the Estonian envoy in Berlin, told the American minister to the Baltic states "that he believed an understanding between Germany and the Soviet Union to be a possibility within the near future," having established this impression from his talks with high German officials and the Soviet ambassador in Berlin.[5]

This contemporary evidence is fully and independently corroborated by Walter Krivitsky, who during that period was in charge of the Soviet military intelligence in Western Europe. Krivitsky relates that in December of 1936 his superior from Moscow, Abram Sloutsky, visited him in The Hague and told him to discontinue immediately all intelligence operations in Germany. Sloutsky told Krivitsky that Stalin "had set our course toward an early understanding with Hitler" and that "in the immediate future we shall consummate an agreement with Germany." And on a visit to Moscow the following spring, Krivitsky learned that David Kandelaki, Stalin's personal emissary, had recently returned from Berlin where he had had talks with the top Nazi leaders, including Hitler himself.[6]

We may guess that at this stage the overtures came almost entirely from Stalin, and that Hitler responded—to the extent he did —with caution and perhaps reluctance. Yet at least one witness testifies that early in 1937, informed by Reinhard Heydrich, chief of the SD, about the alleged plot against Stalin led by Marshal Tukhachevskiy, Hitler decided to back Stalin and ordered Heydrich

---

4. Gilbert to the Department of State, from The State Department File (Washington, D.C.: The National Archives).

5. Lane to Mayer, September 21, 1936, from The Arthur Bliss Lane Collection.

6. Krivitsky, pp. 213–214, 225–226. Kandelaki had been known in Berlin at least since 1935 when he negotiated with Hjalmer Schacht a loan of 500 million reichsmarks to finance Soviet-German trade. See Roediger's memorandum of December 21, 1935, *Documents on German Foreign Policy* (GFP), C, Vol. IV, pp. 931–932.

to provide the Soviet leader with incriminating evidence against Red Army generals.[7]

Although Krivitsky says that Kandelaki had brought some kind of a draft agreement from Berlin, presumably approved by Hitler, no deal was consummated at that time. We can only speculate as to what prevented it. Most likely, Hitler felt that he could accomplish his goals through cooperation with Great Britain and France where the spirit of appeasement ruled supreme. Since this success hinged on his continuing role as an anticommunist crusader, any sign of rapprochement with the Soviet would have been detrimental to his growing understanding with the Western powers.

Given the paranoiac predisposition of the Soviet leadership (*not* of Stalin alone), it can be safely assumed that it began seriously worrying about the "capitalist encirclement," especially after Mu-

---

7. See Walter Schellenberg, *The Labyrinth* (New York: Harper, 1956), Chapter 3. According to Schellenberg (who was Heydrich's right hand in the secret service), Hitler's decision was prompted not only by his wish to see the Red Army purged, but also by a genuine desire to help Stalin for whom, as Walter Laqueur remarked, the Fuehrer had always "had a sneaking admiration." The Tukhachevskiy story still retains fascination. Apparently there was no plot to begin with. Stalin distrusted his generals (as Hitler distrusted *his*) and had in addition a very urgent reason to liquidate them: according to one knowledgeable source, the Tukhachevskiy group had come into possession of evidence that Stalin was once an agent of the Tsarist Okhrana, and planned to confront the Leader at the next Central Committee plenum with their damning discovery. See the article by Alexander Orlov, former chief of the Soviet counterintelligence operations in Spain, in *Life*, April 23, 1956. In order to incriminate Tukhachevskiy, Soviet secret agents in Paris supplied "white" General Skoblin—himself a double agent—with the story of the "plot." The agents in this encounter posed as representatives of the German General Staff, supposedly working hand-in-glove with Tukhachevskiy. See Krivitsky, Chapter VII. Skoblin immediately warned Heydrich, assuming that the "plot" might have bad repercussions for the Nazis as well. We cannot be sure whether Hitler guessed that the idea of the plot actually originated in Stalin's mind, but after he ordered Heydrich to play along, the latter fabricated evidence of Tukhachevskiy's illicit connections with the German General Staff and shrewdly had it delivered to Beneš. The president of Czechoslovakia, greatly alarmed at the possibility of a Soviet-German alliance led by the military, immediately passed the faked papers to the Soviet ambassador in Prague, thus playing straight into the hands of the schemers. The top Red Army generals were executed in June 1937.

nich. With tensions along the Far Eastern frontier of the Soviet Union building up, the specter of a hostile European coalition must have caused considerable concern in Moscow. There was an increased sense of urgency in many government acts, and in the economic field great stress was placed on an early completion of the industrial projects already under way, at the expense of previously announced plans for further expansion.

Yet not everything looked gloomy and there was a realistic hope that the "internal contradictions" within the imperialist camp would provide water for the Soviet mill. Hitler was clearly not satisfied (although he declared he was) with the results of Munich. Czechoslovakia, having lost the Sudetenland, was disintegrating internally, presenting the Fuehrer with further temptations. More significantly, there was lively Nazi agitation in and over Danzig, and all signs pointed to Poland as the next target of Hitler's offensive: beginning with November 1938, the Nazi propaganda against Poland was rapidly reaching an unprecedented pitch. Since both Czechoslovakia and Poland were allies of France, and tantalizing question of whether or not the Western powers would allow them to be gobbled up by Hitler must have often been discussed at the Politburo meetings in Moscow as the year drew to a close.

In the weeks following Munich, the Soviet leadership had to pause, to review its position and come up with a new strategy. Merely to sit on the sidelines and accept exclusion from European affairs was too dangerous. Any further aggrandizement of Germany with the tacit consent of Great Britain and France might lead to the total isolation of the Soviet Union. To forestall this development it was necessary to provoke a crisis which would invalidate the accomplishments of Munich and to show how ephemeral was "peace in our time." In view of the continuing unfriendliness towards the Soviet Union in the British and French "ruling circles" and the exuberant reaction to Munich among the appeasers elsewhere, any move calculated to gain friends in the West appeared impracticable. This left Germany, potentially more dangerous but militarily weak (or so it seemed), but politically in a sense closer and, given the nature of its system of government, more flexible in its choices.

On March 10, 1939, addressing the Party Congress, Stalin indicated that Germany could count on Soviet understanding. Count von der Schulenburg, German ambassador to Moscow, stressed in his report to Berlin that in this speech, "Stalin's irony and criticism were directed in a considerably sharper degree against Britain, i.e., against the reactionary forces in power there, than against the so-called aggressor states, and in particular, Germany."[8] That this was a clear signal to Berlin, and was intended as such, was confirmed several months later by Molotov himself who, cheering the just concluded Nazi-Soviet Pact, "raised his glass to Stalin, remarking that it had been Stalin who—through his speech of March of this year, which had been well understood in Germany—had introduced the reversal in political relations."[9] As if proving to Stalin the soundness of his calculations, within one week after his speech, Hitler declared Slovakia independent and sent his troops to occupy the remaining rump of former Czechoslovakia. Responding to the challenge, Chamberlain and Daladier extended unilateral "guarantees" to Poland, Romania, and Greece. By the end of March the spirit of Munich had completely evaporated, and Europe found itself sharply divided into two implacably hostile camps.

Theoretically, the falling out of the Munich powers gave Stalin a freedom of choice. He could now either approach Great Britain and France, where the signs of alarm and hostility toward Germany were now unmistakable, and join in an effort to contain the Axis, thus ruling out a possibility of war. Or he could come to terms with Hitler, reinsuring him against any threat from the east, thus making war between the two "capitalist" groupings virtually inevitable. In practical terms, however, the first alternative was unsatisfactory. Chamberlain kept insisting that British policy was "not a policy of lining up opposing blocks of powers in Europe animated by hostile

---

8. Schulenburg to the Foreign Ministry, March 13, 1939. GFP, D, Vol. VI, pp. 1–3.

9. *Ibid.*, Vol. VII, p. 228. To Hitler, however, more decisive was the second "signal"—the dismissal of Litvinov on May 3, 1939, which put an effective end to the Soviet negotiations with the Anglo-French delegation. See Hitler's speech to the commanders-in-chief on August 22, 1939. *Ibid.*, p. 204.

intentions toward one another, and accepting the view that war is inevitable. . . . We are trying to build up not an alliance between ourselves and other countries, but a peace front against aggression." [10]

The question remains whether Stalin would have considered a full-fledged alliance with Great Britain and France, accompanied by an unqualified recognition of the Soviet Union as a great power, entitled to a sphere of influence of its own and to territorial expansion at the expense of its western neighbors. That much, at least, the Soviet representatives hinted at in Moscow to the French and British delegates during the talks later in the summer. The critics of appeasement, from Churchill down, have since blamed Chamberlain and Daladier for not exploring this possibility.

Yet it appears doubtful that such a choice in fact existed. To Stalin and his entourage, the principal enemy had always been the democratic West, with its distasteful self-righteousness and its hostility to the Russian Revolution. Although Hitler, too, was an avowed anticommunist, his virulent hostility towards the Versailles system, combined with his growing trouble-making potential, induced Stalin to regard him, on balance, as an asset in the arsenal of Soviet diplomacy. By the late spring of 1939 Stalin knew that Hitler intended to attack Poland: Soviet intelligence in Berlin worked well. And he could reasonably expect that if the attack occurred London and Paris would honor their pledge to come to Poland's rescue. It is simply difficult to believe those of the Soviet writers who kept insisting, in effect, that Moscow failed to see that after the fall of Prague all avenues to Germany's conciliation with the West were closed. For it was precisely this situation which permitted Stalin to encourage Hitler to take the irrevocable step and launch a war which left the Soviet Union sitting happily on the sidelines. Such an outcome, from Stalin's point of view, seemed clearly preferable to the "peace front against aggression" envisioned by Chamberlain.

---

10. Quoted by L. B. Namier, *Diplomatic Prelude, 1938–1939* (London: Macmillan, 1948), pp. 167–168.

The story of the Soviet-German negotiations which culminated in the Nazi-Soviet Pact, signed in Moscow by Molotov and Ribbentrop on August 23, 1939, has been covered extensively by many historians to warrant its repeating here. The early overtures emanated from Moscow, but although the negotiations were conducted with considerable skill by both sides, the terms of the eventual agreement (as recorded in the Secret Protocol to the Pact) met all Stalin's wishes. Thanks mainly to the Soviet ability to sit tight, Hitler finally became so desperate, in view of the scheduled attack on Poland, that in the end he literally begged Stalin to accept Ribbentrop's mission —and a good part of the expected spoils.

There is little reason to doubt that the deal was entered into by both sides in good faith. If at that time Hitler nourished the idea of eventually attacking Russia, we find no evidence of it in the huge assortment of German documents and memoirs published since the war. Nor is there reason to believe that Stalin had any reservations about the deal. The speed with which it was concluded—it took a mere two sessions within one day to resolve both essential and technical matters—was significant. The cynical jokes about the Anti-Comintern Pact being frightening principally to the "City of London and the English shopkeepers" during the gay celebrations in the Kremlin, reflected the absence of any ideological inhibitions on either side. And Stalin's assurance to Ribbentrop that the Soviet government took the new pact "very seriously" and that he "could guarantee on his word of honor that the Soviet Union would not betray its partner," carried a note of unmistakable sincerity.

Perhaps even more convincing in this respect is the trade agreement of February 11, 1940, which grew out of the Soviet-German Boundary and Friendship Treaty, signed in Moscow during Ribbentrop's second visit there from September 27 through 29, 1939. As the chairman of the German economic delegation recorded, the trade negotiations "were difficult and lengthy" both for "material and psychological reasons. . . . The Soviet Union promised far more deliveries than are defensible from a purely economic point of view," often "at the expense of its own supply." In the process of the negotiations he observed that "the desire of the Soviet government to help Germany and to consolidate firmly the political understanding in economic matters as well, became more and more evident." [11]

There were other indications of Soviet sincerity. All anti-Nazi references, even in closed party meetings, ended with the signing of the Pact. All Soviet citizens of German origin were immediately released from prisons and concentration camps, something which was not called for by the Pact or the Treaty. All books and pamphlets containing anti-Nazi propaganda were removed from all libraries and bookstores of the Soviet Union, again, a step which the Germans did not bother to reciprocate. And the expressions of friendship for Germany (and distaste for its "imperialistic" adversaries) filled Soviet radio and periodicals.

Yet the Nazi-Soviet partnership did not survive, and the causes of its dissolution are worth looking into. First, the agreements did not lead to a convergence, psychologically or otherwise, of the two regimes. At no time had there been much cordiality between the leading officials of the two governments and early attempts of Stalin and Molotov to inject a note of intimate rapport into their relations with the Nazis failed because of German standoffishness. The Germans, even the most devoted members of the "Eastern School," were businesslike, exceedingly correct, but nonetheless preferred to talk across the desk and were obviously ill at ease whenever fraternizing was attempted. They did not drink much vodka and did not enjoy noisy Kremlin parties, so much a part of the Moscow scene. Soviet representatives in Berlin had no difficulty in getting appointments with top men in various ministries but were never invited to intimate Nazi gatherings. The Pact of Friendship did not create warm personal friendships on any level.

---

11. Schnurre memorandum, February 26, 1940, GFP, D, Vol. VIII, pp. 814–817. The Soviet Union undertook not only to supply over 3.5 million tons of ores, metals, and grains but also to provide transit for goods going to Germany from the Balkans, the Middle East, and the Far East, as well as to act as a buyer for Germany of raw materials and metals in third countries. The trade deal was in the nature of barter: Germany had to deliver to the Soviet Union a corresponding amount of industrial products and military equipment, but while the Soviets were to deliver their part within eighteen months, German deliveries were to be spread over a period of twenty-seven months.

Second, the partnership concluded in 1939 had not developed into an alliance. The objectives of the two partners remained distinctly different. Hitler wanted to win the war and gain for Germany the position of an undisputed world power. Stalin, while profiting from German victories, considered his political and economic support for Germany adequate contribution to the partnership. He viewed the Soviet Union in an advantageous position: it could not lose even if Germany were bled white in the war or were defeated altogether. This reasoning was sound—but only until the summer of 1940. The fall of France doubtless shook Stalin. But instead of drawing closer to his victorious partner, he chose to assert his independence and, taking advantage of Germany's entanglement in the west, proceeded, in a rather crude fashion, with the outright annexation of the Baltic states and Bessarabia.

Although Stalin stayed essentially within the letter of the agreements, this display of greed and bullishness was a fatal mistake. Hitler never liked to be taken advantage of, and now, at the pinnacle of his power, he was least disposed to view this challenge with magnanimity. In the fall of 1939 he still could regard Stalin as an equal. But in the summer of 1940, the conqueror of the European continent and the leader of the mightiest military machine ever assembled watched with increasing suspicion and impatience the abnormal appetite of his junior partner. He became so furious in fact that Ribbentrop had to remind the Fuehrer that when he was first dispatched to Moscow he was authorized to concede virtually all Eastern Europe (if need be, even Constantinople and the Straits), in exchange for Stalin's benevolence.[12]

Hitler's annoyance with Stalin began with the Soviet attack on Finland: in the Winter War German sympathies were fully on the side of the Finns. The campaigns in the West for a while took Hitler's attention away from eastern affairs. Now that they were in the forefront again, Hitler redefined Germany's interests in Southeast Europe, extending them to all areas not specifically assigned to the Soviet sphere. Simultaneously, he ordered his chief military strategists to start preparing plans for the conquest of Russia.

---

12. Ribbentrop's memorandum, June 24, 1940, GFP, D, Vol. X, pp. 10–11.

Apparently no one in Moscow understood this change in Hitler's attitude. Stalin remained convinced that the German Fuehrer considered the Soviet support indispensable. Although relations had become noticeably cold, this did not disturb the Soviet leaders who were getting the first sweet taste of imperialistic expansion. Great Britain continued to fight and, as they well knew, war on two fronts was a nightmare for the German General Staff.

Following the defeat of France, the Soviet government presented the Germans with a series of demands and sour protests: over a strip of Lithuanian territory initially allocated to Germany, which it wanted to purchase; over the port facilities in Memel (now Klaipeda) which it claimed in the name of former Lithuania; over the presumably excessive compensation it had to pay to the Germans evacuated to Germany from the Baltic states; over the presence of small German contingents in northern Finland; over the inadequate backing of Soviet claims to Romania and, later, over not being recognized as a Danubian power; and over the lag in German deliveries.

We can surmise that this stream of complaints did not help to eliminate the growing chill in Soviet-German relations. Before long, the Soviet government made another psychological error. In July Stafford Cripps, the newly appointed British ambassador, had a long talk with Stalin. After this talk Molotov called in Schulenburg, the German ambassador, and told him pointedly that the British offered their support for the establishment of Soviet political leadership in the Balkans and for the creation of a Soviet military base in the Bosporus Strait. If anything, this hint made Hitler more determined to limit further Soviet expansion. He instructed Ribbentrop to protest the Soviet seizure of Northern Bukovina (not specifically conceded to the Soviet Union by the Pact); and on August 30, having arbitrated the Hungarian-Romanian dispute over Transylvania, he guaranteed the rump of Romania against any further encroachments. This step evoked a sharp Soviet protest.

There are conflicting theories as to precisely when and why Hitler made up his mind to invade Russia.[13] The early planning, and the

---

13. For one theory see Trumbull Higgins, *Hitler and Russia* (New York: Macmillan, 1966), pp. ii–iv.

gradual movement of troops towards the Soviet border which began late in the summer, prove little: no war is "inevitable" until it actually starts. But it seems that early in October, as he invited Molotov to come on a state visit, Hitler decided to make a last attempt to find out how much Stalin's ambitions clashed with his own. That his mind was then still open, is suggested by the fact that on the day of Molotov's arrival in Berlin in November he instructed his military chiefs to resume preparations for the invasion of England "in the spring of 1941," a plan which could be carried out *only* if the attack on Russia were called off.[14]

Molotov and his large delegation were received with top honors. During the lengthy conversations with the head of the Soviet government, Hitler and Ribbentrop outlined to him grandiose plans for joint long-range policies and delimitation of German, Italian, Japanese, and Soviet interests. Molotov listened, visibly unimpressed, and then spelled out, on Stalin's behalf, the Soviet demands: that Germany should completely abandon its interest in the fate of Finland; that it agree to a Soviet protectorate over Bulgaria; and that it facilitate the establishment of Soviet control over the Bosporus and the Dardanelles. If these conditions were met, the Soviet Union would be prepared to join Germany and its allies in a Four Power Pact, Molotov believed. Hitler argued in vain that Finland should be left alone, that Soviet interests in the Black Sea could be secured without violating Turkey's territorial integrity, and that Bulgaria should at least be asked whether it wants the Soviet "guarantee." His eloquence led nowhere. Molotov stood firm, and no decisions were arrived at.

Shortly after he returned to Moscow, on November 26, 1940, Molotov handed to Schulenburg a stiff formal answer to the German proposals. The Soviet Union was prepared to accept the German draft of the Four Power Pact regarding the future political collaboration provided: (a) that the Germans get out of Finland (b) that "within the next few months" Bulgaria is recognized as belonging to the Soviet security area and that Soviet land and military bases are

14. See Directive No. 18, GFP, D, Vol. XI, p. 531.

established "within range of the Bosporus and the Dardanelles"; (c) that the area south of Batum and Baku "is recognized as the center of the aspirations of the Soviet Union"; and (d) that Japan renounce its rights to concessions for coal and oil in Northern Sakhalin.[15]

Hitler did not reply to this note, then or later, in spite of repeated Soviet inquiries. He quietly advised Marshal Antonescu and the Bulgarian minister in Berlin to resist all Soviet pressure, assuring both countries of his support.[16] On December 18, 1940, he issued his Directive No. 21, ordering the German armed forces to be prepared "to crush Soviet Russia in a quick campaign." After that, except for some minor discussions at ambassadorial level, there were no more communications between Berlin and Moscow.

The Soviet government's subsequent reaction to Berlin's ominous silence falls, roughly, into two stages. Up to about the beginning of April 1941, it acted upon the conviction that Hitler would neither want nor dare to attack the Soviet Union under any circumstances. It was during this brief period that Stalin resorted to a power play by putting greater pressure on Bulgaria; by encouraging Turkey to join the anti-Axis "Balkan Front" which the British (and, to a lesser degree, the Americans) struggled to create; and by deliberately slowing down Soviet deliveries to Germany. This Soviet attempt to assert independence from Berlin culminated in the conclusion of a treaty of friendship with the government of Yugoslavia which came to power as a result of a British-sponsored coup d'etat on March 27, 1941. This act infuriated Hitler, removing the last hesitations (if he still had any) to go ahead with the Eastern Campaign.

After the swift German victory in the Balkans—Yugoslavia and Greece collapsed within three weeks—the Soviet leadership began to display signs of concern and, eventually, of mortal fear of a German attack. The enormous concentration of German armies along the Soviet borders could no longer be dismissed as a tactic of intimidation of the erstwhile partner. Yet the reality was too frightening to face, and Soviet policy entered a period of almost total

15. GFP, D, Vol. XI, pp. 714–715.
16. *Ibid.*, pp. 661, 675–676, 767–773.

paralysis, interspersed with a series of pathetic gestures aimed at placating Hitler. Stalin believed nobody who advised him to take precautionary measures, including Churchill, whom he suspected of negotiating with Rudolf Hess a joint Anglo-German operation against the Soviet Union.

When all Soviet attempts to mollify Hitler failed, and in the early hours of June 22, 1941, German motorized divisions began to cross the whole length of the Soviet western border, Molotov had his last meeting with the German ambassador. In reply to the declaration of war read to him by Schulenburg, he could only stutter, "Surely we have not deserved that!"